The Legacy of Elise Hall
Contemporary Perspectives on Gender and the Saxophone

The Legacy of Elise Hall

Contemporary Perspectives
on Gender and the Saxophone

Edited by

Kurt Bertels & Adrianne Honnold

Leuven University Press

Published with the financial support of the KU Leuven Fund for Fair Open Access, LUCA School of Arts, Lewis University, and Royal Conservatoire Antwerp

Published in 2024 by Leuven University Press / Presses Universitaires de Louvain / Universitaire Pers Leuven. Minderbroedersstraat 4, B-3000 Leuven (Belgium).

Selection and editorial matter © Kurt Bertels & Adrianne Honnold, 2024
Individual chapters © The respective authors, 2024

This book is published under a Creative Commons Attribution Non-Commercial Non-Derivative 4.0 Licence. Further details about Creative Commons licences are available at https://creativecommons.org/share-your-work/cclicenses/

Attribution should include the following information: Kurt Bertels & Adrianne Honnold (eds), *The Legacy of Elise Hall: Contemporary Perspectives on Gender and the Saxophone*. Leuven: Leuven University Press, 2024. (CC BY-NC-ND 4.0)

Unless otherwise indicated all images are reproduced with the permission of the rightsholders acknowledged in captions. They are expressly excluded from the CC BY-NC-ND 4.0 licence covering the rest of this publication. Permission for reuse should be sought from the rights-holders.

ISBN 978 94 6270 397 1
eISBN 978 94 6166 547 8 (ePDF)
https://doi.org/10.11116/9789461665478
D/2024/1869/7
NUR: 662

Layout: Crius Group
Cover design: Daniel Benneworth-Gray
Cover illustration: Elise Hall portrait – BSO Archives. http://collections.bso.org/digital/collection/images/id/5514/

In commemoration of

the hundredth anniversary

of Elise Boyer Hall's passing

Contents

9   List of Figures, Music Examples, and Tables

11 Acknowledgments

Introduction

15 Rethinking Elise Hall's Legacy
    Kurt Bertels & Adrianne Honnold

PART I. Histories

29 "Incomparable Virtuoso": A Reevaluation of the Performance Abilities of Elise Boyer Hall
    Andrew J. Allen

57 Paying and Playing? Elise Hall and Patronage in the Early Twentieth Century
    Kurt Bertels

PART II. Critical Organology & Social Identity

81 Exhuming Elise: Rehabilitating Reputations
    Adrianne Honnold

105 Instruments Telling History: Engaging Elise Hall through the Saxophone
    Sarah McDonie

PART III. Beyond Elise Hall: Gender, Media & Culture in the 1920s

127 "He puts the pep in the party": Gender and Iconography in 1920s Buescher Saxophone Advertisements
Sarah V. Hetrick

153 Intersections of Gender, Genre, and Access: The Enterprising Career of Kathryne E. Thompson
Holly J. Hubbs

Epilogue

177 Elise Hall and the Saxophone: Updated Narratives and Future Considerations
Kurt Bertels & Adrianne Honnold

185 About the Authors

187 Index

List of Figures, Music Examples, and Tables

Figures

Figure 1.1. Advertisement for January 1904 Longy Club Concert   36
Figure 1.2. Advertisement for January 1905 Longy Club Concert   39
Figure 1.3. Advertisement for 1909 edition of "MRS. R. J. HALL'S CONCERT"   43
Figure 1.4. Elise Hall following performance with the Boston Symphony Orchestra   46
Figure 1.5. Advertisement for Boston Orchestral Club concert of April 19, 1910   48
Figure 2.1. The announcement of the *Choral Varié*'s publication in *Le Guide Musical*   70
Figure 5.1. Buescher advertisement in *Better Homes and Gardens*, November 1924   140
Figure 5.2. Buescher advertisement in *Cosmopolitan*, April 1927   142
Figure 5.3. Buescher advertisement in *Cosmopolitan*, February 1928   144
Figure 6.1. Kathryne Thompson on the cover of Felix Arndt's *Nola* (New York: Sam Fox Publishing Co., 1924)   162
Figure 6.2. Advertisement for Frank. J. Hart Southern California Music Company offering free lessons from Kathryne E. Thompson for every saxophone purchased at the store. *Los Angeles Times*, July 19, 1921, p. II1.   165
Figure 6.3. Cover of *Bubble and Squeak* by Kathryne E. Thompson (Southern California Music Company, 1923)   170

Music Examples

Example 6.1. From *Valse Minah* by Kathryne E. Thompson
    (Pittsburgh: Volkwein Brothers, 1939)   169
Example 6.2. From *Bubble and Squeak* by Kathryne E. Thompson
    (Southern California Music Company, 1923)   171

Tables

Table 2.1. Elise Hall's musical score collection   63
Table 2.2. Dedications in Hall's musical scores   68

Acknowledgments

This volume is the result of teamwork. We, the editors, are very proud to present a successful international collaboration between scholar-performers from different institutions, such as LUCA School of Arts (KU Leuven), Royal Conservatoire Antwerp, Lewis University, Georgia College, Indiana University Bloomington, University of Arkansas, and Ursinus College. Firstly, we would like to acknowledge the help of all the people involved in this project and, more specifically, the authors who took part in the review process. Without their support and their contributions, this book would not have become a reality. Therefore, our sincere gratitude goes to the author of each chapter who contributed their time and expertise to this book. For this volume, we were fortunate to count on experts with various specializations. They have offered new perspectives as well as a scientific and artistic understanding of the late nineteenth-century saxophonist Elise Hall's legacy. We sincerely thank the co-authors (in the order of the chapters) for this inspiring collaboration: Dr. Andrew Allen, Sarah McDonie, Dr. Sarah Hetrick, and Dr. Holly Hubbs. From the start of this book project, they recognized the urgency of presenting contemporary perspectives on Elise Hall. Despite their own busy academic and/or artistic endeavors they also fully supported our driving force behind this project. Secondly, we wish to acknowledge the valuable contributions of the reviewers for their full support for our initiative, constructive feedback, and many suggestions regarding the improvement of quality, coherence, and content presentation of the chapters. Undoubtedly, they have challenged us to elevate the quality of this volume.

On behalf of the entire team, we are also incredibly grateful to the publisher, Leuven University Press, and in particular Dr. Mirjam Truwant, Acquisitions Editor, for the smooth cooperation in making this publication possible and for all her help with practical concerns.

For financing this volume, we are also indebted to some institutions for their contributions. We express our gratitude to LUCA School of Arts and the KU Leuven Fund for Fair Open Access, and Royal Conservatoire Antwerp. Also, thank you to Lewis University, LUCA School of Arts, and The Research Foundation – Flanders (FWO) for their financial support for travel to the 2023 North American Saxophone Alliance (NASA) Biennial Conference (March 30th

– April 2nd) at The University of Southern Mississippi. Thanks to the NASA programming committee for providing the opportunity to present research from the book to an international cohort of saxophonists and scholars. We are grateful for the opportunity for us, the editors, to be able to finish the book's manuscript in person, thanks to the support of our hotel La Quinta in Hattiesburg, where we could use a work space.

Not surprisingly, some authors also undertook library and archive visits. For these efforts we were each able to count on the appreciated assistance of librarians and archivists, that has provided us with valuable historical resources. We would like to thank Dr. Johan Eeckeloo, head of the music library of the *Koninklijk Conservatorium Brussel*. Also, Maryalice Perri-Mohr, archivist and records manager at the music library of the New England Conservatory, was very eager to support us by providing digital materials of Hall's manuscripts which are preserved in the Elise Hall special collection.

Finally, we are grateful to everyone who in one way or another—perhaps without realizing—contributed to the realization of this book. A special thank you to Prof. Debra Richtmeyer (University of Illinois)—Adrianne Honnold's beloved teacher and mentor—and all of the other women saxophonists who have persevered and managed to thrive in a system that has felt stacked against them. Your artistry and professionalism are an inspiration.

And last but not least: thank you, Derek and Bram, and all of our supportive friends and loved ones, for your endless patience and support for our project.

Kurt Bertels & Adrianne Honnold, editors
Brussels and Chicago, April 2023

Introduction

Rethinking Elise Hall's Legacy

Kurt Bertels & Adrianne Honnold

It was in November 2021 that we shared the intriguing idea of co-editing a book project on the historical figure of saxophonist Elise Hall. After sending several messages back and forth, we finally found a mutually agreeable time for a video meeting. Kurt was at his home in Brussels, while Adrianne was in Chicago, a seven-hour time difference. We had first met at a conference in 2016, "Prepositions in Artistic Research" at the *Vrije Universiteit Brussel*, and instantly connected over our shared experiences as professional saxophonists and researchers; we were both working on doctorates at the time.[1] When our meeting began on Zoom that day in the fall of 2021, Kurt shared his idea for a new edited volume that would bring a twenty-first-century perspective to the life and legacy of Elise Hall. We agreed to embark on this project that day, thrilled with the prospect of critically engaging with aspects of Hall's life and career and excited to begin the journey toward a contemporary exploration that would traverse new avenues of inquiry related to Hall's historiography and largesse.

To commemorate the one-hundredth anniversary of Hall's death in 2024, a modern approach to understanding her legacy forms the thread of this edited volume. This collection of essays is different from existing scholarship related to Hall because it is concerned not with the discrete history of Hall or the saxophone, but with the myriad questions raised from a constellation of factors surrounding this innovative musician, including topics relating to the era in which she lived, the instrument that she played, the music that she performed, and the culture of the time. Just as Hall traveled between Boston and Paris to create opportunities for performance and cultivate repertoire for the saxophone by engaging with European composers, we have embarked on a transatlantic collaboration to present a progressive reassessment of her life and career.

To foreground the essays in this volume, we must first provide some historical and biographical contexts for both Hall and the saxophone. The saxophone was officially presented to the public for the first time in 1841, by the Belgian inventor Antoine-Joseph ('Adolphe') Sax during the Industrial Exhibition in Brussels. Sax moved to Paris to establish his musical instrument business, and after some lobbying by the inventor, the first ensembles to adopt the saxophone were European military bands. The development of the pedagogy soon followed, necessitated by the increase in the number of saxophone players and a methodical approach to learning how to play it. Quickly thereafter, the rise of higher music institutions in Europe and the United States created possibilities for the initial introduction of the saxophone into the academy, and the first generation of saxophone educators was created.[2] In addition to the needs of the military musicians, the very first saxophone classes at universities necessitated the creation and dissemination of early repertoire and instructional methods.[3] As this saxophone education evolved and the number of players increased, the advancement of the repertoire quickly accelerated. This growth became a way to promote the lyrical and technical possibilities of the new instrument and stimulated its acceptance in the first decades after its invention. The historical repertoire not only played a crucial role in the world's very first educational opportunities for saxophonists, but also in the process of promoting the instrument and ensuring its positive reception by the public.

To date, details of Hall's life have been presented in the works of William Street, Stephen Cottrell, James Noyes, and a few others, but deserve a brief overview here as a frame of reference for the reader.[4] Elizabeth Boyer Swett Coolidge was born in Paris in 1853, to a wealthy family from Boston, Massachusetts. Throughout her life, she would continue to travel back and forth, actively engaging in the musical communities of both cities. Elise, as she came to be known, married Dr. Richard J. Hall in 1879, and they took up residence first in New York City, and later in Santa Barbara, California, where she began playing the saxophone and embarked on a journey toward her life in music. While on the West Coast—so goes the often repeated anecdote—Hall began playing the saxophone on the suggestion of her husband, who had 'prescribed' the playing of a wind instrument to counteract a hearing impairment and to capitalize on her love for music.[5] While this narrative is widely known in and beyond the saxophone community, saxophonist-scholar James Noyes questioned this assumption with his article "Elise Hall in Santa Barbara (1889-1898): The Amateur Musical Club and Philharmonic Society" in *The Saxophone Symposium* (2022).[6] Noyes argues that although Hall did lose her hearing at an advanced age, her choice to play the saxophone was "certainly keeping with the late nineteenth-century zeitgeist and consistent with Léon Vallas's understanding that her playing was for sustaining health."[7] In other words, she likely took up the saxophone because it was in vogue to do so, not in an attempt to address a specific ailment or impairment as other historians had presumed. Further, the author also rightly points out that journals at the time did not at all address Hall's presumed disability.

Despite reviews on her entrepreneurship and musicianship, there was no "hint of deficiency."[8] Noyes' investigation of the longstanding speculation about Hall's hearing impairment is a welcome and long overdue reconsideration of her life story, and it exposes some of the ways that the facts of her life have not always been closely scrutinized from a modern viewpoint.

The choice to play the saxophone was not obvious; rather, it was quite unexpected for a woman at the time. Yet it is important to acknowledge that Hall's devotion to the saxophone at the turn of the twentieth century was not an isolated phenomenon. Scholar(-performers) such as Thomas Smialek, L.A. Logrande, and Holly Hubbs have demonstrated that the first prominent American saxophone soloists—in sharp contrast to Europe—were women who were mainly active in popular musical genres.[9] Their pioneering investigations serve as compelling evidence of the leadership and impact of women musicians in promoting and disseminating the new instrument. The saxophone would go on to develop strong associations with masculinity and male performers through the social and cultural environment of the 1920s and 1930s in the United States, which relegated the contributions of women to the background.

Dr. Hall died a few years later in 1897, and Mrs. Hall moved the family to Boston where she quickly resumed her status as a member of the wealthy, elite society at the time. Back in the Northeast, she quickly established herself within the musical community. She took up lessons with Georges Longy, oboist of the Boston Symphony Orchestra, and she began working with the Boston Orchestral Club. From 1900 until approximately 1920, Hall worked to develop a repertoire that she could perform with members of the Orchestral Club and actively participated in the production of concerts. Her efforts were incredibly consequential to the history of the saxophone, the development of its concert repertory, and the recognition of the cultural contributions of the Orchestral Club writ large. Her activities further had an impact on the saxophone community and on the musical life of communities in France and the United States. She became the dedicatee of works primarily by French composers in the first two decades of the twentieth century, and as such, she was responsible for several commissions of internationally renowned composers which resulted in significant contributions to the classical saxophone repertoire. Before she became involved with the instrument, the repertoire was almost non-existent; due to her efforts, it was extended to include works by composers Claude Debussy, Vincent d'Indy, Charles Martin Loeffler, Florent Schmitt, André Caplet, and Paul Gilson, to name a few.

Hall possessed the privilege of wealth and time that opened doors and allowed her to pursue various musical endeavors, but the patriarchal system and the marginalization of the novel saxophone that existed in the nineteenth century undoubtedly colored perceptions regarding her efforts and the instrument's reputation. Her work to create classical music and formal performance opportunities for the saxophone coincided with the instrument's growing reputation as a central ingredient in popular music and jazz. Indeed, her accomplishments are astonishing considering the obstacles that existed.

At this point it is essential to recognize the problematic parts of Hall's life, despite the fact that she was one of the very first female saxophone soloists and a well-known benefactor. Critical engagement with certain aspects of her life and career has mostly been neglected in previous research and, in the spirit of understanding her as a whole person, must be briefly explored here in order to frame the reader's perspective on the subsequent chapters. Firstly, Hall came from a family of colonizers. This term was used with pride by members of her illustrious family, the Coolidges, who originally came to the United States from England. In the twenty-first century, this assertion is appalling and offensive.[10] Families like hers considered themselves to be some of the first "Americans," a complete untruth that refutes the violent subjugation and casting out of indigenous peoples who inhabited North America prior to its colonization by Europeans. Thus, although it is difficult to unequivocally state that she actively engaged in discriminatory or violent behavior in her daily life, she was a party to systems of oppression that existed in the United States at the time. Hall's socioeconomic status provided the platform from which to engage in forms of cultural hegemony; she was a member of the elite, wealthy ruling class that manipulated the production of culture in society and delineated who was worthy of participating in it and/or enjoying it.

Secondly, the status that Hall maintained in society likely imparted her with a sense of privilege and entitlement.[11] Evidence that supports this claim can perhaps be seen in her persistence with the composers whom she worked with (as outlined in Debussy's letters) or in the abundance of favorable reviews of her performances—and lack of uncomplimentary critiques—by critics and journalists.[12] In the case of her commission from Debussy, it is difficult to determine whether she was acting imperiously by showing up at his home in France unannounced, or whether she was exercising due diligence on her investment with the renowned composer.[13] The narratives that have described Hall's experiences with Debussy are clouded by a distinctly sexist tone, magnanimously supporting Debussy's reticence in completing the work, so it is almost impossible to determine the exact nature of their interactions.[14] In terms of the positive reviews that Hall received following several of her performances in Boston, it is important to keep in mind that she exerted a great deal of influence—socially and financially—on the musical culture of Boston. Because of her financial support of institutions in the city at the time, it is possible that the reviews of Hall's performances may have been generously interpreted to favor her and her musical colleagues. Again, it is very difficult to place ourselves within the social and cultural environment of the time and to read between the lines of the reviews that were published, but it is plausible to think that the cultural capital she possessed may have had an effect on the media. Andrew Allen's chapter later in this volume speaks to this subject and lays out noteworthy evidence to support the idea that Hall was a very accomplished performer, but it is important to acknowledge the power that she possibly wielded in order to understand Hall as a human being and not a sacrosanct historical figure of the past.

A great deal of long overdue attention has been paid to the topic of women in music since the 1990s, and this recuperation has resulted in positive strides toward representation in the arts and increased discovery of historical information about women's work and their abundant contributions to musical practices and cultures.[15] However, as Catherine Strong and Sarah Raine noted in their research on gender equality in the music industry in 2019, people who identify as women have historically been marginalized in many ways, including through sexist attitudes towards their perceived lack of ability to play instruments, as well as through "mechanisms of taste-making that create canons and histories that focus on men."[16] Almost thirty years before Strong and Raine, Susan McClary published the first edition of *Feminine Endings* (1991), a pioneering volume that was one of the first to substantively bring forth musicological approaches to the investigation of "gendered metaphors prevalent in discourse about music."[17] As McClary observed, musicology as a discipline had been quite conservative up to that point (the 1990s) and had failed not only to examine gender and sexuality as they relate to music but also had managed to disengage from "cultural interpretation of any sort."[18] Although this volume does not explicitly utilize methods from feminist musicology as outlined in McClary's research of the 1990s, the spirit of her approach calls us to action and informs our interpretation of the subject of this volume.

Three principles culled from the two sources discussed above provide inspiration for the inquiries in this volume and are connected to the structure of this book: the exclusion of women from "taste-making" or the development and allocation of aesthetic value and the canon; sexist attitudes towards women playing instruments; and the study of music and musicians through the lens of gender and sexuality. Just as technology has evolved to allow us, the co-editors, to collaborate on a book project from two different continents, a great expansion of scholarly research and interpretation in diverse areas of music has been carried out since the first biography of Hall was published forty years ago. For women that have been "discovered" and studied for their contributions to music (for example, the rediscovery of Hildegard von Bingen in the late 1980s), their histories are often told using language and methodologies that continue to subordinate their skills and marginalize them and their music. We, as saxophonists and scholars, are now an objective distance away from Hall's historiographies and are thus positioned to answer questions about her from new vantage points featuring fresh voices.

The three lines of inquiry outlined above specifically relate to the pioneering saxophonist from Boston. This volume aims to contribute substantively to the existing scholarship surrounding Hall's life and career by analyzing historical and sociocultural factors that have not been thoroughly explored in the past. The following chapters discuss various aspects using Hall as the point of departure, but the predominant through line in each scholar's work is gender, considered in combination with the saxophone. In terms of music studies, these two factors separately warrant thorough investigation from various perspectives and paradigms, but when combined, the significance is magnified for several reasons that are discussed in each chapter. Hall's career and the works that she commissioned around the turn of the twentieth century were neglected for over fifty years. The first published biography of Hall was a doctoral thesis completed by William Street in 1983 entitled "Elise Boyer Hall: America's First Female Concert Saxophonist: Her Life as Performing Artist, Pioneer of Concert Repertory for Saxophone and Patroness of the Arts."[19] In the years since this thesis was completed, additional investigations of a heuristic nature have been carried out concerning her life embedded in a historical context and the musical scores she commissioned from internationally renowned composers.[20] Anecdotally, there is some misinformation circulating in the saxophone community that has gone unchallenged, and from a research stance, there has been little to no rehabilitation of commonly held perceptions about Hall.

In order to examine the three foundational principles listed above, this volume aims to answer questions regarding the implications of Hall's patronage, participation in "amateur" music-making, and considerations of gender on the legacy of the saxophone and its repertoire, broadly conceived. How did intersectional factors that form her identity shape perceptions of the saxophone in the early twentieth century and now, in the twenty-first century?[21] How can we translate or understand her legacy today?

To answer these questions, we encouraged scholars to submit abstracts outlining their chosen approaches. With an international call for papers, we invited scholars with diverse, interdisciplinary backgrounds to link various inquiries into Hall's impact with broader perspectives on early twentieth-century music from a contemporary standpoint. Possible research perspectives were proposed, such as Hall's repertoire, saxophone and gender, instrumental performance practice, and patronage in music.

This book is important, then, because it contributes to research and knowledge of the saxophone and one of the world's first women saxophone soloists, two subjects that warrant thorough investigation. Saxophonists have been preoccupied with performing and pushing the boundaries of what the instrument can do technically and musically, which has been essential to its development. However, in the twenty-first century, it is vital to reflect on what has already been accomplished by researching the key figures and their contributions while utilizing theoretical approaches from outside the musical sphere to connect to broader academic communities.

Questions relating to gender and identity have been carried out in some areas of music studies, but there has not been a great deal of discourse on this topic as it relates to the saxophone. This status is interesting because—despite the fact that several women of the late nineteenth century played pivotal roles in the nascent instrument's history—the saxophone maintains an implicitly masculine gender association. This connection is due to a combination of factors, including the enduring tradition of the prohibition of women from wind instrument performance in the nineteenth century and the impact of male-dominated jazz and popular music on the instrument's historical trajectory. A significant detail that sets this volume apart from other research is that the majority of the contributors involved in this project are women. Therefore, this book highlights the perspectives and scholarly voices that have not been heard before in relation to the topic of Hall. While experience as a saxophonist is certainly not a requirement to participate in or understand this volume, the fact that saxophonists were involved in its creation brings unique perspectives shaped by an intimate knowledge of the instrument and its performance.

The saxophone is globally popular yet has a shorter history than other woodwind instruments that were invented decades or even millennia earlier, like the flute. And yet, in the years since the saxophone was introduced in the mid-1840s, the instrument has become a recognizable iconographic artifact with a distinct collection of connotations acquired from the people who have played it and the genres in which it is featured. Indeed, the saxophone is the prism through which we view Hall. There have been many renowned saxophonists that have contributed to the development of pedagogical and performance conventions throughout its relatively brief history, yet there remains a lack of reflexivity and a dearth of research that uses the instrument as its subject in broader contexts outside of the saxophone community.[22] This condition is partially evidenced by the number of times that each of the authors refers to a small collection of source material. Indeed, there is some repetition and crossover of information in the chapters below, but it is to be expected in the examination of a subject that has received a relatively small amount of scholarly attention in the past. Even so, each author presents a unique approach to discussing some of the previously held assumptions about Hall.

This volume is comprised of a collection of methodologies that reflect the variety of views chosen by each contributing scholar. Individual research paradigms are thoroughly explored in the following chapters, including methodologies from critical organology, material culture, cultural studies, patronage studies, feminist musicology, media studies, and performance practices/performance-based research. These approaches are indicative of the far-reaching implications of a study on a woman saxophonist of the late nineteenth and early twentieth centuries and serve to comprehensively investigate Hall, the structures surrounding her, and other concerns facing women in music.

To answer the queries stated above, the book is organized into three main parts. Part I, 'Histories,' includes two chapters that consider performance and patronage, Hall's most enduring impact on the history of the saxophone aside from gender considerations. The first chapter is entitled "'Incomparable Virtuoso': A Reevaluation of the Performance Abilities of Elise Boyer Hall" by Andrew J. Allen and presents an overview of a representative selection of Hall's public performances and their reception from media outlets of both the United States and France. Narrative analysis of these musical reviews presents an updated assessment of Hall's reputation as a saxophonist. The second chapter, "Paying and Playing? Elise Hall and Patronage in the Early Twentieth Century" by Kurt Bertels, presents different perspectives on Hall's efforts in performing and commissioning music in their full complexity. Whereas existing scholarship frames her straightforwardly as a rich lady who paid composers to write works that she could perform herself, the present chapter seeks to go beyond the clichés and highlight several aspects of Hall as a patron and performer. It situates her efforts against the background of early saxophone repertoire and the central role of female patrons at the turn of the nineteenth century.

Part II, 'Critical Organology & Social Identity,' features two chapters. Musical instruments are influential actors, responsible for the mediation of the "act of sound-making between the musician and the music."[23] Critical organology is therefore primarily concerned with investigating the "morphological, metaphorical, and historical contexts" in which instruments acquire and embody socially assigned characteristics.[24] Using this approach in tandem with an exploration of Hall's social identity allows us to illuminate the interconnected nature of the relationship between the saxophonist and the saxophone.

The first chapter that explores these themes is "Exhuming Elise: Rehabilitating Reputations" by Adrianne Honnold. This chapter explores Hall and the saxophone through a sociocultural, intersectional lens, examining how the convergence of gender, class, race, and hierarchical structures have influenced her narrative history and reputation and, by proxy, the saxophone's history. In the next chapter, "Instruments Telling History: Engaging Elise Hall through the Saxophone," Sarah McDonie uses Hall as a case study to explore how instruments actively participate in our engagement with the past, framing our viewpoints on the role that material culture plays in investigations of instrumentalists. In this part, a combination of methods is used from cultural studies, material studies, critical organology, and feminist musicology.

Part III, 'Beyond Elise Hall: Gender, Media & Culture in the 1920s,' includes two chapters that examine proximate topics correlating to the historical, social, and cultural environment of the United States in the 1920s, the end of the era in which Hall was active. Specifically, Sarah Hetrick's chapter "'He puts the pep in the party:' Gender and Iconography in 1920s Buescher Saxophone Advertisements" explores the ways that advertisements—a substantial part of the burgeoning mass media industry of the 1920s in the United States—were a catalyst for constructing some of the sociocultural connotations associated with the saxophone. The subsequent chapter, "Intersections of Gender, Genre, and Access: The Enterprising Career of Kathryne E. Thompson" by Holly Hubbs, presents a brief survey of the marginalization of other notable women in music and segues into a historical overview of an entrepreneurial saxophonist of the era named Kathryne E. Thompson.

This volume aims to reach an audience of scholars and instrumentalists from a broad range of disciplines within and adjacent to music and includes historical, social, and cultural perspectives. In terms of gender studies, there are a few examples of valuable discourse surrounding the saxophone's association with male players and masculinity that have been carried out in recent years, but this area of research requires further examination. Accordingly, this volume is poised to move the conversation on gender forward.

Spatial and temporal contexts illuminate an examination of Hall, as she was actively engaged in musical endeavors that contributed to the development of the burgeoning cultural institutions of the United States during the Gilded Age. Thus, readers are able to gain specific knowledge concerning one of the innovative women actively involved in arts organizations at the turn of the twentieth century, as well as a case study example of one individual's contributions to establishing the highbrow/lowbrow dichotomy that was being codified at the time.

The authors that have contributed chapters are saxophonists, and therefore others interested in critical organology and its general aim of understanding how musical instruments operate as actors with agency in human social environments will find worthwhile information here. The saxophone is an almost universally recognized instrument, but there are few critical examinations of the reciprocal exchange of influences that flow between it and the people—such as Hall—who play(ed) it. Hall's decision to choose the saxophone is a defining characteristic of her life in music, but her wealth, patronage, and position in society potentially would have earned her a place in the history books even if she had chosen a different instrument to play. Therefore, a general population of saxophonists will likely also be interested in this volume, especially considering that the global community is quite active in its engagement with saxophone-related investigations from both academic and applied domains. Indeed, Hall and the work she carried out performing, commissioning, and producing concerts is a somewhat mythological forebear (or spirit animal) to many members of the saxophone community who follow in her entrepreneurial footsteps. In many saxophonists' continued pursuit of a more permanent and revered position in classical music, we find Hall's career to be aspirational in some ways. In other ways, it is important to contextualize her life and career as simultaneously problematic (due to her family's history of colonization and perpetuation of hegemonic power relations), innovative (she was an impresario and the first woman to play the saxophone with an orchestra in the United States), and subject to the gender-based discrimination that prevailed at the turn of the twentieth century.

The scholarly inquiries in this volume are by no means exhaustive, but they do a meaningful job of pushing the boundaries of research into women and the saxophone by revisiting and re-contextualizing Elise Hall. One of the ways that this work is valuable is because four of the six chapters are written or co-written by women, and that has never been done before in studies of Hall and/or the saxophone.

We, the editors, hope that this volume will initiate conversations and inspire new avenues of inquiry into the way language is used, narratives are told, and histories are written, in addition to playing a crucial part in promoting equitable futures for saxophonists and scholars of all types. We hope that several of these essays will serve as a springboard to increase engagement with the saxophone in a broad range of scholarly studies and, conversely, bring methodologies from broader academic disciplines to illuminate saxophone studies.

NOTES

1. This international conference was organized by the *Koninklijk Conservatorium Brussel* and aimed at presenting the ongoing research by doctoral students, including a focus on the policy of practice-based ("artistic") research and historically informed performance practice.
2. For investigations into the early foundation of saxophone schools see for instance Kurt Bertels and Kristin Van den Buys, "The Brussels Saxophone School," *The Saxophone Symposium* 43 (2020): 71–87; Erik Abbink, "Saxophone Education and Performance in British Columbia: Early History and Current Practices" (PhD diss., The University of British Columbia, 2011); Joseph M. Murphy, "Early Saxophone Instruction in American Educational Institutions" (PhD diss., Northwestern University, 1994).
3. For an investigation into the history of saxophone pedagogy, see Pascal Terrien, *A History of the Saxophone Through Methods Published in France: 1846-1942*, trans. Sylvia Kahan (Sampzon: Éditions Delatour France, 2015); Gail Beth Levinsky, "An Analysis and Comparison of Early Saxophone Methods Published between 1846-1946" (PhD diss., Northwestern University, 1997).
4. Stephen Cottrell, *The Saxophone* (New Haven: Yale University Press, 2013), 243–246; Frederick Hemke, "The Early History of the Saxophone" (PhD diss., University of Wisconsin, 1975); William Henry Street, "Elise Boyer Hall, America's First Female Concert Saxophonist: Her Life as Performing Artist, Pioneer of Concert Repertory for Saxophone and Patroness of the Arts" (DMA diss., Northwestern University, 1983).
5. Street, "Elise Boyer Hall," 21. As Street notes, the hearing impairment was believed to be a result of typhoid fever.
6. James R. Noyes, "Elise Hall in Santa Barbara (1889-1898): The Amateur Musical Club and Philharmonic Society," *The Saxophone Symposium* 45 (2022): 75–93.
7. As stated by Noyes, Léon Vallas was one of the first to address Hall's deafness in his biography *Claude Debussy*. "He maintains that 'for the sake of her health,' she 'devoted herself' to the saxophone" (Noyes, "Elise Hall in Santa Barbara," 77–78).
8. Noyes, "Elise Hall in Santa Barbara," 78.
9. Holly J. Hubbs, "American Women Saxophonists From 1870-1930: Their Careers and Repertoire" (PhD diss., Ball State University Indiana, 2003); Thomas Smialek and L. A. Logrande, "Mrs. B. L. Hackenberger: Bessie Mecklem as Progressive-Era Clubwoman," *The Saxophone Symposium* 45 (2022): 50-74; Thomas Smialek and L. A. Logrande, "Asenath Mann: Boston's Gilded-Age Saxophonist," *The Saxophone Symposium* 45 (2022): 7–41; Thomas Smialek and L. A. Logrande, "Louise Linden: America's First Saxophone Virtuoso," *The Saxophone Symposium* 38-39 (2015-2016): 1–29.
10. Street, "Elise Boyer Hall," 4.
11. Street, "Elise Boyer Hall," 1–26.
12. For more information on Debussy's letters, see Street, "Elise Boyer Hall," 44–50; James R. Noyes, "Debussy's 'Rapsodie Pour Orchestre et Saxophone' Revisited," *The Musical Quarterly* 90, no. 3/4 (Fall – Winter 2007): 416–445, http://www.jstor.org/stable/25172879; Léon Vallas, *Claude Debussy: His Life and Works*, trans. Maire O' Brien and Grace O' Brien (Oxford: Oxford University Press, 1933).
13. Street, "Elise Boyer Hall," 26.
14. Vallas, *Claude Debussy*, 161–162.
15. References include: Ellen Koskoff, "When Women Play: The Relationship Between Musical Instruments and Gender Style," *Canadian University Music Review/Revue de Musique des Universités Canadiennes* 16, no. 1 (1995): 114–127; Veronica Doubleday, "Sounds of Power: An Overview of Musical Instruments and Gender," *Ethnomusicology Forum* 17, no. 1 (2008): 3–39; Karen J. Blair, *The Torchbearers: Women and Their Amateur Arts Associations in America, 1890-1930* (Bloomington: Indiana University Press, 1994); Naomi Schor, *Reading in Detail: Aesthetics and the Feminine* (New York: Routledge, 2013); Rita Steblin, "The Gender Stereotyping of Musical Instruments in the Western Tradition," *Canadian University Music Review/Revue de Musique des Universités Canadiennes* 16, no. 1 (1995): 128–144.
16. Catherine Strong and Sarah Raine (eds.), *Towards Gender Equality in the Music Industry: Education, Practice and Strategies for Change* (Bloomsbury: Publishing USA, 2019).
17. Susan McClary, *Feminine Endings: Music, Gender, and Sexuality* (Minneapolis: University of Minnesota Press, 2002).
18. McClary, *Feminine Endings*, x.
19. For the full reference, see footnote 3.
20. Paul Cohen, "The Saxophone Music of Charles Martin Loeffler," *The Saxophone Symposium* 6, no. 4 (Fall 1981): 10–17; Paul Cohen, "Vintage Saxophone Revisited: Early Professional Women Saxophonists," *Saxophone Journal*, no. 4 (July/August 1990): 8–13; Kurt Bertels, "Performing Dedications. A Contextual and Artistic Reflection on the Dedication of the World's First Saxophone Concerto," *FORUM+* 29, no. 3 (2022): 47–

53; Noyes, "Debussy's 'Rapsodie Pour Orchestre et Saxophone' Revisited."
21. For more information on intersectionality, see Kimberlé Crenshaw, "Demarginalizing the Intersection of Race and Sex: A Black Feminist Critique of Antidiscrimination Doctrine, Feminist Theory, and Antiracist Politics," *The University of Chicago Legal Forum* 7989, no. 1, Article 8 (1989): 139–67. This concept is also defined and further explored by Adrianne Honnold in part II.
22. For research on the performance practice of the nineteenth and early twentieth century, see Kurt Bertels, *Een ongehoord geluid* (Brussels: ASP Editions, 2020); Bertels, "Performing Dedications," 47–53.
23. Maria Sonevytsky, "The Accordion and Ethnic Whiteness: Toward a New Critical Organology," *The World of Music* 50(3) (2008): 101–118.
24. Ibid.

WORKS CITED

Abbink, Erik. "Saxophone Education and Performance in British Columbia: Early History and Current Practices." PhD diss., The University of British Columbia, 2011.

Bertels, Kurt. *Een ongehoord geluid. De saxofoonklas van het Koninklijk Conservatorium Brussel tussen 1867 en 1904*. Brussels: ASP Editions, 2020.

———. "Performing Dedications. A Contextual and Artistic Reflection on the Dedication of the World's First Saxophone Concerto." *FORUM+* 29, no. 3 (2022): 47–53.

Bertels, Kurt, and Kristin Van den Buys. "The Brussels Saxophone School." *The Saxophone Symposium* 43 (2020): 71–87.

Blair, Karen J. *The Torchbearers: Women and Their Amateur Arts Associations in America, 1890-1930*. Bloomington: Indiana University Press, 1994.

Cappabianca, Michael. "Elise Hall: An Interview with Paul Cohen." March 19, 2021. Accessed February 8, 2023. https://wam.rutgers.edu/elise-hall-an-interview-with-dr-paul-cohen/.

Cohen, Paul. "The Saxophone Music of Charles Martin Loeffler." *The Saxophone Symposium* 6, no. 4 (Fall 1981): 10–17.

Cohen, Paul. "Vintage Saxophone Revisited; Early Professional Women Saxophonists." *Saxophone Journal*, no. 4 (July/August 1990): 8–13.

Cottrell, Stephen. *The Saxophone*. New Haven: Yale University Press, 2013.

Crenshaw, Kimberlé. "Demarginalizing the Intersection of Race and Sex: A Black Feminist Critique of Antidiscrimination Doctrine, Feminist Theory, and Antiracist Politics." *The University of Chicago Legal Forum* 7989, no. 1, Article 8 (1989): 139–167.

Doubleday, Veronica. "Sounds of Power: An Overview of Musical Instruments and Gender." *Ethnomusicology Forum* 17, no. 1 (2008): 3–39.

Koskoff, Ellen. "When Women Play: The Relationship Between Musical Instruments and Gender Style." *Canadian University Music Review/Revue de Musique des Universités Canadiennes* 16, no. 1 (1995): 114–127.

Levinsky, Gail Beth. "An Analysis and Comparison of Early Saxophone Methods Published between 1846-1946." PhD diss., Northwestern University, 1997.

McClary, Susan. *Feminine Endings: Music, Gender, and Sexuality*. Minneapolis: University of Minnesota Press, 2002.

Murphy, Joseph M. "Early Saxophone Instruction in American Educational Institutions." PhD diss., Northwestern University, 1994.

Noyes, James R. "Debussy's 'Rapsodie Pour Orchestre et Saxophone' Revisited." *The Musical Quarterly* 90, no. 3/4 (Fall – Winter 2007): 416–445.

———. "Elise Hall in Santa Barbara (1889-1898): The Amateur Musical Club and Philharmonic Society." *The Saxophone Symposium* 45 (2023): 75–93.

Schor, Naomi. *Reading in Detail: Aesthetics and the Feminine*. New York: Routledge, 2013.

Sonevytsky, Maria. "The Accordion and Ethnic Whiteness: Toward a New Critical Organology." *The World of Music* 50(3) (2008): 101–118.

Steblin, Rita. "The Gender Stereotyping of Musical Instruments in the Western Tradition." *Canadian University Music Review/Revue de Musique des Universités Canadiennes* 16 (1) (1995): 128–144.

Street, William Henry. "Elise Boyer Hall, America's First Female Concert Saxophonist: Her Life as Performing Artist, Pioneer of Concert Repertory for Saxophone and Patroness of the Arts." DMA diss., Northwestern University, 1983.

Strong, Catherine, and Sarah Raine, eds. *Towards Gender Equality in the Music Industry: Education, Practice and Strategies for Change*. New York: Bloomsbury Academic, 2019.

Terrien, Pascal (ed.). *A History of the Saxophone Through Methods Published in France: 1846-1942*. Edited and translated by Sylvia Kahan. Sampzon: Editions Delatour France, 2015.

Vallas, Léon. *Claude Debussy: His Life and Works*. Translated by Maire O'Brien and Grace O'Brien. Oxford: Oxford University Press, 1933.

PART I

Histories

"Incomparable Virtuoso"
A Reevaluation of the Performance Abilities of Elise Boyer Hall

Andrew J. Allen

ABSTRACT

Although Elise Hall's efforts at commissioning and performing with high-quality amateur groups have been thoroughly documented and examined, anecdotally her performance skills are frequently underrated by the saxophone community. She participated in several high-profile professional performances starting in 1904, including appearances with the Longy Club, the Paris performances of 1904-1906, a concert with the Boston Symphony Orchestra in 1909, and her all-professional "Mrs. Hall's Concerts" of 1908 onward. The attendant positive reviews from all of the above point to the fact that Hall has often been critically undervalued as a saxophonist. Through the examination of advertisements, concert announcements, and periodicals of the era, this chapter demonstrates that Hall was an artist of the highest caliber.

Introduction

Many saxophonists who are acquainted with historical accounts of Elise Hall's life and career have developed the opinion that she was an eccentric novice who was, at best, a mediocre performer. She is commonly presented in historical accounts of the past as a wealthy white woman with the time and ambition to take up the saxophone and commission several renowned composers to write music for the nascent instrument. It is the intention of this chapter to forever lay the negative assessments to rest, using primary source materials contemporary to Hall's career, especially from the time period of 1904 onward. In order to reevaluate the prevalence of unfavorable assessments of Hall's saxophone skills, newspaper and magazine accounts and concert advertisements found in programs of the Boston Symphony Orchestra from the time period are examined.

These examples illustrate that Hall was consistently recognized for her performance abilities as well as her commissioning and concert production activities.

From the beginning, Hall received praise for her playing, far above that of her peers. Following the financial and social freedom accorded her with the death of her husband, she quickly progressed from skilled amateur to professional-level performer, commissioned widely, and played in prominent concert halls in the United States and France. She increasingly surrounded herself with the best musicians available as her collaborators. Throughout her career, she exhibited an extremely high seriousness of purpose, both in her activities as a performer and as an impresario of concerts of contemporary music. In some ways, her efforts toward creating new works and performing them compare favorably to those of other prominent saxophonists and dedicatees of canonic works of a later era, such as Sigurd Raschèr and Marcel Mule.[1] While there is no evidence that Mrs. Hall was paid for her performances, this chapter offers evidence that she, indeed, consciously pursued a career as a professional-level performer from 1904 until near the end of her life. For her efforts, she was lauded in the highest terms by critics, especially from 1905 onward, and many of her performance activities from this period forward were undertaken largely with professional musicians. The previous dismissive considerations of Hall's work have been due partially to a lack of pertinent information and partially to the blatant misogyny of early sources which appears to have warped perceptions of the saxophonist in otherwise well-intentioned studies of her life and work; in this regard, the influence of Vallas has been especially pernicious and is noted below. No matter the cause, the solution is clear: we must evaluate the true historical record and place Hall in the pantheon (or, due to her pioneering spirit and courage, at the head) of the great early saxophone performers.

Several sources have traced Hall's musical activities, but many have positioned her as either a dilettante or as a well-meaning benefactor of the saxophone, rather than as a serious musician, and these sources provide a foundation for the saxophone community's general dismissal of her abilities. One of the earliest treatments of Hall appears in Léon Vallas's *Claude Debussy: His Life and Works*, originally published in English in 1933. Vallas is conspicuously misogynistic in his description of the saxophonist. He imagines Debussy's reaction to the *Société Nationale* performance of 1904 (discussed below) as follows: "He thought it ridiculous to see a lady in a pink frock playing on such an ungainly instrument; and he was not at all anxious that his work should provide a similar spectacle."[2] Vallas's defamation is countered effectively in an article by James Noyes, "Debussy's 'Rapsodie Pour Orchestra et Saxophone' Revisited," in which the author discusses correspondence from Debussy that speaks of Hall in a positive manner.[3]

In Frederick Hemke's 1975 dissertation, "The Early History of the Saxophone," the author sheds valuable light on many of Hall's most prominent commissions but pays little attention to her role as performer. Since historical sources influencing his work appear to have been minimal, he sometimes ornamented his account of Hall's life, injecting his subjectivities and drawing negative conclusions. For example, he assumes she took up the saxophone due to her life becoming "extremely listless and apathetic."[4] Later, he asserts that the compositions written for Hall were "geared for a performer who has not mastered a great deal of technique."[5]

Hemke also makes a claim at knowing the thoughts and emotions of a person long-dead when he states that "Alfred Cortot…led a nervous Mrs. Hall through the concert of the *Société nationale*," whereas contemporary accounts (noted below) point to a confident and assured performance.[6] In general, Hemke seems unaware of American performances by Hall outside of those with the Boston Orchestral Club. Indeed, he assumes her concert of March 11, 1912, discussed below, was performed with the amateur ensemble, instead of with a cast of professionals. He also implies that her career came to a close after this performance. This idea is thoroughly refuted in the paragraphs to follow here.[7] Hemke's 1977 article "The Fairer Sax," is a re-packaging of the account of Hall found in the dissertation.[8] Two of the standard saxophone references, Cottrell's *The Saxophone* and *The Cambridge Companion to the Saxophone* are both heavily influenced by Hemke's approach in their accounts of Hall's life and activities.[9] They make no mention of Hall's performance abilities, rather, they only discuss her efforts at commissioning literature.

David Whitwell's book *The Longy Club: A Professional Wind Ensemble in Boston (1900-1917)* offers invaluable context regarding a fully professional ensemble, led by Georges Longy, that called upon Hall as a performer at least three times on public concerts across eight years.[10] In addition, Valerie Gudell's dissertation, "Georges Longy: His Life and Legacy," offers additional context for the professional relationship between Hall and her frequent colleague and collaborator.[11]

Any research on Hall is deeply indebted to the work of William Street. In his dissertation, he laid the groundwork for explorations of the pioneer that would follow.[12] While Street fully acknowledged Hall's role as a performer, as well as that of patron, he did not explore the particulars and implications of her professional-level performances. A comprehensive examination of Hall's reception, sociocultural considerations, and performance practices were likely outside the purview of the thesis and subject to the constraints of the time period in which it was written.

A review of some of the works that feature a sociological approach to examining women's music clubs of the Gilded Age has been extremely helpful in framing Hall's activities. Her first public performances took place in the context of music clubs. Carol Neuls-Bales (in the book *Women in Music*) observed,

> The women's club movement, which gained striking momentum late in the nineteenth century both in Europe and the United States, was an unprecedented phenomenon that provided middle- and upper-class women with the opportunity for self-development and the betterment of their communities, as well as a means of overcoming isolation at home… In the United States, where men by default "left culture to the ladies," club women were the chief promoters of cultural interests throughout the nation.[13]

While Hall's initial work, especially in Santa Barbara, seems to mirror the description above, the increasing professionalization of both her own performances and those concerts that she organized show that Hall departed from this model in enterprising ways.

Anna Bull's *Class, Control, and Classical Music* gives a great deal of context to the artistic world that Hall inhabited. In the English-speaking nations of the late nineteenth- and early twentieth-centuries, a model of bourgeois womanhood emerged that centered on a life of childbearing and domestic labor. Due to upper-class moral hegemony, any other work was viewed as suspect. As a result, most professional women musicians in the nineteenth- and early twentieth-centuries were from the lower or middle classes.[14] Hall's wealth may have actually freed her to do something novel: to pursue a professional-level musical career, while being able to do without any actual pay for her labor. While unjust, this, along with her social class and wealth, would have allowed the saxophonist to sidestep the moral strictures of her time.

Bull also states that musical achievement for the upper classes in Hall's era was mainly viewed as being for recreation or for the entertainment of male relatives.[15] Due to the gender stereotypes established primarily to appease the "hypervigilant" male gaze, women were largely prohibited from playing wind instruments.[16] Hall subverted both of these norms, performing in and producing concerts intended for large paying audiences, and she proudly embraced the saxophone, despite the antagonistic nature of Vallas and the uncritical reviewers that followed.

Bull also contends that the Romantic-era orchestra was "a bourgeois fantasy of male control," with one dictatorial leader directing the masses of the ensemble. In fact, she gives an example of the abuses of this system in Hall's own city: in the late 1880s, Henry Higginson, the founder of the Boston Symphony, would summarily fire musicians for performing in any capacity outside of his orchestra.[17] The example of Hall and Longy (in his role as conductor of the Boston Orchestral Club and "Mrs. Hall's Concerts") again subverts the dominant model: Hall and Longy were at the very least equals in the execution of administrative duties. Evidence suggests that, in the end, Hall may have been the more dominant personality and musical force, as explored below.

Performances that are considered to be representative of Hall's overall career are further explored in the part that follows, with a focus on those that featured professional musicians who collaborated with the saxophonist. Contemporary reviews, from both the American and French media, serve as contemporary accounts of her playing ability.

The Earliest Performances

By March 1892, Hall was already playing saxophone and performing as a member of the Santa Barbara Amateur Music Club.[18] In September 1895, her husband, Dr. Hall, was elected president of the Santa Barbara Philharmonic Club, but by January 30, 1896, Mrs. Hall had taken over these duties.[19] That evening in January, she performed Köhler's *Bon Soir* and Messler's *It Was Not So to Be* on a program of the Society, accompanied by a string quartet. She was met by "the universal applause of the audience."[20] On October 28 of the same year, she performed excerpts from Flotow's *Martha* on another program of the Philharmonic Society.[21]

Hall's future as a producer of serious concerts is foreshadowed by an event interrupted by tragedy. In January 1897, Mrs. Hall was preparing for a music festival. It was billed as the "society event of the week" of January 18, and it was to feature two evenings filled with concerts.[22] Mrs. Hall had engaged professional vocal soloists and a chorus of seventy local musicians for a grand performance.[23] Rehearsals with a large orchestra were scheduled to begin at seven in the evening on Wednesday, January 20, but, suddenly, all came to a halt: Dr. Hall became violently ill with a case of pneumonia that quickly spiraled out of control.[24] He would succumb in a matter of days, with his funeral held on Tuesday, January 26. Hall was suddenly a widow.[25]

On February 6, 1897, Richard Hall's last will and testament was filed with the probate court, and Hall petitioned for appointment as the executor of the estate. The will stated that all of Dr. Hall's property would go directly to Mrs. Hall to do with as she pleased.[26] Notably, contemporary accounts indicate that Dr.

Hall's estate was of a nominal value.[27] While she may not have received much in the way of financial resources from her late husband, she was endowed with legal and social freedom due to the dictates of his will, and her family's money assured her a consequential amount of economic comfort. In 1898, Hall and her daughters moved back east into her mother's Beacon Street townhome in Boston.[28] Her true musical career would soon begin.

The Boston Orchestral Club

In 1899, Hall began her association with Georges Longy, a French oboe player and conductor newly arrived in Boston for a position with the Boston Symphony Orchestra. What initially started as a student-teacher relationship, with Longy serving as a musical coach for Hall, soon turned into a quarter-century-long musical partnership and friendship. Hall reorganized a dormant organization, the Boston Orchestral Club, in the fall of 1899, and recommended Longy for the position of conductor.[29]

The membership of the Boston Orchestral Club was amateur and decidedly upper-class.[30] While Hall organized and funded the group, she initially served only as a performer and member of the music committee. She became committee chair in 1902, and, finally, president in 1904. As Hall gained more authority within the organization, however, a peculiar thing happened: it went from being an ensemble playing classics to one performing contemporary works, mostly by French composers. In fact, under Hall's leadership, the local media often treated the club as the city's second orchestra. It gave the Boston and American premieres of several works.[31] Indeed, Debussy's *Prélude à l'après-midi d'un faune*, *Hamlet* by Berlioz, and Mussorgsky's *Night on Bald Mountain* all received their first performances in the United States by the ensemble.[32] Hall's ambitions were far above those of most musicians associated with club life.

On the first concert of the reconstituted Boston Orchestral Club on January 31, 1900, Hall was singled out for her performance on *L'Arlésienne, Suite 1* by Bizet. The *Musical Courier* wrote that "Mrs. Hall played the saxophone solo admirably."[33] By the group's April 27, 1900 performance, the reviewer wrote that "of the soloists, Mrs. Hall with her warm, authoritative playing, and her unusual, beautiful instrument, led."[34] Writing of a March 1903 chamber concert hosted by Julia Terry, the correspondent for the *Boston Evening Transcript* stated, "In these works Mrs. Hall displayed to advantage the breadth and musical beauty of her phrasing, and likewise the wonderful sonority of her instrument."[35] These favorable appraisals seem to indicate that she was more than a dilettante.

1904 Longy Club Performance

The year 1904 potentially marked a turning point in the career of Hall. Along with the amateur Boston Orchestral Club, she increasingly appeared with all-professional groups. The Longy Club had been founded by Hall's friend, collaborator, and ally Georges Longy in 1900. From the beginning, the club was a novel, mutable wind chamber ensemble whose normal members included pairs of flutists, oboe players, clarinetists, bassoonists, and horn players. All regular performers were also full-time members of the Boston Symphony Orchestra, and Longy would often call upon other professional musicians from the BSO to perform works for larger forces.[36]

On January 25, 1904, Hall made her first appearance with the group, on the second concert of their fourth season. She played Charles Martin Loeffler's *Ballade Carnavalesque* for flute, oboe, saxophone, bassoon, and piano. While the reviewer was critical of the work, they stated, "the most strikingly beautiful passage was one for saxophone solo, with pianoforte accompaniment."[37] Hall's playing had attracted praise from a professional critic, on a professional concert, even when the writer was critical of the local composer on the program. It seems that the work fell far short of the player, in contrast to the usual judgments levied against Hall.

Despite the minimal coverage of Hall, it is remarkable that the reviewer had kind words for her performance. The concert also featured two vocalists, "Mr. and Mrs. Charles Gilibert." Charles Gilibert was lauded on two continents as an operatic baritone. Trained at the Paris Conservatory, he had performed at the *Opéra-Comique*, the Metropolitan Opera, and Covent Garden.[38] Despite his prestige, however, the reviewer for *The Boston Evening Transcript* harshly criticized him and his wife, stating:

> Of Mr. Gilibert it is necessary to say only that he was by no means at his best. Not in good voice, he sang with much art, which, however, frequently degenerated into artfulness, so unspontaneous did it seem. Extravagance, too, was not absent from his work. Of Mrs. Gilibert it is necessary to say still less. She has a very small voice, the lower and middle tones of which are not disagreeable. Despite the fact that she produces this thread of a voice very unskillfully and sings frequently out of tune, Mrs. Gilibert has at her disposal a certain cleverness such as we imagine most French people to have. She sings facilely, making rhetorical points with some skill, and, in short, might well have received what artistic training she has had on the opera bouffe stage.[39]

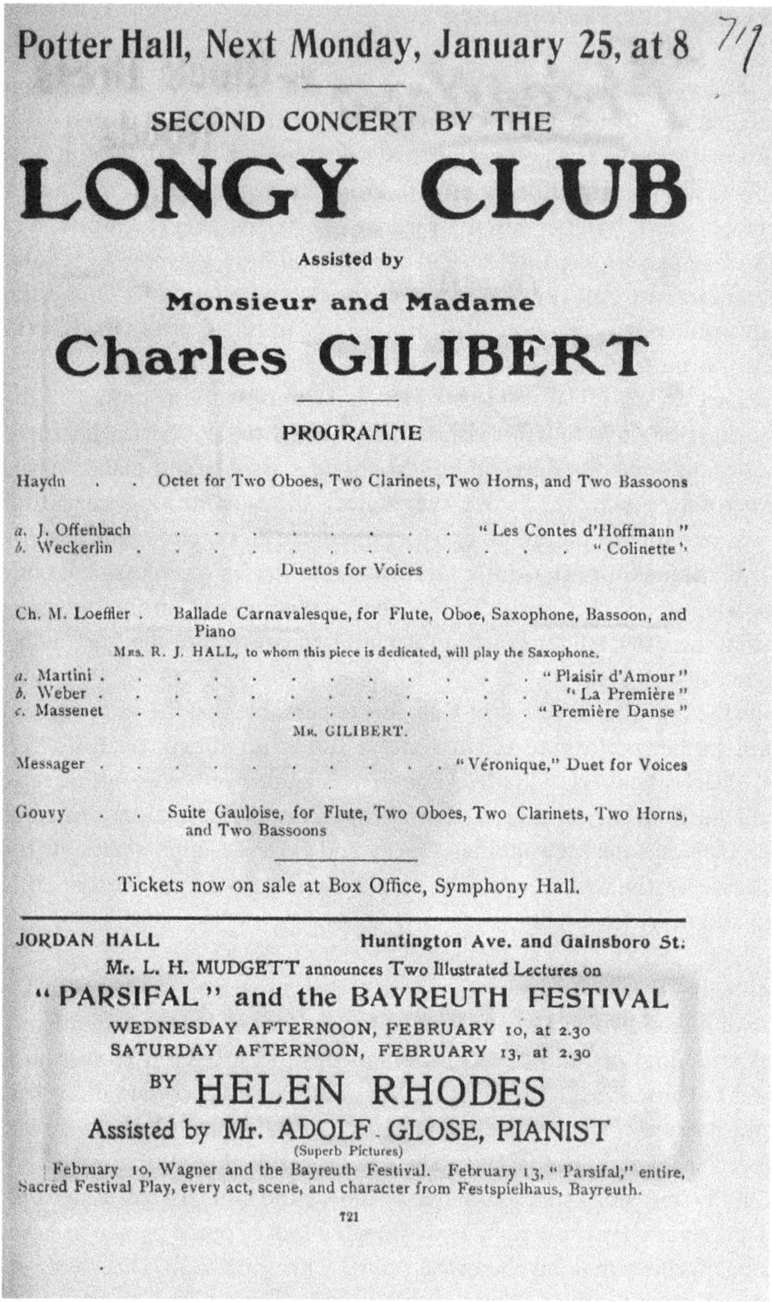

Potter Hall, Next Monday, January 25, at 8

SECOND CONCERT BY THE

LONGY CLUB

Assisted by

Monsieur and Madame

Charles GILIBERT

PROGRAMME

Haydn . . Octet for Two Oboes, Two Clarinets, Two Horns, and Two Bassoons

a. J. Offenbach . . . . "Les Contes d'Hoffmann"
b. Weckerlin . . . . "Colinette"
Duettos for Voices

Ch. M. Loeffler . Ballade Carnavalesque, for Flute, Oboe, Saxophone, Bassoon, and Piano
Mrs. R. J. HALL, to whom this piece is dedicated, will play the Saxophone.

a. Martini . . . . "Plaisir d'Amour"
b. Weber . . . . "La Première"
c. Massenet . . . . "Première Danse"
Mr. GILIBERT.

Messager . . . . "Véronique," Duet for Voices

Gouvy . . Suite Gauloise, for Flute, Two Oboes, Two Clarinets, Two Horns, and Two Bassoons

Tickets now on sale at Box Office, Symphony Hall.

JORDAN HALL   Huntington Ave. and Gainsboro St.
Mr. L. H. MUDGETT announces Two Illustrated Lectures on
"PARSIFAL" and the BAYREUTH FESTIVAL
WEDNESDAY AFTERNOON, FEBRUARY 10, at 2.30
SATURDAY AFTERNOON, FEBRUARY 13, at 2.30

BY HELEN RHODES
Assisted by Mr. ADOLF GLOSE, PIANIST
(Superb Pictures)
February 10, Wagner and the Bayreuth Festival. February 13, "Parsifal," entire, Sacred Festival Play, every act, scene, and character from Festspielhaus, Bayreuth.

Figure 1.1. Advertisement for January 1904 Longy Club Concert[40]

One thing appears manifest: in her first outing with a professional ensemble, Hall did more than survive. She performed admirably with professional musicians, and, at least in the case of the Giliberts, her performance exceeded expectations.

The 1904 *Société Nationale* Concert

On May 17, 1904, Elise Hall gave a remarkable performance by some accounts. Firstly, she played Vincent d'Indy's *Choral Varié* with a professional orchestra for the musical cognoscenti of France, at a concert of the *Société Nationale de Musique*. The *Société* was founded in 1871 by Camille Saint-Saëns to improve the quality of French concert music. By 1904, the organization represented the highest ideals of the French musical tradition, and often spoke for the more conservative elements in musical society; yet here was an American woman, playing the saxophone, on this most august of French stages.[41] Secondly, looking beyond the unfettered misogyny of the French critics, one can detect a respect that they begrudgingly bestowed upon Hall after the performance. The correspondents could find nothing to fault in her playing, so instead they resorted to non sequitur, ad hominem attacks:

> I would never have imagined that the fancy would come to a lady to practice the saxophone and become a *virtuoso* [emphasis added] in this thankless specialty. Mrs. Elise Hall made the trip from America to France on purpose to prove to us that the thing was possible. This forms a rather bizarre and, to tell the truth, ungraceful spectacle, which does little to show off feminine graces. But Mrs. Hall does not care and blows imperturbably into her copper pipe, like a man.[42]

As another critic decried: "M. d'Indy's chorale for saxophone is very good, and Mrs. Elise Hall *played it very well, with a beautiful sound* [emphasis added], but frankly, this instrument hardly befits the fair sex."[43] The Paris correspondent for *The New York Times* was laudatory without the chauvinism, presumably because it was written for an American audience:

> Mme Elise Hall, an American musician and conductress, was the chief attraction this evening at a grand orchestral concert given at the Nouveau Theatre by the Société Nationale de Musique. She played a saxophone solo in Vincent d'Indy's *Choral Varié* for saxophone and orchestra, which was

produced tonight for the first time. *The composition was much applauded, as was also Mme. Hall's masterly execution.* [emphasis added][44]

As of May 1904, the month of this performance, the Parisian musical scene was unquestionably male-dominated. No woman had ever been admitted to any of the wind instrument classes of the Paris Conservatory, effectively barring them from professional life as brass and woodwind players.[45] And yet, there was Hall, performing as a soloist with a professional orchestra on her saxophone: A "virtuoso" with "masterly execution."

1905 Longy Club Performance

At the Longy Club's January 19, 1905 concert, Hall joined the ensemble for the world premieres of Longy's *Lento in c# minor* for saxophone solo, two clarinets, bassoon, double bass, three kettledrums, and harp; and Caplet's *Legende*.[46] The *Boston Evening Transcript's* reporter spent the majority of the review on Hall and the new works:

> The interest of the occasion was mostly aroused by the two pieces for saxophone, both of which were written to be performed by Mrs. Hall. Heretofore there has been little literature for the saxophone, and it is the art of Mrs. Hall that has inspired such composers as Caplet, Mr. Longy, and Mr. Loeffler to make experiments for the instrument, to see what may be done with it in the way of chamber music. Mr. Longy's piece is peculiar in that it requires greater bravura in saxophone playing than we have been accustomed to hear. The music is practically a saxophone solo, the other instruments being used chiefly for color or dramatic effect… [A]lthough it may be doubted if either Mr. Longy's or Caplet's piece will ever gain a place in the repertory of chamber music, there is no question that both composers have done useful service in providing to the world the value of the saxophone in chamber music. Mrs. Hall, who has gained appreciably in her art since she last appeared in public, played admirably indeed, with very beautiful tone, with frequent exquisite phrasing, and often with extreme brilliance of execution. If the saxophone ever gains recognition as an instrument for chamber concerts, it will be largely due to Mrs. Hall.[47]

Works featuring Hall made up half the program for this concert. Again, the reviewer praises her more highly than the pieces she performed.

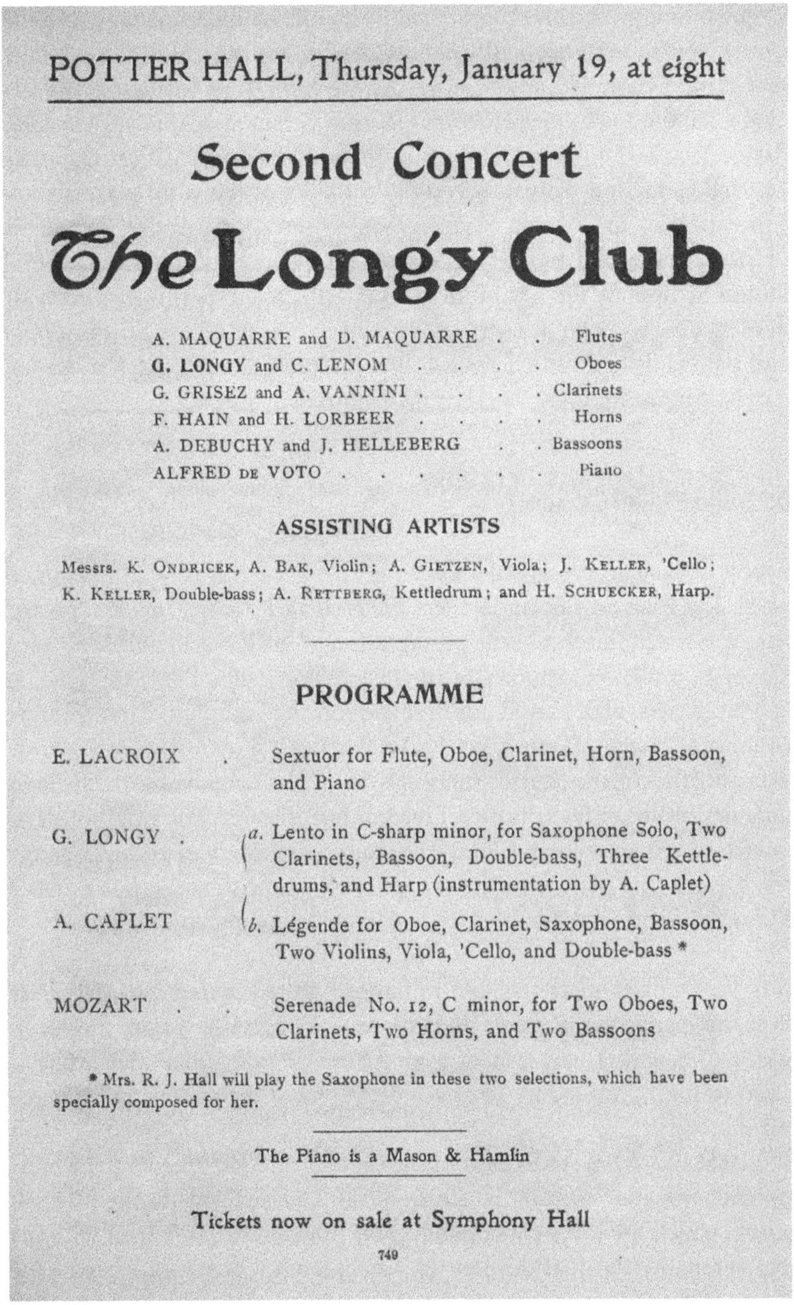

POTTER HALL, Thursday, January 19, at eight

Second Concert

The Longy Club

A. MAQUARRE and D. MAQUARRE . . Flutes
G. LONGY and C. LENOM . . . . Oboes
G. GRISEZ and A. VANNINI . . . . Clarinets
F. HAIN and H. LORBEER . . . . Horns
A. DEBUCHY and J. HELLEBERG . . Bassoons
ALFRED DE VOTO . . . . . . Piano

ASSISTING ARTISTS

Messrs. K. ONDRICEK, A. BAK, Violin; A. GIETZEN, Viola; J. KELLER, 'Cello; K. KELLER, Double-bass; A. RETTBERG, Kettledrum; and H. SCHUECKER, Harp.

PROGRAMME

E. LACROIX . Sextuor for Flute, Oboe, Clarinet, Horn, Bassoon, and Piano

G. LONGY . *a.* Lento in C-sharp minor, for Saxophone Solo, Two Clarinets, Bassoon, Double-bass, Three Kettle-drums, and Harp (instrumentation by A. Caplet)

A. CAPLET *b.* Légende for Oboe, Clarinet, Saxophone, Bassoon, Two Violins, Viola, 'Cello, and Double-bass *

MOZART . Serenade No. 12, C minor, for Two Oboes, Two Clarinets, Two Horns, and Two Bassoons

* Mrs. R. J. Hall will play the Saxophone in these two selections, which have been specially composed for her.

The Piano is a Mason & Hamlin

Tickets now on sale at Symphony Hall

749

Figure 1.2. Advertisement for January 1905 Longy Club Concert[48]

Hall's collaborators on this program were all professional musicians, and she was the only woman included in the concert.[49] The core members of the Longy Club were as follows: flutists and brothers André and Daniel Maquarre, oboists Longy and Clément Lenom, clarinetists Georges Grisez and Augusto Vannini, horn players Frank Hain and Heinrich Lorbeer, bassoonists Albert Debuchy and John Helleberg, and pianist Alfred de Voto. All of the wind players were regular members of the Boston Symphony Orchestra, and André Maquarre, Longy, Grisez, and Debuchy were all principal chairs.[50] In addition, several other Boston Symphony Orchestra members participated on this concert: violinists Karl Ondricek (who also served as concertmaster of the Boston Pops) and Adolf Bak, violist Alfred Gietzen, cellist Joseph Keller, bassist Karl Keller, percussionist August Rettberg, and harpist Heinrich Schuecker.[51]

1905 Salle Pleyel Concert

In May 1905, Hall again presented a Paris performance, this time in the famed Salle Pleyel. The Paris correspondent for *The New York Daily Tribune* reported that "there was much interest in the presentation to the Parisian public by Mrs. Elize [sic] Hall, a Boston virtuoso, of the instrument called the saxophone, at the Salle Pleyel. Mrs. Hall played admirably upon the saxophone, interpreting compositions of Vincent d'Indy and Charles Loeffler."[52]

Concerning the concert, the journal *Paris Musical et Dramatique* published a congratulatory profile of Hall. Its direct recounting of her artistic ambitions and performance career are telling. Clearly, the journalist interviewed both Longy and Hall directly. The picture of the saxophonist is unequivocal: not a casual amateur, but, rather, a "remarkable artist," and an "incomparable virtuoso."

> And if we are particularly pleased to have to write the name of Mrs. Elise Hall at the beginning of these lines today, it is because we are aware, in speaking of her work, not only of paying homage to a remarkable artist … but also to fulfill[ing] a duty of gratitude to one of the noblest benefactors of our musical art.
>
> Mrs. Elise Hall … came to Paris at the age of twelve. After receiving the most comprehensive education at the Couvent des Oiseaux, she devoted herself to music, which she loves passionately. This innate taste combined with the ardent sympathy she had devoted to our country, encouraged her to the in-depth study of our masters. At the same time … she assiduously studied the saxophone, and became an incomparable virtuoso.

If the names and works of our illustrious musicians are now better known on the other side of the Atlantic, it is to the perseverance of Mrs. Hall and Mr. Longy that we owe it.[53]

1906 Salle Pleyel Concert

On June 1, 1906, Hall gave yet another concert in the Salle Pleyel as an orchestral soloist.[54] As one Parisian critic recorded:

> It was a delicate treat for the distinguished and numerous public who had flocked to this manifestation of art, that the hearing of the symphonies and melodies composed by the elite of our experienced musicians for Mrs. Hall and interpreted by her masterfully on the saxophone, the orchestra, composed of our most remarkable solo musicians from the Opéra and the Opéra-Comique, being conducted by M. Longy with that certainty and that sense of nuance which characterizes him…
>
> We had the rare pleasure of hearing *Impression d'Automne* … by André Caplet; *Malagnegna*, by G. Pessard; *La Tompe des Alpes*, by A. Chauvet, and an exquisite composition by M. G. Longy entitled *Impression*, very warmly applauded.[55]

Julien Torchet, writing for *Le Guide Musical* gave even greater detail, as well as warm plaudits for Hall:

> If you were a great lady, passionate about music and mistress of a very large fortune, would you come up with the idea of diverting part of it to the propagation of the saxophone; I doubt it. You would think that this instrument does not yet have enough nobility to deserve this sacrifice, and you would rather reserve the surplus of your wealth for the glory of the organ, the violin, or the piano. An American, Mrs. Hall, in love with the saxophone, has dedicated herself to the study of this instrument and plays it as a talented virtuoso. But, as there is little ad hoc music, she commissions, every year, from young musicians special works where, of course, the main part is reserved for the saxophone, and has them edited and performed at her expense… Mrs. Hall comes to Paris every year to give a hearing of new compositions of this genre… For Mrs. Hall, I have only one word to say about her talent: her virtuosity is undeniable, her very pure style and the sound she draws from her instrument is both soft and full; her success has therefore been lively and deserved.[56]

While this was the last recorded Parisian concert, Hall had established herself as an international soloist. She performed with accompanying ensembles of established professionals. Finally, she garnered critical acclaim from members of the media. Hall was a serious artist, drawing unprecedented attention for her instrument from the musical establishment. This recognition would not be replicated for twenty-five years, until the rise of the aforementioned soloists Mule and Raschèr.

A New Tradition: The 1908 "Mrs. Hall's Concert"

On January 21, 1908, Hall organized a concert. Instead of calling on the amateur forces of the Boston Orchestral Club, she assembled a ninety-member orchestra (fifty of whom were regular members of the Boston Symphony Orchestra) for a program of contemporary music, to be conducted by Georges Longy. After the concert, the reviewer for *The Boston Evening Transcript* stated: "Mrs. Hall is well known for her sincere devotion to French music of the modern school, as well as her untiring efforts on behalf of musical progress." Hall performed as soloist on d'Indy's *Choral Varié* on this concert.[57] The evening also featured the Boston premieres of Balakirev's *In Bohemia* and Rabuad's *Symphony in e minor*.[58]

This event could be seen as the beginning of a new era for Hall. From this point, she seems to have gradually reduced the activities of the Boston Orchestral Club, with its amateur performers and stodgy social requirements, in favor of calling upon professional-caliber musicians. It can also be seen as a change in Hall's role. With the Boston Orchestral Club, she was the leader of a part-artistic, part-social organization. With the establishment of "Mrs. Hall's Concert," she can be viewed instead as an impresario, a producer of professional contemporary music performances.

1909 "Mrs. Hall's Concert"

While records are spotty, it appears that these concerts became at least a semi-annual tradition: the 1909 edition was dedicated to the works of Henry Woollett; it also included pieces by César Franck and Nikolai Rimsky-Korsakov and was a novel mix of orchestral and chamber music.[59] Hall herself appears to have only performed on one piece: Woollett's *Danses Païennes* for saxophone, two flutes, cello, and harp.[60] Her fellow musicians on the work were flutists André Maquarre and Arthur Brooke, cellist Josef Keller, and harpist Heinrich

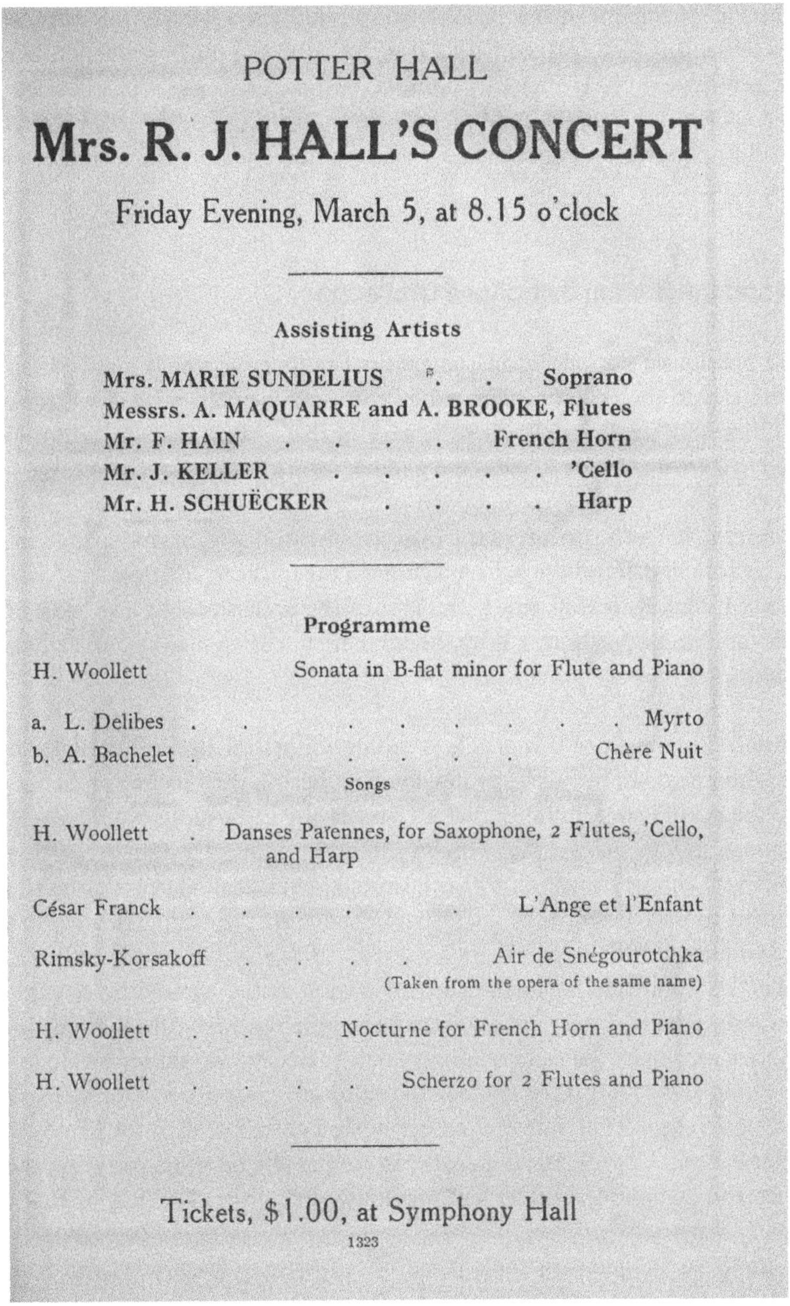

POTTER HALL

Mrs. R. J. HALL'S CONCERT

Friday Evening, March 5, at 8.15 o'clock

Assisting Artists

Mrs. MARIE SUNDELIUS . . . Soprano
Messrs. A. MAQUARRE and A. BROOKE, Flutes
Mr. F. HAIN . . . . French Horn
Mr. J. KELLER . . . . 'Cello
Mr. H. SCHUËCKER . . . . Harp

Programme

H. Woollett — Sonata in B-flat minor for Flute and Piano

a. L. Delibes . . . . Myrto
b. A. Bachelet . . . . . Chère Nuit
Songs

H. Woollett . Danses Païennes, for Saxophone, 2 Flutes, 'Cello, and Harp

César Franck . . . . . L'Ange et l'Enfant

Rimsky-Korsakoff . . . . Air de Snégourotchka
(Taken from the opera of the same name)

H. Woollett . . . Nocturne for French Horn and Piano

H. Woollett . . . Scherzo for 2 Flutes and Piano

Tickets, $1.00, at Symphony Hall
1325

Figure 1.3. Advertisement for 1909 edition of "MRS. R. J. HALL'S CONCERT"[61]

Schuecker, all members of the Boston Symphony. The reviewer for *Musical America* stated that Hall "played with a rich, full tone and much brilliance. She was recalled several times after this number."[62] Thus, while she was still a featured soloist on this concert and received praise from the press, this concert shows a shift towards an equal capacity as a producer and artistic director of concerts, expanding Hall's role.

Hall and the Boston Symphony Orchestra

Hall had previously performed in professional settings in which many musicians with ties to the BSO participated, but in 1910 she collaborated with the orchestra in an official capacity. In February of that year, a startling editorial appeared in *The New Music Review and Church Music Review*:

> We observe that at a concert of the Boston Symphony Orchestra ... the saxophone solo in Bizet's *Suite No. 1*, taken from the music to "L'Arlésienne" was played by Mrs. R. J. Hall, not a member of the orchestra, but a woman of wealth and social position… Why should there not be women in our leading orchestras, if they are proficient?[63]

While brief, the subtext of this article is profound: first of all, Hall performed onstage with a regular, full-time, professional orchestra, for a paying audience. Second, she played so admirably that a critic of the early 1900s would use it as an opportunity to suggest that women should be allowed to join orchestras when this was almost unheard of in the United States. Hall appears to be the first woman to ever perform as an instrumentalist in the orchestra with the Boston Symphony.[64]

While this editorial was unsigned, it was apparently astounding enough to be picked up by wire services and reprinted in newspapers throughout the country. In a reprint by the *Deseret News* of Salt Lake City, the author was identified as Philip Hale.[65] If this is true, then the editorialist was a first-hand witness to this historic event. Hale was the regular Boston correspondent for *The New Music Review and Church Music Review*, as well as the program notes writer for the Boston Symphony, and he had previously written approvingly of Hall's activities.[66]

The program in question took place on Christmas Eve, 1909, and was repeated the next day.[67] Hale is credited with writing the program notes for these concerts, and they were led by the conductor Max Fiedler.⁶⁸ An unidentified review in Allen Brown's *Boston Symphony Orchestra Scrapbooks* paints a more complete picture:

> Mrs. R. J. Hall of Bay State Road is the first woman to play an instrument in the Boston Symphony Orchestra. Yesterday afternoon, when a saxophone player was taken suddenly ill, Mrs. Hall consented to take his place. Mrs. Hall played the difficult solo parts in the "L'Arlesienne" of Bizet without the slightest hesitation and was warmly applauded.
> It was a novel sight and one which was thoroughly appreciated by the lovers of good music, for it required superb pluck and courage as well as skill to carry through the performance. Had Mrs. Hall not proved equal to the task, the orchestra would have been seriously embarrassed… The fact that this social leader was such an adept at the saxophone was known to but comparatively few people and there was considerable surprise when she took her place in the orchestra yesterday.⁶⁹

Olin Downes, writing in *Musical America* in January 1910, stated:

> In the … first suite from Bizet's music to "L'Arlesienne" Mrs. R. J. Hall of this city played the saxophone solo… Mrs. Hall, a musician of uncommon attainments, has been for years a pupil of Georges Longy, the first oboeist [sic] of the orchestra. She played her solo in the prelude of the suite with a beauty of tone and a sense of style which seems peculiar to French musicians and their disciples.⁷⁰

Later, in another article, the correspondent for *Musical America* wrote:

> [S]he played her solo in the first movement with a beauty of tone and legato which more than did justice to the tradition of the orchestra, she maintained balance of tone in a hall to which she was not accustomed, and her intonation … was true.⁷¹

In addition to the vital information above, this article gives us a rare opportunity; the correspondent includes Hall's own words through an interview. She advocated for publicly-funded American conservatories on the French model, with merit reigning in admissions. She also made a passionate appeal for high standards and the introduction of extensive solfège training for musicians.⁷²

Figure 1.4. Elise Hall following performance with the Boston Symphony Orchestra[73]

Her words and attitudes paint a picture of someone deeply committed to her art with the highest artistic standards. When reflecting on the state of classical music in America, Hall decried the attitude of many of the salaried musicians she encountered:

> Take, for instance, the orchestral players. How often are they seen enthusiastic over their music? It is business. They are paid by the hour—not a bad provision for their welfare, yet how disheartening it can be, during an earnest rehearsal, to see a player stop, look at his watch and leave... For all the pleasant things [that] could be said on the subject I cannot say that I consider America in its present state compares well with Europe as a place for artistic development.[74]

"Mrs. Richard J. Hall, President"

A Boston Orchestral Club advertisement for an April 19, 1910 concert gives an interesting view of Hall's stature. Immediately below the name of the ensemble are the words "Mrs. Richard J. Hall, President." Hall's name comes before Longy's on the program, and is featured in larger type—a remarkable and conspicuous development, albeit perhaps a natural progression considering her financial support of the Club. Hall's artistic direction of the ensemble is clear: the relatively modernist program goes beyond Longy's slightly more conservative preferences. Concertgoers at this 1910 performance could be treated to works by Balakirev (billed as "Balakireff"), Franck, Ducasse, Lazzari, and Lalo, in addition to a saxophone work by Moreau. Hall seems to have gained artistic control.[75]

In the 1910 *Musical America* interview, the writer made Hall's position clear. A caption to a portrait of the saxophonist reads: "Mrs. R. J. Hall, One of Boston's Best Known Musicians, Who Has Introduced Much of the Modern-day Music at Concerts Under Her Direction."[76] No matter that Longy held the baton, it was Hall's artistic vision that he was fulfilling.

1912 Performance with the Longy Club

On New Year's Day, 1912, Hall performed the world premiere of Woollett's *Octuor* for saxophone, oboe, clarinet, and string quintet. In addition to the regular Longy Club musicians, the other performers on the work were violinists Sylvain Noack and Adolf Bak, violist Emile Ferir, cellist Josef Keller, and bassist

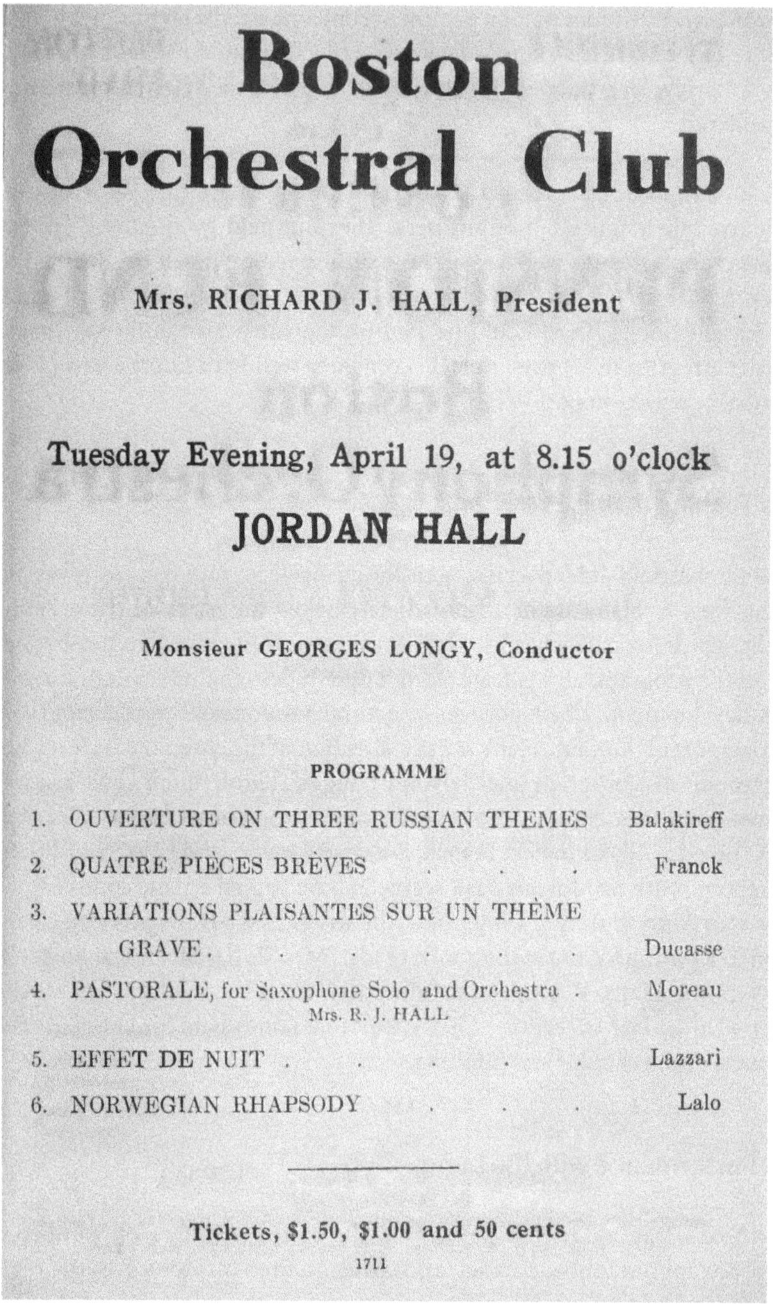

Boston Orchestral Club

Mrs. RICHARD J. HALL, President

Tuesday Evening, April 19, at 8.15 o'clock

JORDAN HALL

Monsieur GEORGES LONGY, Conductor

PROGRAMME

1. OUVERTURE ON THREE RUSSIAN THEMES — Balakireff
2. QUATRE PIÈCES BRÈVES — Franck
3. VARIATIONS PLAISANTES SUR UN THÈME GRAVE — Ducasse
4. PASTORALE, for Saxophone Solo and Orchestra — Moreau
   Mrs. R. J. HALL
5. EFFET DE NUIT — Lazzari
6. NORWEGIAN RHAPSODY — Lalo

Tickets, $1.50, $1.00 and 50 cents

1711

Figure 1.5. Advertisement for Boston Orchestral Club concert of April 19, 1910[77]

Ernest Huber—all members of the Boston Symphony. Noack served as assistant concertmaster of the orchestra while Ferir was principal viola.[78] *The Boston Globe*'s critic said, "Mrs. Hall's playing is always to be enjoyed, as it was last night, for the purity and sympathy of her tone and for her excellent style."[79]

1912 "Mrs. Hall's Concert"

In 1912, the Boston Orchestral Club was disbanded. This is, perhaps, a function of familial strife interfering with Hall's artistic calling. In 1911, her son-in-law, attorney Benjamin Young, established a deed-in-trust that limited the amount of money available to Hall at any one time. It is difficult to surmise, but perhaps he viewed her professional activities as a drain on his own potential earnings from her estate. No matter his motivations, this restriction on virtually unlimited funds probably made it impossible to continue running an organization that produced an entire season of concerts.[80]

With these limitations, Hall seems to have turned her attention wholeheartedly to an annual or semi-annual professional showcase of contemporary music. On the March 11, 1912 edition of "Mrs. R. J. Hall's Concert," she programmed Florent Schmitt's *Rhapsodie Viennoise*, Albert Roussel's *Poeme de la Foret*, three movements from Roger-Ducasse's *Petite Suite*, and Philippe Gaubert's *Poeme élégiaque*. Hall joined the ensemble for the last piece, and then performed with them again for the encore, Woollett's *Siberia*. Regarding the saxophonist's playing, the correspondent for the *Boston Evening Transcript* remarked that "Mrs. Hall played the saxophone parts in both these works with authority, skill, artistic sensibility to tonal effect, and musicianly sentiment."[81]

The Boston Globe's reviewer gave even more telling details of the performance. Perhaps unaware of the earlier iterations of "Mrs. Hall's Concert," they took the new format to be a re-imagining of the concept of the Boston Orchestral Club. As the correspondent wrote, "A marked and improving trend toward a symphonic and away from semi-professional or amateur personnel may have occasioned the change of title."[82] The orchestra consisted primarily of musicians from the Boston Symphony, but Hall made a striking move in hiring her professional ensemble: the entire first violin section, as well as the principal flute and viola, were women. It would be another forty years before the Boston Symphony itself admitted a female principal player.[83] *The Globe* also thought to add that Hall's "tone upon the saxophone is of uncommon beauty."[84]

The Last Years: 1916 "Mrs. Hall's Concert," 1917 Jean Huré Concert, and Hall's 1920 Home Concert

The coverage of the 1916 "Mrs. Hall's Concert" included a revealing introduction by the critic. They did not write "Mrs. Richard J. Hall, patron of the arts…" or "Mrs. Richard J. Hall, music lover…" Rather, the correspondent started simply and directly:

> Mrs. Richard J. Hall, saxophone player, gave a delightful concert of chamber music in Jordan Hall on the evening of March 21. She was assisted by Povla Frisch, the wonderfully gifted soprano… Mrs. Hall is a mistress of her instrument and on this occasion played with a great variety of expression.[85]

The ensemble for the evening was made up entirely of members of the Boston Symphony, conducted by Longy.[86] Povla Frisch was a Danish-born, Paris-trained professional vocalist who would teach at Julliard from 1940 onward.[87] The concert featured Woollett's *Octuor* and *Danses Païennes*, both of which used Hall on the saxophone, and an unnamed piece by Grovlez.[88]

On February 8, 1917, Georges Longy presented a recital of works by Jean Huré. Hall was a featured soloist on the composer's *Andante* for alto saxophone, strings, harp, tympani, and organ. She was supported entirely by members of the Boston Symphony Orchestra.[89] As the First World War began to curtail performances in the United States, and as Hall's son-in-law continued to restrict her activities, it would be one of the saxophonist's last public performances.

Street has recorded her final concert as taking place with the MacDowell Club Orchestra, in a performance of Caplet's *Impression d'Automne*, conducted by Longy, on January 28, 1920.[90] However, the February 7, 1920 edition of *Musical America* lists another musical triumph. As the correspondent relayed:

> An unusual and interesting musicale was given last week at the home of Mrs. Richard Hall, well known in Boston as a patron of music and player upon the saxophone. Those taking part were Mrs. Richard Hall, saxophone; Mrs. Morgan Butler, soprano; Renee Longy Miquelle, piano; Henry Gideon, piano; Verne Powell, flute, and eight members of the Boston Symphony… The program included such unique pieces as Woollett's Danse Paiennes [sic] and Pessard's "Malaguena" and "Andalouse," all with saxophone solos.[91]

To the end, Hall held the highest standards, and surrounded herself with professionals.

Conclusion

Hall's skill has been historically undervalued as a performing saxophonist due to the unmediated subjectivities and biases of previous historiographers. According to the documentary evidence found in contemporaneous reviews, she played at a professional level commensurate with other saxophonists of the era. Indeed, she, in many ways, seems to have been an artist of a higher caliber.

Hall operated in a wide variety of capacities as an orchestral saxophonist, chamber musician, and soloist, with the finest classical musicians of Boston and Paris, and received high praise from critics. In nearly all circumstances, she was the only female instrumentalist performing in any of these professional spaces. In addition, she possessed a broader artistic ambition than the band soloists of her era. Rather than playing theme-and-variation-based, diatonic-scale-laden light music, she sought mature, contemporary repertoire by the finest composers of the era that she could engage. Although she was not a pedagogue, Hall's performances and the works she commissioned warrant consideration on a level commensurate with well-known male saxophonists and teachers of the early twentieth century.

The previous negative perception of Hall as a performer is a miscarriage of justice. Since Vallas, it has been assumed that Hall was a middling performer. Generations of saxophone historians have unwittingly transmitted these biased views. As a result, Hall has been severely underestimated in saxophone historiography. Her performances were consistently covered by professional reviewers in some of the most respected journals in the United States and France. While the reviews were sometimes overshadowed by misogyny, they were overwhelmingly positive. More often than not, her performance abilities were singled out for applause over those of professionals on the same program.

From 1904 onward, Hall increasingly performed with professional musicians of the highest caliber. Many of her frequent collaborators were principal players in the Boston Symphony Orchestra, and many of these musicians chose to perform with Hall and take part in concerts with her repeatedly. It appears obvious that prior assessments of Hall's skills were inaccurate. How much of this was brought on by gender-based implicit bias? The goal is to learn from this case study and avoid repeating discriminatory assumptions about today's performers.

NOTES

1. Sigurd Raschèr was a German-American soloist who, beginning in the 1930s, commissioned works from Alexander Glazunov, Jacques Ibert, and many others. Marcel Mule was a French soloist and pedagogue who established the first saxophone class of the twentieth century at the Paris Conservatory in 1942. For more biographical information, see Stephen Cottrell, *The Saxophone* (New Haven: Yale University Press, 2013), 246–253.
2. Léon Vallas, *Claude Debussy: His Life and Works*, trans. Maire and Grace O'Brien (New York: Dover, 1973), 162.
3. James R. Noyes, "Debussy's 'Rapsodie Pour Orchestre et Saxophone' Revisited," *The Musical Quarterly* 90, no. 3/4 (Fall – Winter 2007): 416–445.
4. Frederick Hemke, "The Early History of the Saxophone" (PhD diss., The University of Wisconsin, 1975), 429.
5. Hemke, "The Early History of the Saxophone," 440.
6. Hemke, "The Early History of the Saxophone," 442.
7. Hemke, "The Early History of the Saxophone," 443–445.
8. Frederick Hemke, "The Fairer Sax," *The Saxophone Symposium* 2, no. 1 (Winter 1977): 7–11.
9. Stephen Cottrell, *The Saxophone* (New Haven: Yale University Press, 2013); Richard Ingham (ed.), *The Cambridge Companion to the Saxophone* (Cambridge: Cambridge University Press, 1999).
10. David Whitwell, *The Longy Club: A Professional Wind Ensemble in Boston (1900-1917)* (Northridge, CA: Winds, 1988).
11. Valerie M. Gudell, "Georges Longy: His Life and Legacy" (PhD diss., The University of Houston, 2001).
12. William Henry Street, "Elise Boyer Hall, America's First Female Concert Saxophonist: Her Life as Performing Artist, Pioneer of Concert Repertory for Saxophone and Patroness of the Arts" (DMA diss., Northwestern University, 1983).
13. Carol Neuls-Bales (ed.), *Women in Music*, revised edition (Boston: Northeastern University Press, 1996), 188.
14. Anna Bull, *Class, Control, and Classical Music* (Oxford: Oxford University Press, 2019), 36–39.
15. Bull, *Class, Control, and Classical Music*, 39.
16. Bull, *Class, Control, and Classical Music*, 42.
17. Bull, *Class, Control, and Classical Music*, 105–106.
18. "Santa Barbara Brevities," *The Los Angeles Times*, March 12, 1892.
19. "Santa Barbara," *The Los Angeles Herald*, September 19, 1895, 4.
20. "Last Night's Concert," *The Independent* (Santa Barbara, California), January 31, 1896.
21. "The Orphan's Fair," *The Independent* (Santa Barbara, California), October 28, 1896.
22. "Santa Barbara," *The Los Angeles Times*, January 17, 1897, 24.
23. "The Music Festival," *The Los Angeles Times*, January 16, 1897, 13.
24. "Santa Barbara Brevities," *The Los Angeles Times*, January 19, 1897, 13; "Serious Illness of Dr. R. J. Hall Stops the Festival," *The Los Angeles Times*, January 21, 1897, 13.
25. "Sketch of the Life of the Late Dr. R. J. Hall," *The Los Angeles Times*, January 26, 1897, 11.
26. Ibid.
27. "Findings in the Charter Contest—Dr. Hall's Will," *The Los Angeles Times*, February 7, 1897, 25.
28. Street, "Elise Boyer Hall," 25.
29. Street, "Elise Boyer Hall," 28; Gudell, *Georges Longy*, 53.
30. Street, "Elise Boyer Hall," 29.
31. Street, "Elise Boyer Hall," 30–31.
32. Whitwell, *The Longy Club*, 8.
33. Emilie Frances Bauer, "Music in Boston," *Musical Courier*, February 7, 1900, 34.
34. "Copley Hall: The Orchestral Club," *The Boston Evening Transcript*, April 28, 1900.
35. R.R.G., "Chickering Hall: Miss Terry's Concert," *The Boston Evening Transcript*, March 12, 1903.
36. Whitwell, *The Longy Club*, 5.
37. "Potter Hall: Longy Club," *The Boston Evening Transcript*, January 26, 1904, 11.
38. J. B. Steane, "Gilibert, Charles," Grove Music Online, accessed July 20, 2022, https://www.oxfordmusiconline.com/grovemusic/view/10.1093/gmo/9781561592630.001.0001/omo-9781561592630-e-5000011455
39. "Potter Hall: Longy Club," *The Boston Evening Transcript*, January 26, 1904, 11.
40. Philip Hale, *Programme of the Twelfth Rehearsal and Concert* (Boston: Boston Symphony Orchestra, 1904), 721.
41. "Best Premieres at the Société Nationale de Musique," *Interlude*, accessed July 20, 2022, https://interlude.hk/best-premieres-at-the-societe-nationale-de-musique/
42. P.D. "Chronique Musicale: Les Concerts," *La Chronique des Arts* 22 (May 28, 1904), 182. "Je n'aurais jamais supposé que la fantaisie pât venir à une dame de s'exercer sure le saxophone et de devenir virtuose dans cette spécialité ingrate. Mme Elise Hall a fait tout exprès le voyage

d'Amérique en France pour nous bien prouver que la chose était possible. Cela forme un spectacle assez bizarre et, à vrai dire, peu gracieux, qui fait mal valoir les graces féminines. Mais Mme Hall n'en a cure et souffle imperturbablement dans sa pipe de cuivre, comme un homme."

43. "Societé Nationale de Musique," *Le Guide Musical* 50, nos. 23 & 24 (June 5 & 12, 1904), 483. "Le choral pour saxophone de M. d'Indy est fort bien, et Mme Elise Hall l'a très bien joué, avec une belle sonorité, mais franchement, cet instrument ne sied guère au beau sexe."

44. "Mme Hall's Paris Success," *The New York Times*, May 18, 1904.

45. Street, "Elise Boyer Hall," 76; Karen J. Blair, *The Torchbearers: Women and Their Amateur Arts Associations in America, 1890-1930* (Bloomington: Indiana University Press, 1994). Women were not included in the "pipeline" of conservatory training to professional orchestra.

46. Boston Symphony Orchestra, *Program of the Eleventh Rehearsal and Concert* (Boston: Boston Symphony Orchestra, 1905), 749.

47. R.R.G., "Porter Hall: Longy Club," *The Boston Evening Transcript*, January 20, 1905, 10.

48. Boston Symphony Orchestra, *Program of the Eleventh Rehearsal and Concert* (Boston: Boston Symphony Orchestra, 1905), 749.

49. Boston Symphony Orchestra, *Program of the Eleventh Rehearsal and Concert* (Boston: Boston Symphony Orchestra, 1905), 749.

50. "A Listing of All the Musicians of the Boston Symphony Orchestra from its Founding in 1881," *The Stokowski Legacy*, accessed July 19, 2022, https://www.stokowski.org/Boston_Symphony_Musicians_List.htm

51. R.R.G., "Porter Hall: Longy Club," *The Boston Evening Transcript*, January 20, 1905, 10; "A Listing of All the Musicians of the Boston Symphony Orchestra from its Founding in 1881."

52. C.I.B., "Topics in Paris," *The New York Daily Tribune*, May 28, 1905.

53. Edmond-Achille Frank, "Mme Elise Hall," *Paris Musical et Dramatique* 2, no. 6 (May 1905), 1-2. "Et si nous nous félicitons particulièrement d'avoir à écrire aujourd'hui le nom de Mme Elise Hall en tête de ces lignes, c'est que nous avons conscience, en parlant de son oeuvre, non seulement de rendre hommage à une artiste remarquable … mais aussi d'accomplir un devoir de reconnaissance envers une des plus nobles bienfaitrices de notre art musical. Mme Elise Hall … vini à Paris à l'age de douze ans. Après avoir reçu une éducation des plus complètes au couvent des Oiseaux, elle s'adonna à la musique qu'elle aime passionnément. Ce goût inné confondu à l'ardente sympathie qu'elle avait vouée à notre patrie. l'incita à l'étude approfondie de nos maitrès. En même temps … elle étudiait avec assiduité le saxophone, et devenait une incomparable virtuose… Si les noms et les ouvrages de nos musiciens illustres sont mieux connus à présent de l'autre côté de l'Atlantique, c'est à la persévérance de Mme Hall et de M. Longy que nous le devons."

54. "Concerts Annoncés," *Le Courrier Musical* 9, no. 11 (June 1, 1906), 400.

55. Edmond-Achille Frank, "Le Concert de Mme. Elise Hall," *Paris Musical et Dramatique* 3, no. 18 (June 1906), 3. "Ce fut un délicat régal pour le public distingué et nombreux qui s'était empressé à cette manifestation d'art, que l'audition des symphonies et des melodies composes par l'élite de nos musiciens expès pour Mme Hall et interprétés magistralement par elle sur le saxophone, l'orchestre, composé de nos pus remarquables musiciens solistes de l'Opéra et de l'Opéra-Comique, étant conduit par M. Longy avec cette sûreté et ce sentiment de nuances qui le caractérisent… Nous eûmes le rare Plaisir d'entendre *Impression d'Automne* … André Caplet; *Malagnegna*, de G. Pessard; *La Tompe des Alpes*, de A. Chauvet, et une exquise composition de M. G. Longy initulée *Impression*, très chaleureusement applaudie."

56. Julien Torchet, "Salle Pleyel," *Le Guide Musical* 52, no. 25-26 (June 24 and July 1, 1906), 460-461. "Si vous étiez grande dame, passionnée pour la musique et maitresse d'une très grosse fortune, vous viendrait-il l'idée d'en distrire une partie à la propagation du saxophone; J'en doute. Vous penseriez que cet instrument n'a pas encore assez de quartiers de noblesse pour mériter ce sacrifice et vous réserveriez plutôt le superflu de vos richesses à la gloire de l'orgue, du violon ou du piano. Une Américaine, Mme Hall, éprise du saxophone, s'est vouée à l'étude de cet instrument et en joue en virtuose de talent. Mais, comme il existe peu de musique ad hoc, elle commande, chaque année, à de jeunes musiciens des oeuvres spéciales où, naturellement, la partie principale et réservée au saxophone, et les fait éditer et exécuter à ses frais… Mme Hall vient tous les ans à Paris donner une audition des compositions nouvelles de ce genre… Pour Mme Hall, je n'ai qu'un mot à dire de son talent: sa virtuosité est indéniable, son style très pur et la sonorité qu'elle tire de son instrument à la fois douce et pleine; son succès a donc été vif et mérité."

57. E.B.H., "Jordan Hall: Mrs. Hall's Concert," *The Boston Evening Transcript*, January 22, 1908.

58. Boston Symphony Orchestra, 8 (Boston: Boston Symphony Orchestra, 1909), 610.

59. "Longy Club Concert," *The Boston Globe*, January 2, 1912.
60. Boston Symphony Orchestra, *16* (Boston: Boston Symphony Orchestra, 1909), 1323.
61. Boston Symphony Orchestra, *16*, 1323.
62. D.L.L., "Gives Saxophone Recital," *Musical America*, March 13, 1909, 26; "A Listing of All the Musicians of the Boston Symphony Orchestra from its Founding in 1881."
63. Editorials, *The New Music Review and Church Music Review* 9, no. 99 (February 1910), 135.
64. Lydia Savitzkaya would be the first regular female member in the 1924-1925 season as a harpist. The second woman, Louise Came, also a harpist, would not join the orchestra until 1937. See "A Listing of All the Musicians of the Boston Symphony Orchestra from its Founding in 1881."
65. "Sharps and Flats," *Deseret News* (Salt Lake City, Utah), February 19, 1910.
66. Philip Hale, "Music in Boston," *The New Music Review and Church Music Review* 5, no. 51 (February 1906), 706.
67. O.D., "The Saxophone, Her Medium of Musical Expression," *Musical America*, February 26, 1916, 15.
68. Philip Hale, *10* (Boston: Boston Symphony Orchestra, 1909), 3.
69. Unidentified press clipping in Allen A. Brown, *Boston Symphony Orchestra Scrapbooks, 1881-1882 to 1859-1960*, 110, accessed August 3, 2022, https://archive.org/details/bostonsymphonyor2931brow
70. Olin Downs, "'Messiah' Feature of Boston Concerts," *Musical America*, January 1, 1920, 27.
71. O.D., "The Saxophone, Her Medium of Musical Expression," 15.
72. O.D., "The Saxophone, Her Medium of Musical Expression," 15.
73. Allen A. Brown, *Boston Symphony Orchestra Scrapbooks, 1881-1882 to 1859-1960*, 109, accessed August 3, 2022, https://archive.org/details/bostonsymphonyor2931brow
74. O.D., "The Saxophone, Her Medium of Musical Expression," 15.
75. Boston Symphony Orchestra, *22* (Boston: Boston Symphony Orchestra, 1910), 1711.
76. O.D., "The Saxophone, Her Medium of Musical Expression," 15.
77. Boston Symphony Orchestra, *22*, 1711.
78. "A Listing of All the Musicians of the Boston Symphony Orchestra from its Founding in 1881."
79. "Longy Club Concert," *The Boston Globe*, January 2, 1912.
80. Street, "Elise Boyer Hall," 89.
81. E.B.H., "Novel French Music Under Mr. Longy," *The Boston Evening Transcript*, March 12, 1912.
82. "Mrs. Hall's Concert," *The Boston Globe*, March 12, 1912.
83. Barbara Jepson and David Atkinson Wells, "Dwyer, Doriot Anthony," Grove Music Online, accessed July 21, 2022, https://www.oxfordmusiconline.com/grovemusic/view/10.1093/gmo/9781561592630.001.0001/omo-9781561592630-e-1002284269
84. "Mrs. Hall's Concert," *The Boston Globe*, March 12, 1912.
85. "Mrs. Hall's Delightful Concert," *Musical Courier*, April 6, 1916, 33.
86. "Mrs. Hall's Delightful Concert," 33.
87. "Povla Frisch (1881-1960)," Mahler Foundation, accessed July 16, 2022, mahlerfoundation.org/Mahler/contemporaries/povla-frisch/
88. "Mrs. Hall's Concert," *The Boston Globe*, March 22, 1916.
89. "Jean Hure's Music at First of Longy Concerts," *The Boston Globe*, February 4, 1917.
90. Street, "Elise Boyer Hall," 37.
91. C.R., "Boston Welcomes New Conductor," *Musical America*, February 7, 1920, 20.

WORKS CITED

Bull, Anna. *Class, Control, and Classical Music*. Oxford: Oxford University Press, 2019.

Cottrell, Stephen. *The Saxophone*. New Haven: Yale University Press, 2013.

Gudell, Valerie M. "Georges Longy: His Life and Legacy." DMA diss., The University of Houston, 2001.

Hemke, Frederick. "The Fairer Sax." *The Saxophone Symposium* 2, no. 1 (Winter 1977): 7–11.

———. "The Early History of the Saxophone." DMA diss., The University of Wisconsin, 1975.

Ingham, Richard, ed. *The Cambridge Companion to the Saxophone*. Cambridge: Cambridge University Press, 1999.

Jepson, Barbara, and David Atkinson Wells. "Dwyer, Doriot Anthony." Grove Music Online. Accessed July 21, 2022. https://www.oxfordmusiconline.com/grovemusic/view/10.1093/gmo/9781561592630.001.0001/omo-9781561592630-e-1002284269

Neuls-Bales, Carol, ed. *Women in Music*. Revised edition. Boston: Northeastern University Press, 1996.

Noyes, James R. "Debussy's 'Rapsodie Pour Orchestre et Saxophone' Revisited." *The Musical Quarterly* 90, no. 3/4 (Fall-Winter, 2007): 416–445.

"Povla Frisch (1881-1960)." Mahler Foundation. Accessed July 16, 2022. mahlerfoundation.org/Mahler/contemporaries/povla-frisch/

Steane, J. B. "Gilibert, Charles." Grove Music Online. Accessed July 20, 2022. https://www.oxfordmusiconline.com/grovemusic/view/10.1093/gmo/9781561592630.001.0001/omo-9781561592630-e-5000011455

Street, William Henry. "Elise Boyer Hall, America's First Female Concert Saxophonist: Her Life as Performing Artist, Pioneer of Concert Repertory for Saxophone and Patroness of the Arts." DMA diss., Northwestern University, 1983.

Vallas, Léon. *Claude Debussy: His Life and Works.* Translated by Maire and Grace O'Brien. New York: Dover, 1973.

Whitwell, David. *The Longy Club: A Professional Wind Ensemble in Boston (1900-1917).* Northridge, CA: Winds, 1988.

Mediography

B., C. I. "Topics in Paris." *The New York Daily Tribune*, May 28, 1905.

Bauer, Emilie Frances. "Music in Boston." *Musical Courier*, February 7, 1900.

"Benjamin Young, Lawyer, 78, Dies." *The New York Times*, June 5, 1964.

"Best Premieres at the Société Nationale de Musique." Interlude. Accessed July 20, 2022. https://interlude.hk/best-premieres-at-the-societe-nationale-de-musique/

Boston Symphony Orchestra. *8.* Boston: Boston Symphony Orchestra, 1909.

Boston Symphony Orchestra. *16.* Boston: Boston Symphony Orchestra, 1909.

Boston Symphony Orchestra. *22.* Boston: Boston Symphony Orchestra, 1910.

Boston Symphony Orchestra. *Program of the Eleventh Rehearsal and Concert.* Boston: Boston Symphony Orchestra, 1905.

Brown, Allen A. *Boston Symphony Orchestra Scrapbooks, 1881-1882 to 1859-1960.* Accessed August 3, 2022. https://archive.org/details/bostonsymphonyor2931brow

"Concerts Annoncés." *Le Courrier Musical*, June 1, 1906.

"Copley Hall: The Orchestral Club." *The Boston Evening Transcript*, April 28, 1900.

"Cottage Hospital." *The Independent* (Santa Barbara, CA), November 9, 1891.

"The Country Club." *The Independent* (Santa Barbara, CA), April 4, 1896.

D., O. "The Saxophone, Her Medium of Musical Expression." *Musical America*, February 26, 1916.

D., P. "Chronique Musicale: Les Concerts." *La Chronique des Arts*, May 28, 1904.

Downs, Olin. "'Messiah' Feature of Boston Concerts." *Musical America* January 1, 1920.

Editorials. *The New Music Review and Church Music Review*, February 1910.

"Findings in the Charter Contest—Dr. Hall's Will." *The Los Angeles Times*, February 7, 1897.

Frank, Edmond-Achille. "Le Concert de Mme. Elise Hall." *Paris Musical et Dramatique*, June 1906.

———. "Mme Elise Hall." *Paris Musical et Dramatique*, May 1905.

G., R. R. "Chickering Hall: Miss Terry's Concert." *The Boston Evening Transcript*, March 12, 1903.

———. "Porter Hall: Longy Club." *The Boston Evening Transcript*, January 20, 1905.

H., E. B. "Jordan Hall: Mrs. Hall's Concert." *The Boston Evening Transcript*, January 22, 1908.

———. "Novel French Music Under Mr. Longy." *The Boston Evening Transcript*, March 12, 1912.

Hale, Philip. *10.* Boston: Boston Symphony Orchestra, 1909.

———. "Music in Boston." *The New Music Review and Church Music Review*, February 1906.

———. *Programme of the Twelfth Rehearsal and Concert.* Boston: Boston Symphony Orchestra, 1904.

"Jean Hure's Music at First of Longy Concerts." *The Boston Globe*, February 4, 1917.

L., D. L. "Gives Saxophone Recital." *Musical America*, March 13, 1909.

"A Listing of All the Musicians of the Boston Symphony Orchestra from its Founding in 1881." *The Stokowski Legacy*. Accessed July 19, 2022. https://www.stokowski.org/Boston_Symphony_Musicians_List.htm

"Last Night's Concert." *The Independent* (Santa Barbara, California), January 31, 1896.

"Longy Club Concert." *The Boston Globe*, January 2, 1912.

"Mme Hall's Paris Success." *The New York Times*, May 18, 1904.

"Mrs. Hall's Concert." *The Boston Globe*, March 12, 1912.

"Mrs. Hall's Concert." *The Boston Globe*, March 22, 1916.

"Mrs. Hall's Delightful Concert." *Musical Courier*, April 6, 1916.

"The Music Festival." *The Los Angeles Times*, January 16, 1897.

"The Orphan's Fair." *The Independent* (Santa Barbara, California), October 28, 1896.

"Potter Hall: Longy Club." *The Boston Evening Transcript*, January 26, 1904.

R., C. "Boston Welcomes New Conductor." *Musical America*, February 7, 1920.

"Santa Barbara." *The Los Angeles Herald*, September 19, 1895.

"Santa Barbara." *The Los Angeles Times*, January 17, 1897.

"Santa Barbara Brevities." *The Los Angeles Times*, March 12, 1892.

"Santa Barbara Brevities." *The Los Angeles Times*, January 19, 1897.

"Serious Illness of Dr. R. J. Hall Stops the Festival." *The Los Angeles Times*, January 21, 1897.

"Sharps and Flats." *Deseret News* (Salt Lake City, Utah), February 19, 1910.

"Sketch of the Life of the Late Dr. R. J. Hall." *The Los Angeles Times*, January 26, 1897.

"Societé Nationale de Musique." *Le Guide Musical*, June 5 & 12, 1904.

Torchet, Julien. "Salle Pleyel." *Le Guide Musical*, June 24 and July 1, 1906.

"Viva, Flora." *The Los Angeles Times*, April 16, 1896.

Paying and Playing?
Elise Hall and Patronage in the Early Twentieth Century

Kurt Bertels

ABSTRACT

The overall objective of this chapter is to study Elise Hall's patronage in early twentieth-century saxophone music. By commissioning new musical works for the saxophone from sixteen (mostly European) composers, Hall not only established transatlantic musical networks in the beginning of the twentieth century, but she also expanded the repertoire significantly and laid the foundations for the most canonical works in saxophone performance to the present day. This chapter aims to approach Hall's efforts for the saxophone in their full complexity. Whereas existing scholarship frames her straightforwardly as a wealthy woman who paid composers to write works that she could perform herself, the present chapter seeks to go beyond the clichés and highlight several aspects of Hall as a patron and performer. It situates her efforts against the background of early saxophone repertoire and the central role of female patrons at the turn of the nineteenth century. I also aim to analyze crucial historical documents testifying to Hall's contributions, including Hall's reception in the contemporary press and the function of the dedications in the compositions written for her. Finally, building on theories from the field of patronage studies, this chapter also invites present and future scholars to reflect more conceptually on the intricacies of Hall's life and work.

Introduction

It was in 2005 that, for the very first time, I came across the historical figure of Hall while studying Paul Gilson's *Concerto No. 1* at the age of 16.[1] Extremely intrigued by a Belgian composer who wrote the world's first concerto for the saxophone in 1902, I immediately started exploring the cultural-historical context in which Gilson composed his work.[2] The more I discovered the broader context of Gilson's composition, the more I experienced how an individual work of art is determined by various contextual, social, and institutional factors, as Linda Whitesitt summarizes effectively in the following quote:

> Far from the Romantic ideal of art as the product of individual and isolated genius, music culture is the outcome of actors in socially defined roles playing parts in socially constructed institutions. It is the result of performers, listeners, teachers, instrument makers, publishers, critics, ticket purchasers, managers, helpmates, fundraisers, administrators, and volunteers interacting- in private and public institutions—family, church, court, salon, concerts, symphony orchestras, festivals, and conservatories. By transcending the myth of the great artist and looking at systems rather than individuals as the architects of art, women become visible as starring actors in the institutional creation musical culture.[3]

I soon learned that the French-American Hall was exactly this type of influential actor in the creation of Gilson's first saxophone concerto, an insight that increased my interest to approach saxophone history through Gilson's work as a transatlantic endeavor.[4] Gradually, several conversations with fellow saxophonists brought up the anecdote that she was an affluent saxophonist who spent a part of her fortune generating new music at the beginning of the twentieth century. This image of Hall, quite widespread in saxophone studies, is what this chapter generally seeks to revisit and refine.

Gilson's *Concerto No. 1* is not the only composition that can be linked to Hall. Indeed, all of the musical works from Hall's collection occupy a remarkable place in the early history of the saxophone. Her efforts to prompt composers to write new saxophone music resulted in the expansion of the early saxophone repertoire with new works from mainly European composers, such as Claude Debussy and Vincent d'Indy. A part of this collection, the manuscripts of which are preserved at the New England Conservatory (NEC), have become some of the most canonical saxophone repertoire.[5] It includes settings ranging from chamber music to concertante works for saxophone and orchestra. By soliciting and performing new saxophone compositions, Hall took up an extraordinary position in the international field of the saxophone which might have inspired the budding Belgian composer Gilson. Again, bearing Whitesitt's quote in mind, Hall's story captures the imagination as she was not only influenced by a cultural-historical context, but also by direct and indirect influences such as her saxophone teacher Georges Longy, other renowned patrons of the era, and the composers that wrote music for her to perform.

Whereas Hall is still perceived—and usually depicted today—as a true patron who conceived and realized the plan to request new saxophone music from contemporary composers, the present chapter sheds new light on Hall's role as a promoter of the saxophone. It aims to approach Hall's work in its full complexity, with attention to the historical context, gender-based discriminatory practices of the era, patronage theory, and the reception of Hall. For that purpose, this chapter seeks to contextualize Hall's music collection, which consists of foundational scores and thus remains relevant for today. The ambition is to reassess Hall's influential role in saxophone history by revisiting existing scholarship, analyzing the framing of Hall in contemporary newspapers and journals, and interpreting the dedications on the manuscripts in her collection. By approaching Hall's story through the lens of patronage theory and more general historical reflections on women musicians in the nineteenth and early twentieth century, this chapter shows the relevance of Hall's case outside the saxophone community.

Extant scholarship within saxophone studies vaguely refers to Hall's specific contribution as patronage, without further discourse stemming from this notion and without a nuanced reflection on the intricacies of her work. According to saxophonist Frederick Hemke in one of the first studies on the early saxophone history, Hall was "one of the truly enigmatic personalities of saxophone history" and "a Boston society woman who became avidly interested in the saxophone and undertook the commissioning of compositions for saxophone and orchestra by several prominent composers of her day."[6] William Street, Hall's biographer, describes her as a "patron and performer," the "first woman to take a serious interest in saxophone performance and the development of saxophone concert repertory."[7] In addition to an overview of her concert programs from the Boston Orchestral Club, Street was the only one to provide an overview of the composers who dedicated works to Hall and of the manuscripts still available today based on the inventory of the Elise Hall Collection of Saxophone Music by 20th-Century Composers (NEC).

The viewpoints of Hemke and Street have often been cited by scholars without critical examination in the decades since their respective publications in 1975 and 1983. In *The Saxophone*, Stephen Cottrell expresses admiration for Hall's contribution: "the list of French composers whom Elise Hall approached to write new pieces for the saxophone ... is quite remarkable." Antonino Mollica also refers to Hall as a French-American patron, "franco-américaine mecène," to whom he owes "commissions that are the first great concertante pieces for saxophone."[8] Contrary to the aforementioned studies on the broader context of Hall's entire collection, only three contributions have focused on the genesis of specific musical scores such as d'Indy's *Choral Varié*, Gilson's *Concerto no. 1*, and Debussy's *Rapsodie*.[9]

Surprisingly, Hall's music collection has not yet attracted the attention of historians of patronage in music. Despite the framing of Hall as a wealthy "patroness" who might have paid composers to compose new music, her career as a performer who commissioned new music from composers has not yet been the subject within the study of female patronage in the long nineteenth century. The authors of *Cultivating Music in America*, Ralph Locke and Cyrilla Barr, examine the different roles that women played in American music culture, for instance, and stress that female patrons of Western classical music have been overlooked since 1800.[10] Although these authors focus on female American patrons, Hall's efforts are not examined, perhaps because she was active in a transnational context, both in North America and in Europe.[11] In a list of patrons, Hall is only briefly mentioned as "Elise Boyer Hall (of Boston), who commissioned works for saxophone from Debussy and others."[12] A reference work on patronage, Myriam Chimenès' *Mécènes et Musiciens*, discusses the salon culture during the Third Republic in France and explores how composers such as Gabriel Fauré, Igor Stravinsky, d'Indy, and Debussy maintained close ties with patrons in order to participate in Parisian high society and further their careers. During the Third Republic (1870-1940), French politics had no policy regarding the dissemination and creation of new music, so private initiatives and public events by patrons and the construction of networks within Parisian art salons, among others, represented a milestone in music history.[13] Interestingly, Hall is not mentioned in this investigation, either. Indeed, she was left out of this study because she was American and mainly active in the United States. Perhaps she was an outsider as she was commissioning new music for saxophone, which was novel and relatively unknown in Western art music.

Paul Dimaggio has investigated how cultural entrepreneurship, as part and parcel of the transitioning economy in nineteenth-century Boston—the environment in which Hall operated—formed the basis for the development of high culture in America.[14] Additionally, Bill Faucett's *Music In Boston* focuses on how the city, in the period before World War I, made conscious efforts to strengthen its musical culture. In doing so, he focuses on how national and international trends influenced the activities of composers and musicians and how the work of philanthropists enhanced Boston's artistic life. In his book the author shows, for example, how it became an important place for contemporary composers such as Richard Strauss. Again, though, Hall's contributions are excluded from these discussions.

Before focusing on the perception of Hall's activities in the early twentieth-century press, it is important to briefly sketch the rise and evolution of nineteenth-century saxophone music from a historical perspective.

Why New Saxophone Music?

In all periods of music history, women have played influential roles as performers, educators, entrepreneurs, composers, and patrons. Even today, as this book shows, Hall is fondly remembered as a woman who combined various roles in the cultural field during the long nineteenth century. Studies of the first generation of women saxophonists indicate that Hall's artistic practice was colored by the developments of her time: in the United States—in contrast to Europe—women explicitly identified themselves as saxophonists in both classical and popular music genres.[15] Therefore, it is a mistake to place Hall and her saxophone practice in isolation; she and her music did not exist in a vacuum. Society dictated that instruments such as the harp, piano, or guitar were considered appropriate for girls and women to play during the nineteenth and early twentieth centuries. Hall, as a young girl from a wealthy family, initially learned to play the piano. Those instruments were believed not to detract from the imposed ideal of a woman's grace and elegance. Only men were encouraged to play orchestral and wind instruments and to pursue professional development opportunities in music. However, this view of musicianship changed over time; by the end of the nineteenth century women dedicated themselves to learning instruments—including wind instruments—that had previously been socially unacceptable for them to play. The burgeoning saxophone culture was also a party to this movement.

Hall's shift to the saxophone posed challenges, primarily because the instrument did not have a wealth of repertoire with orchestra or in chamber music ensembles. She started encouraging contemporary composers to write for the ensemble as a benefactor of the Orchestral Club of Boston because she also wanted to become an active saxophonist within the same association. To better understand this position, it is necessary to outline the historical trajectory of the saxophone repertoire during the second half of the nineteenth century.

Hall became artistically active at the turn of the twentieth century, around sixty years after the saxophone was officially introduced in 1841. After the famous contest between the ensembles the *Saxons* and *Carafons* on the Champ de Mars in Paris on April 22, 1845, Adolphe Sax's instruments were officially adopted by the French military bands. Consequently, the saxophone was officially introduced into the military music education of the *Gymnase musical militaire*.[16] The adoption of the instrument in these organizations represented the first form of institutionalized saxophone education, and inspired the Belgian musical field soon after. At the *Royal Conservatoire de Bruxelles*, the first director, François-Joseph Fétis, founded the first Belgian saxophone class in 1867, one of the world's first conservatory classes for the young instrument.[17] The emergence of both the French and Belgian educational traditions for the saxophone in the nineteenth century provided the first important incentive for the rise of the repertoire, which was mostly comprised of works for solo saxophone or saxophone and piano. The music was mainly composed for solo or duo ensembles at this time because this gave the students the best opportunity to establish themselves as soloists.[18] Within the context of both classes, new music scores fulfilled a pedagogical function whether or not they were considered compulsory work.[19]

In general, one can divide the nineteenth-century saxophone repertoire into two main successive phases. Until the 1870s, in the first two decades after the presentation of the saxophone in 1841, composers such as Jules Demersseman and Jean-Baptiste Singelée created some of the very first saxophone scores. These composers were mainly active as performers who were close acquaintances of Adolphe Sax and wrote music to support his new invention. Both composers were responsible for a great deal of early saxophone repertoire. Demersseman and Singelée, respectively a flutist flautist and violinist, were neither saxophone specialists nor players and created the first saxophone music from their own instrumental practices. Thus, the saxophone's unique characteristics did not necessarily serve as an inspiration during the compositional process.

In the second period—in the last decades of the nineteenth century—the very first teachers and professional saxophone players published music scores and instructional methods not solely to help saxophone students, but also to augment their own concert repertoire. Important figures among them include Louis Mayeur, Charles Soualle, and Edouard Lefebre.[20] These saxophonists were mainly active as teachers in France and Belgium and as professional practitioners of the instrument, and therefore this music was not created solely to function as pedagogical material. Soualle, Lefebre, and Mayeur, who significantly contributed to the early saxophone repertoire, were primarily performers.

The existing "early" saxophone repertoire didn't offer Hall the possibility to perform with an orchestra or in the context of chamber music. At the beginning of the twentieth century, composers started dedicating their compositions to her when she became active as a saxophonist. Hall was thus compelled to encourage contemporary composers to include the saxophone in their own compositions and was able to establish connections and collaborate with composers because she had become independent in the late nineteenth century. When her husband died, she was able to create the space for herself to organize her passion for music-making in various ways, not only for herself but also for the benefit of others.

During the first two decades of the twentieth century, between 1900 and 1920, sixteen composers dedicated one or more compositions to Hall. Table 2.1 displays the full list of her collection and each manuscript's place of preservation.

Table 2.1. Elise Hall's musical score collection

	Composer	Composition	Year	Place of preservation
1	André Caplet	Légende	1903	NEC
2		Impressions d'automne	1905?	Lost
3	François Combelle	Fantaisie Mauresque	Publication in 1920	Unknown
4	Claude Debussy	Rapsodie	1903-1908	NEC
5	Paul Dupin	Chant	1910	NEC
6	Philippe Gaubert	Poème Élégiaque	1911	NEC
7	Paul Gilson	Concerto no. 1	1902	Royal Conservatory Brussels
8	Gabriel Grovlez	Suite	1915	NEC
9	Jean Huré	Andante	1915	NEC
10		Concertstück	After 1915	NEC
11	Vincent d'Indy	Choral varié	1903	Unknown
12	Charles Martin Loeffler	Carnavalesque	1903	NEC
13		Divertissement Espagnol	1900	NEC
14		Rapsodie	/	Destroyed
15	Georges Longy	Rhapsodie	1904	NEC
16		Impression	1902	Lost
17	Léon Moreau	Pastorale	/	NEC
18	Jules Mouquet	Rapsodie	1907	NEC
19	Florent Schmitt	Légende	1918	Unknown
20	Georges Sporck	Légende	1905	Unknown
21	Henri Woollett	Siberia	1909-1910	NEC
22		Octuor	1909	NEC

At the beginning of the twentieth century, Europe set the tone for the cultural/entrepreneurial sector in the United States, with wealthy American patrons primarily recruiting artists of European origin to create works for them. At the time, it was fashionable to prioritize the musical works of European culture and to dismiss music by American composers. The idea that European music (and other art forms) symbolized "sophistication and cultivation" influenced various art institutions such as the Metropolitan Museum of Art, the Metropolitan Opera, the New York Philharmonic, and Carnegie Hall, as well as several institutions in Boston.[21] It was in the same vein that Hall actively promoted French culture and established collaborations with European composers. As the above list of compositions indicates, fourteen of the sixteen composers who dedicated their music to Hall were French, one was Belgian, and one composer had American nationality. Each of them had obtained the *Premier Prix de Rome*, which was widely considered the most prestigious composition prize for young composers. Although Hall was behaving very American in her tenacity and spirit as an entrepreneur in Boston, her Orchestral Club in Boston was profoundly Francophile as she and several members were French or French-American themselves. It thus seems that Hall wanted to connect with the most prominent French composers at that time to promote what was considered the best contemporary European music in America. This goal would have also served as an opportunity for Hall to show off the Boston Club's good taste and affinity for all things modern in France. In *Cultivating Music in America*, the authors mention that Charles Martin Loeffler, an American composer who received support from Isabella Stewart Gardner and also dedicated a composition to Elise Hall, was one of the exceptions.[22]

Hall's Patronage in the Press

To this day, it is almost impossible to retrace Hall's precise steps in generating new music. Such research is hampered in part because no personal notes or diaries—often crucial sources in patronage studies—have so far been recovered from her estate. As a result, for the time being, we do not know how Hall conceived of her own role and how she intended to fulfill that role. Was she following a deliberately sophisticated strategy or was she unintentional in her approach to creating repertoire? So far, the contemporary research which consistently frames her as a patron who financially supported her composers has not dealt with these critical questions regarding her method to gather new music. As Andrew Allen's chapter in this book demonstrates, analysis of print media helps us to gain more insights into the perception of Hall's role. Indeed, the era's periodicals took note of Hall's entrepreneurial endeavors and frequently highlighted her accomplishments in the music industry. Her initiatives gained public visibility and had the potential to spark discussion thanks to the media, which we can consider in this case to also be a promotional channel. A few articles discuss Hall's pursuit of new music as well as her efforts to increase American awareness of European music, particularly that of French composers. We find two instances of this in *Musical America* and *The Musical Courier* of 1910:

> To her Boston is deeply indebted for a remarkable series of orchestral concerts of modern French music, a series which will be continued during the latter half of this season.[23]
> Mrs. Hall has placed the musical community of Boston under a debt of gratitude, not alone by submitting the newest of the French school of composition each season (this being the eighth), but in creating by means of this club a school for wind instruments, as she procures every new instrument required by the wind choir for the performance of the new compositions.[24]

As indicated, the question remains unanswered how Hall would assess her own role. Newspaper articles and reviews show us how the work of Hall, both as someone who commissioned composers and as a dedicatee, was perceived in different ways. The difference is that someone who explicitly commissions music from a composer may not necessarily finance the composer's work. In this way, people who commission musical works can be distinguished from patrons who also support the artist financially.

For the first category, which is about Hall who commissioned new music, journalists and reviewers talk about repertoire that was composed expressly/specifically for Hall. For this venture, Hall herself took the initiative. There are also articles that less explicitly mention whether Hall was responsible for commissioning, which discuss new music dedicated to Hall, yet do not clearly indicate that she functioned as a patron. There are several examples of this sort. *The Musical Courier* of 1904 discusses composer d'Indy, who would have "composed expressly for Mrs. Richard J. Hall." In 1905 the same paper states "the pieces by Longy and Caplet … were composed especially for Mrs. R. J. Hall."[25] Two articles explicitly mention how Hall sought out composers every summer abroad—presumably in France—to request new works for the saxophone. Regarding d'Indy's *Choral Varié*, an article from *Le Guide Musical* describes how the American patron visited the composer in Paris and even begged him "to write a piece for this instrument [saxophone]. She recently came to France to show her talent and proposes to play the composition of M. d'Indy." Another 1910 article in *The Musical Courier* goes into more detail about it. The same article also mentions that composer Léon Moreau composed (and dedicated) his "Pastorale" for Hall:

> As Mrs. Hall gives almost her entire time to this work, going abroad every summer in search of the best musical literature, it may be easily seen that a work conducted as a labor of love, and fostered by such lofty musical ideas, must in time become in its way, even as the great Boston Symphony Orchestra has become, a standard for the highest in the field of musical culture. In the program of Tuesday evening, the "Pastorale", of Leon Moreau, composed for and dedicated to Mrs. Hall ...[26]

In 1916 *The Musical Courier* positively reports "Mrs. Hall's delightful concert" which literally states that the music performed was "especially composed for Mrs. Hall."[27] Even after Hall's active period as a saxophonist, an article titled 'D'Indy Work Originally Written for Mrs. R. J. Hall of Boston' states that the French composer composed his Choral Varié at Hall's request.[28] In the article 'Boston hears much new French music' in *Musical America* of 1912, the journalist writes about Hall as commissioner and dedicatee: "these compositions were presented for the first time in this city: [...]; 'Poème Elegiaque' (composed for and dedicated to Mrs. Hall) for saxophone and orchestra, Gaubert; [...]."[29]

In other instances, Hall is also labeled and portrayed as a patron. "An unusual and interesting musicale was given last week at the home of Mrs. Richard Hall, well known in Boston as a patron of music and player upon the saxophone."[30] As far as Hall's role as the one who commissioned the works, it has remained unclear to the present day what compensation she offered the composers. Unlike articles in which Hall appears as commissioner or as dedicatee, there is almost no information to be found about Hall's services in return. There is only one article from 1906 in *Le Guide Musical*—a newspaper that was prominent in the French and Belgian musical communities—that claims that Hall might have paid for new compositions.[31] Moreover, at the end of her artistic career, Hall is described in *Musical America* as "well known in Boston as a patron of music and player upon the saxophone." Likewise, we do have evidence that Hall paid Debussy for his work: "when he [Debussy] accepted Elise Hall's prepaid commission" and "the composer certainly needed the money."[32]

For the second category, Hall is perceived both as a commissioner of music and as the dedicatee. Some other newspaper articles regularly mention Hall as the performer/producer—as president of the Boston Orchestral Club—to whom the composers dedicate their works, although it does not necessarily mean that she commissioned them. Of the newspaper articles in which Hall was mentioned purely as a dedicatee there are two examples in *Musical America*. In 1906 an article appears in which we read that "Mrs. R. G. [J.] Hall, President of Society, gives Charming Rendition of Saxophone Solo dedicated to Her … " and that "An 'Elegie for Saxophone, Impression d'Automne,' composed by Audre Caplet, and dedicated to Mrs. Hall, was played by her most delightfully and intelligently."[33] In 1911 we read that "The saxophone solo in the work of Woollett was played by Mrs. Hall, to whom the composition is dedicated."[34] The evidence presented here indicates that Hall's relationship with the composers and the works is complicated, and there is not conclusive evidence to confirm the exact nature of her role in the production of the musical scores.

Hall as a Dedicatee

Building on the reception analysis of Hall's role in (contemporary) newspaper articles, in this section the compositions' paratexts are analyzed in order to examine how Hall's name appears in the manuscripts of her collection.[35] In so doing, I leave aside for a moment the question of whether or not Hall functioned as the commissioner or merely as the dedicatee. Instead, the issue is raised as to which composers mention Hall's name in their manuscripts and why it is necessary for those composers to do so. With this section, we also situate the scores dedicated to Hall in a broader context of dedicating music at the beginning of the twentieth century.

Dedications in musical scores can have multiple meanings, drawn from the composer's act of dedicating a composition to a performer and the performer's act of commissioning a work from a composer. Neither instance of dedication necessarily corresponds to the other; it is perfectly conceivable that a composer dedicates a composition to one person but the work has been commissioned by someone else. In music history, dedication is an important practice that can serve several functions. Firstly, studies highlight especially the composers' and publishers' commercial strategies involved in the phenomenon of dedication. Explicit mentions of famous dedicatees, moreover, increased the commercial and public success of the scores and thus afforded composers the opportunity "to assert power over the reception of their works."[36] According to Emily Green, for instance, the act of dedicating culminated during the nineteenth century as an important part of the print culture. Published scores prominently displayed the names of dedicatees in large and ornate script on the title page. Interestingly, scholarship on dedications in music restricts itself mainly to music before 1900, focusing the examination of dedications on the oeuvre of more canonized composers such as Mozart, Brahms, Liszt, and Haydn.[37] Secondly, patterns of dedications during the nineteenth century suggest a composer's engagement with new trends in biography, celebrity, and sociability. Composers were increasingly searching for novel ways to distinguish and position themselves as genuine celebrities, without particularly chasing commercial objectives.[38] This phenomenon could be understood in Bourdieu's terms as an organization of the gift economy with the goal of an accumulation of symbolic capital. Simultaneously, this entrepreneurship gave rise to the beginning of the music industry—the idea of considering music as a commercial product in the networks of publishers and composers.[39]

There are some interesting facts about the music associated with Hall: the manuscripts of her music collection show that most composers dedicated their score to Hall. Of the 22 works dedicated to Hall, fourteen manuscripts are held in the New England Conservatory archives. Gilson's *Concerto*, whose manuscript was rediscovered in the south of France in 2017, is archived in the music library of the Royal Conservatory Brussels.[40] From the entire collection, five manuscripts have been destroyed or lost. Of two works from the whole list, whose manuscripts are not in the archive, we can only rely on the print edition by a publishing house. Table 2.2 lists the dedications as they appear in the scores together. Here we notice that not all works bear a dedication. Of the seventeen works we can consult in manuscript or print edition, ten musical scores contain a literal dedication to the saxophonist. In these dedications Hall's name is mentioned, and sometimes Boston is mentioned as well as her position as president of the Boston Orchestral Club.

Table 2.2. Dedications in Hall's musical scores

Composer	Score	Dedication
Claude Debussy	*Rapsodie*	A Madame E. Hall avec l'hommage respectueux de Claude Debussy
Paul Dupin	*Chant*	Dédié à Madame Elise Hall
Philippe Gaubert	*Poème Élégiaque*	à madame Elise Hall, président de l'orchestral club de Boston (bien respectueux hommage)
Paul Gilson	*Concerto no. 1*	A madame B. Hall de Boston
Gabriel Grovlez	*Suite*	A Madame Elise Hall A Madame Elise Hall, artiste émérite, l'auteur offre respectueusement la dédicace de cette "suite"

Composer	Score	Dedication
Jean Huré	Andante	A madame Elise Hall
Charles Martin Loeffler	Divertissement Espagnol	Dédié à madame R. J. Hall
Georges Longy	Rhapsodie	Pour Madame E. Hall Présidente de l'Orchestral Club de Boston, en respectueux hommage
Léon Moreau	Pastorale	à madame richard hall
Henri Woollet	Siberia	à madame Elise Hall

Through the Lens of Patronage Theory

After contextualizing approaches that build on historical documents, the final section of this chapter provides tools to reflect more conceptually on Hall's activities. These concepts are borrowed from the field of patronage theory, which generally studies the arts from an institutional perspective as a particular economy in which several types of capital can circulate.

When Hall explicitly requests a composer, a relationship is initiated—a patronage dynamic—between the patron ("the giver") and the artist ("the demander"). Patronage studies talk about complex and non-uniform relationships and negotiations between both parties. According to patronage expert Helleke van den Braber's model, the "giver" and "demander" face each other with the artwork between them.[41] Without this work of art, which connects both parties, there is no relationship. That relationship is not merely maintained by a patron who "invests" and a creator who "profits," but rather is founded on a form of reciprocity. Both parties invest and benefit; there is a gift exchange. Moreover, it is a misconception that the investment on the part of the demander can only be financial. Van den Braber talks about the patron who can support the artist economically, socially, and with narrative capital. On the artist's side, the investment is mainly by means of cultural and narrative capital.

We can use Van den Braber's theory of patronage dynamics to gain more insights into the relationship between Hall and her composers. The example of d'Indy's *Choral Varié* serves as an excellent case in point: in the first step, both the patron and the artist develop plans and set expectations, and they agree on the nature of the artwork that will be created. For example, Hall asks the composer d'Indy to write a work for her in which the saxophone will play a role, and she mentions that she herself as a performer wants to perform this new composition. With regard to the *Choral Varié*, an article from *Le Guide*

> LE GUIDE MUSICAL 639
>
> A. DURAND et fils, éditeurs, 4, place de la Madeleine, Paris
>
> Vient de paraître :
>
> # VINCENT D'INDY
>
> Op. 54. — **Marche du 76ᵉ Régiment d'Infanterie**
> Piano à quatre mains. . . Net : fr. 3 50
>
> Op. 55. — **Choral varié,** pour saxophone solo (ou alto) et orchestre :
> Edition *A*. Saxophone et piano. . Net : fr. 3 50
> Edition *B*. Alto et piano . . . » » 3 50
> Partition d'orchestre . . . . » » 6 —
> Parties d'orchestre . . . . » » 8 —
> Chaque partie supplémentaire . . » » 0 75

Figure 2.1. The announcement of the *Choral Varié*'s publication in *Le Guide Musical*

Musical describes how the American patron visited the composer in Paris and even begged him "to write a piece for this instrument [saxophone]. She recently came to France to show her talent and proposes to play the composition of M. d'Indy."[42] In addition, the influential music journal *Le Guide Musical* paid attention to this specific commission. This journal mentioned that d'Indy considered the composing of *Choral Varié* as a way to relax while he was working on his "admirable" *Symphony No. 2* (1903). He started composing the *Choral Varié*, as *Le Guide Musical* suggests, at the request of a gifted American woman, "une Américaine dont le talent sur cet instrument est notoire."[43] By September 1903, two months before the very first edition of the piece, the journal *Le Guide Musical* alluded to the future edition of the *Choral Varié* (see fig. 2.1).[44]

In November 1903 the same journal announced the first edition of the saxophone piece by Durand et fils:

> La maison Durand et fils, qui sait peu à peu s'attacher la plupart des musiciens français contemporains de véritable valeur vient de faire paraître, luxueusement éditées, deux œuvres nouvelles signées de compositeurs dont aucune production ne saurait passer inaperçue: MM. Vincent d'Indy et Claude Debussy.[45]

The second step is about the gift exchange between both the patron and the artist. To this day, we know nothing concrete about Hall's financial contribution. However, we can distill various forms of social and narrative capital.

When it comes to social capital, Hall herself was active in Boston's high society. She opened up her network there to d'Indy, providing both visibility and an interesting network for future projects of the artist. Apparently, the French composer had kept his patron informed of the publication of his *Choral Varié* since the very first performances, which were announced by *The Musical Courier* and were played by Hall herself. Soon after the release by the publisher she delivered the very first performance of the *Choral Varié* with her Orchestral Club on January 4, 1904, in Boston. *The Musical Courier* advertised this concert on January 6, 1904:

> The first concert of the Boston Orchestral Club, George Longy conductor, will be on Tuesday evening in Jordan Hall, and the program will be of interest. Vincent d'Indy's new chorale and variations for saxophone and orchestra, composed expressly for Mrs. Richard J. Hall of this city, and dedicated to her, will be performed for the first time. Mrs. Hall will play the saxophone part, and in the spring she will introduce the work in Paris at a concert conducted by the composer.[46]

Indeed, as mentioned in this review, Hall, too, managed to perform d'Indy's saxophone work outside the United States after her premiere in Boston, in close collaboration with the composer himself, who, as the quote above reveals, conducted the performance. At the composer's request she appeared in a concert series organized by the Parisian *Société nationale de musique*. This Parisian performance should not surprise us, as she was actively engaged in the musical communities in both Boston and Paris. By consulting prominent newspapers, we know that Hall was quite a well-known figure in the French capital, where she used to perform the compositions that were written for her. According to Julien Torchet in *Le Guide musical,* Hall visited Paris every year to present the new compositions commissioned by her. Also, the swift international performance of the work is rather surprising in the context of the early saxophone. On January 17, 1904, the Brussels journal *Le Guide Musical* mentioned a performance by another saxophonist, "Monsieur Kühn," which took place only one week after Hall's premiere, on January 9 and 10, 1904, at the *Concerts populaires* in Brussels. This concert was advertised in *Le Guide Musical* on January 3, 1904.[47] The Belgian Kühn was a well-known saxophonist who was already praised by *Le Guide Musical* in November 1877.[48] However, the short reference to his performance from the *Choral Varié* was rather negative: "the *Choral Varié*, for saxophone and orchestra, by V. d'Indy seemed a bit severe in theme and pace, despite the intonation of the soloist Mr. Kühn."[49]

What Van den Braber's model does not allow us to take into account, however, is the crucial role of actors serving as intermediaries. In Hall's case, George Longy, Hall's saxophone teacher, friend, and colleague, was a well-documented liaison between the musician Hall and the composers. Before actively working in Boston as an oboist for the Boston Symphony Orchestra, Longy was a member of the Paris *Société de Musique de Chambre pour instruments à vent*, an ensemble that collaborated with composers on a regular basis. In Boston, Longy, who was inspired by the Paris ensemble, founded the Longy Club, which allowed him to work closely with contemporary (French) composers. His concert programs demonstrate that he was experienced through his numerous collaborations with contemporary composers. Not coincidentally, several composers in Longy's network also dedicated work to Hall. Longy himself dedicated two works to Hall, and he collaborated with at least seven of the fifteen other European composers including d'Indy, Huré, Moreau, Mouquet, Schmitt, Woollett. However, it remains uncertain what role Longy exactly played, how exactly he assisted Hall, and if he was the one to approach the French composers. Consequently, earlier reflections on Longy's contribution have remained limited to mere suppositions. Cottrell briefly claims that "she was undoubtedly advised by Longy,"[50] whereas Gudell, Hemke, and Noyes already go a step further, as their following statements respectively indicate:

> Longy assisted Elise Hall in contacting composers to write works for her and as a result, increased the repertoire of chamber and concerto pieces for her instrument.[51]

> Through the help of her teacher, Georges Longy, then solo oboist with the Boston Symphony, she received advice on how to expend her new enthusiasm and her money in a practical and positive manner.[52]

> with Georges Longy acting as intermediary between saxophonist and composer.[53]

Regarding the narrative capital, Hall makes it possible for the artist to construct a narrative. As a saxophonist from the United States, she asked d'Indy to write a new work for her. This means that Hall selected him as a composer, and that she values his work highly. From d'Indy's side, the composer offers various types of cultural capital, among which Van den Braber distinguishes three different types: knowledge, proximity, and impact. Firstly, the composer maintained a close relationship with his patron and he informed her with inside information about the composition. Secondly, as indicated previously, d'Indy and Hall performed together in Paris. In this way, Hall—the "giver"— became involved in d'Indy's artistic network. Thirdly, the composer might have engaged the patron to determine certain aspects of his piece of art. However, except for these testimonies in music journals, it has remained uncertain until today to what extent Hall might have influenced the composer's artistic process; it is unknown whether the composer asked for Hall's technical advice for his saxophone composition. Yet we can assume that d'Indy had the occasion to attend one or more performances by Hall and therefore would have been somewhat familiar with her playing.[54]

Conclusion

At the end of the nineteenth century, Elise Hall learned to play the saxophone at a time when women in the United States, as opposed to Europe, were emerging as saxophonists in a variety of genres. This saxophone practice presented new challenges to Hall. In the decades immediately following the official introduction of the saxophone by inventor Adolphe Sax, the first repertoire developed in three phases. In the initial phase, acquaintances of the inventor primarily composed the first works for saxophone. These composers were not experts and wrote the works on the basis of their own experience with other instruments they knew. In the second phase, it was mainly the first saxophone teachers and international soloists who composed the repertoire from their own experiences teaching and/or performing. In this period, the emergence of the first saxophone education, Sax's saxophone class at the Paris *Gymnase musical militaire* and of the Royal Conservatory of Brussels played a major role. In a third phase, the impetus of the French-American Elise Hall expanded the saxophone repertoire between 1900 and 1920. In doing so, she realized a break with the nineteenth-century repertoire composed mainly for saxophone solo or saxophone and piano. The scores that Hall collected have a variety of settings, from chamber music to concertante works for saxophone and orchestra.

In total, Hall's collection consists of 22 compositions, and most of these manuscripts reside in the archives of the New England Conservatory. All of the composers were of European descent—fourteen French, one Belgian, and one German-American—and, almost without exception, all had won the prestigious Premier Prix de Rome. Through the engagement with these composers, Hall reinforced the trend of promoting primarily European art of international standing in the United States, whether by individuals or institutions. Hall belonged to the high society of her time and inhabited both North American and French circles of influence. After the death of her husband Dr. Richard Hall, she lived an independent life. A wealthy widow who invested her money in a private club, the Boston Orchestral Club, she joined other female patrons of the era.

Today, we lack historical evidence to support the claim that Hall specifically commissioned all of the aforementioned composers. Dedications to Hall do not explicitly prove that she always took the initiative. It is conceivable, for instance, that composers spontaneously dedicated a work to this famous American saxophonist, so as to establish their own reputation as internationally oriented composers or to encourage a potential collaboration with Hall. Moreover, the paratextual analysis of the available scores (in manuscript or edition) has shown that not all composers dedicated their musical works to Hall. However, it does not mean that Hall did not commission them.

When it comes to patronage dynamics, Hall's relationships with composers differ fundamentally from those of other patrons. In addition to possibly commissioning composers, as an active saxophonist she was also able to perform scores. Hall's productive combination of patronage and performance thus offers food for thought food for reflection on complex practices of patronage which go beyond the classic model of a wealthy woman who supports artists financially; throughout her activities, Hall invested in others, in saxophone music, and in her own musical career. Future research can hopefully build on the questions raised and the ideas offered in this chapter, as well as fruitfully combine musicological, historical, and artistic methodologies to better understand Hall's fascinating story.

NOTES

1. The autograph and a handwritten copy of it only surfaced more than one hundred years after its composition date, respectively in 2017 and 2019.
2. Yet Gilson was not the first to compose for solo saxophone and orchestra. By 1879 the American composer Caryl Florio (1843-1920) wrote his *Introduction, Theme and Variation* for saxophonist Edward Lefebre (1835-1911), which might be the first composition for solo saxophone and chamber orchestra in the saxophone's history. In 1900, Charles Martin Loeffler (1861-1935) composed his *Divertissement Espagnol* for Elise Hall, staging a saxophone solo and orchestra. For more cultural-historical information and information about the rediscovery, see Kurt Bertels, "Gevonden: 's werelds eerste saxofoonconcerto," *De Moderne Tijd* 3, no. 4 (2019) 352–359; Kurt Bertels, "Brussels Connection: An Outline of Research into Early Belgian Saxophone Music, Including the World's First Saxophone Concerto Composed by Paul Gilson," *Clarinet and Saxophone Society of Great Britain* 47 (June 2022): 22–24.
3. Linda Whitesitt, "Women's Support and Encouragement of Music and Musicians," in *Women and Music: A History*, ed. Karin Pendle (Bloomington: Indiana University Press, 1991), 301. The second version was published in 2001.
4. Gilson's saxophone concerto was performed and recorded for the very first time in its original form in 2020. For the recording, see Kurt Bertels, Jan Latham-Koenig, Flanders Symphony Orchestra, *Works for Saxophone and Orchestra by Paul Gilson (1865-1942)*, Etcetera Records, 2020; "Paul Gilson saxophone," Spotify, accessed July 27, 2022; Kurt Bertels, "Performing Dedications. A Contextual and Artistic Reflection on the Dedication of the World's First Saxophone Concerto," *FORUM+* 29, no. 3 (2022): 47–53.
5. The musical works from Hall's collection are performed and recorded by internationally renowned saxophonists such as Arno Bornkamp and Claude Delangle.
6. Frederick Hemke, "The Early History of the Saxophone" (PhD diss., The University of Wisconsin, 1975), 429.
7. William Henry Street, "Elise Boyer Hall, America's First Female Concert Saxophonist: Her Life as Performing Artist, Pioneer of Concert Repertory for Saxophone and Patroness of the Arts" (DMA diss., Northwestern University, 1983), iii.
8. "commandes que l'on doit les premières grandes pièces concertantes pour saxophone" (translation by the author). Antonino Mollica, "Le saxophone exotique aux XIXe et XXe siècle," in *Une histoire du saxophone par les méthodes parues en France 1846-1942*, ed. Pascal Terrien (Sampzon: Editions Delatour France, 2014), 168.
9. Kurt Bertels, "Performing Dedications: A Contextual and Artistic Reflection on the Dedication of the World's First Saxophone Concerto," *FORUM+* 29, no. 3 (2022): 47–53; Kurt Bertels, "Attuned to the 'Saxophone Lady': Vincent d'Indy's *Choral Varié*, its context, and its performance," *The Saxophone Symposium* (forthcoming in 2023); James R. Noyes, "Debussy's 'Rapsodie Pour Orchestre et Saxophone' Revisited," *The Musical Quarterly* 90, no. 3/4 (Fall – Winter 2007): 416–445, http://www.jstor.org/stable/25172879.
10. Ralph P. Locke and Cyrilla Barr (eds.), *Cultivating Music in America: Women Patrons and Activists since 1860* (Berkeley: University of California Press, 1997).
11. Ralph P. Locke and Cyrilla Bar, "Introduction: Music Patronage As a 'Female-Centered Cultural Process,'" in *Cultivating Music in America*, ed. Ralph P. Locke and Cyrilla Bar (Berkeley: California University Press), 6. "[This book] would deal only with women patrons in the United States. Patrons who were active in other countries are therefore not discussed."
12. Locke and Bar, "Introduction," 7.
13. Myriam Chimènes, **Mécènes et musiciens. Du salon au concert à Paris sous la IIIe République** (Paris: Librairie Arthème Fayard, 2004).
14. Paul Dimaggio, "Cultural Entrepreneurship in Nineteenth-Century Boston: The Creation of an Organizational Base for High Culture in America," *Media, Culture and Society* 4 (1982): 33–50.
15. For studies on female saxophone players see Holly J. Hubbs, "American Women Saxophonists from 1870-1930: Their Careers and Repertoire" (PhD. diss., Ball State University, 2003); Thomas Smialek and L. A. Logrande, "Louise Linden: America's First Saxophone Virtuoso," *The Saxophone Symposium* 38/39 (2016): 1–29; Thomas Smialek and L. A. Logrande, "America's 'Young Lady Saxophonist' of the Gilded Age: The Performances, Repertoire, and Critical Reception of Bessie Mecklem," *The Saxophone Symposium* 36/37 (2014): 90–123; Thomas Smialek and L. A. Logrande, "Mrs. B. L. Hackenberger: Bessie Mecklem as Progressive-Era Clubwoman," *The Saxophone Symposium* 45 (2022): 50–74; Thomas Smialek and L. A. Logrande, "Asenath Mann: Boston's Gilded-Age Saxophonist," *The Saxophone Symposium* 45 (2022): 7–41.

16. After inventor Adolphe ("Antoine-Joseph") Sax obtained his French patent in 1846, Sax himself led a saxophone class between 1857 and 1870.
17. As in Paris, the existence of the Brussels saxophone class was only temporary. In 1904, after 37 years, the class was taken out of the curriculum. See Kurt Bertels and Kristin Van den Buys, "The Nineteenth-Century Brussels Saxophone School," *The Saxophone Symposium* 43 (2020): 71–87.
18. The saxophone quartet attains its full development in the twentieth century. Saxophonist Alfonso Padilla presented this topic during the International Palmela Saxophone Festival 2021 (*Repertorio para cuarteto de saxofones: evolución histórica y perspectivas de futro*); Cottrell, *The Saxophone*, 138–142.
19. For research on the repertoire of these classes, see Bruce Edward Ronkin, "The Music for Saxophone and Piano Published by Adolphe Sax" (DMA diss., University of Maryland, 1987); Kurt Bertels, *Een ongehoord geluid. De saxofoonklas van het Koninklijk Conservatorium Brussel tussen 1867 en 1904* (Brussels: ASP Editions, 2020), 47–74.
20. Stephen Cottrell, "Charles Jean-Baptiste Soualle and the Saxophone," *Journal of the American Musical Instrument Society* XLIV (2018): 179–208; Nancy Lynne Greenwood, "Louis Mayeur, His Life and Works for Saxophone Based on Opera Themes" (PhD diss., University of British Columbia, 2005); James R. Noyes, "Edward A. Lefebre (1834-1911): Preeminent Saxophonist of the Nineteenth Century" (PhD diss., Manhattan School of Music, 2000).
21. Carol J. Oja, "Women Patrons and Crusaders for Modernist Music: New York in the 1920s," in *Cultivating Music in America*, ed. Ralph P. Locke and Cyrilla Barr (Berkeley: California University Press), 239.
22. Oja, "Women Patrons," 239. "With the exception of Isabella Stewart Gardner, who in Boston at the turn of the century subsidized Charles Martin Loeffler, patrons paid little attention to native composers."
23. *Musical America*, January 1, 1910, 27.
24. *The Musical Courier*, April 27, 1910, 40.
25. *The Musical Courier*, January 6, 1904, 19; *The Musical Courier*, January 25, 1905, 37.
26. *The Musical Courier*, April 27, 1910, 40.
27. *The Musical Courier*, April 6, 1916, 33.
28. *Musical America*, May 14, 1921, 32.
29. *Musical America*, March 23, 1912, 24.
30. *Musical America*, February 7, 1920, 20.
31. *Le Guide musical*, June 24, 1906, 460–461. "Salle Pleyel—Si vous étiez grande dame, passionée pour la musique et maîtresse d'une très grosse fortune, vous viendrait-il l'idée d'en distraire une partie à la propagation du saxophone? J'en doute. Vous penseriez que cet instrument n'a pas encore assez de quartiers de noblesse pour mériter ce sacrifice et vous (…)."
32. Noyes, "Debussy's 'Rapsodie Pour Orchestre et Saxophone' Revisited," 420.
33. *Musical America*, April 28, 1906, 12.
34. *Musical America*, February 4, 1911, 31.
35. For research on the role of dedications, see Mary S. Lewis, "Introduction: The Dedication as Paratext," in *Cui Dono Lepidum Novum Libellum: Dedicating Latin Works and Motets in the Sixteenth Century*, ed. Ignace Bossuyt (Leuven: Leuven University Press, 2008), 1–11; Nancy November, "Marketing Ploys, Monuments and Music Paratexts: Reading the Title Pages of Early Mozart Editions," in *Late Eighteenth-Century Music and Visual Culture*, ed. C. Eisen and A. Davison (Turnhout: Brepols, 2017), 155–172; Stephen Rose, "The mechanisms of the music trade in Central Germany 1600-1640," *Journal of The Royal Musical Assocation* 130 (2005): 1–32.
36. Emily H. Green, *Dedicating Music 1785-1850* (Rochester: University of Rochester, 2019), 37.
37. Studies have focused on composers such as Haydn: Tom Beghin, *The Virtual Haydn* (Chicago: University of Chicago, 2015); Mozart: Mark Evan Bonds, "Replacing Haydn: Mozart's 'Pleyel Quartets,'" *Music and Letters* 88 (2007): 201–225; and James Webster, "One More Time: Mozart's Dedication to Haydn," in *Widmungen bei Haydn und Beethoven*, ed. Bernhard R. Appel and Armin Raab (Beethovenhaus Verlag, 2015), 121–138; Brahms: Andrea Hammes, *Brahms gewidmet: ein Beitrag zu Systematik und Funktion der Widmung in der zweiten Hälfte des 19. Jahrhunderts* (Göttingen: V&R Unipress, 2015); Liszt: Alan Walker, *Reflections on Liszt*. (New York: Cornell University Press, 2005); and Rossini: Denise Gallo, "Selling 'Celebrity': The Role of the Dedication in Marketing Piano Arrangements of Rossini's Military Marches," in *The Idea of Art Music in a Commercial World, 1800-1930*, ed. Christina Bashford and Roberta Montemorra Marvin (Suffolk: Boydell Press, 2016), 8–26.
38. Green, *Dedicating Music*, 3.
39. Bashford & Marvin, *The Idea of Art Music in a Commercial World*.
40. For an article on the rediscovery of Gilson's manuscript, see Kurt Bertels, "Gevonden: 's werelds eerste saxofoonconcerto," *De Moderne Tijd* 3, no. 4 (2019): 351–359. Gilson's first saxophone concerto was performed and recorded for the very first time in its original form in 2020. For the recording, see Bertels, Latham-Koenig, Flanders Symphony Orchestra, *Works for Saxophone and Orchestra by Paul Gilson (1865-1942)*.
41. Helleke Van den Braber, *Van maker naar mecenas (en weer terug)*, Universiteit Utrecht.

42. *Le Guide Musical*, July 31 and August 7, 1904, 575. "Elle a fait prier M. Vincent d'Indy d'écrire un morceau pour cet instrument [saxophone]. Elle est venue récemment en France afin de faire apprécier son talent et se propose de jouer la composition de M. d'Indy."
43. Gustave Samazeuilh, "Bibliographie," *Le Guide Musical*, November 22, 1903, 820.
44. *Le Guide Musical*, September 6, 1903, 631; *Le Guide Musical*, September 13, 1903, 639.
45. *Le Guide Musical*, November 22, 1903, 820. "The firm Durand et Fils, which has gradually been able to attract the majority of contemporary French musicians of real value, has just published two new works signed by composers whose work cannot go unnoticed: Vincent d'Indy and Claude Debussy."
46. *The Musical Courier*, January 6, 1904, 19.
47. *Le Guide Musical*, January 3, 1904, 14.
48. *Le Guide Musical*, January 10, 1878, 13-14. "Le jeune Kühn, âge de 11 ans, joue du saxophone de la façon la plus brillante; il nous a été donné d'apprécier son style correct et élégant, la facilité étonnante avec laquelle il triomphe des plus grandes difficultés. Il a interpreété d'une manière tout à fait supérieure une fantaisie pastorale de Singelée, et un solo de Klosé; il a su tenir l'assistance sous le charme de ses sons, tantôt suaves et mélodieux, tantôt graves et sonores. Aussi la salle entière lui a-t-elle fait une ovation justement méritée." (Translation by the author: "The 11-year-old Kühn plays the saxophone in the most brilliant way; we have been given to appreciate his correct and elegant style, the astonishing ease with which he triumphs over the greatest difficulties. He interpreted in a quite superior way a pastoral fantasy of Singelée, and a solo of Klose; He knew how to hold the audience under the spell of his sounds, sometimes sweet and melodious, sometimes serious and sonorous. So the whole room gave him a well-deserved ovation.")
49. *Le Guide Musical*, January 17, 1904. "le *Choral Varié*, pour saxophone et orchestre, de V. d'Indy a paru un peu sévère de thème et d'allure, malgré la justesse d'éxécution du soliste M. Kuhn."
50. Cottrell, *The Saxophone*, 244.
51. Gudell, "Georges Longy,"
52. Hemke, *The Early History of the Saxophone*, 430.
53. Noyes, *Debussy*.
54. In his historical study on The Longy Club, David Whitwell shows that d'Indy collaborated closely with the Parisian musician Longy, who served as Hall's private teacher and founded his own ensemble *The Longy Club* in Boston.

WORKS CITED

Beghin, Tom. *The Virtual Haydn*. Chicago: University of Chicago, 2015.

Bertels, Kurt. "Gevonden: 's werelds eerste saxofoonconcerto." *De Moderne Tijd* 3, no. 4 (2019): 352–359.

———. "Performing Dedications. A Contextual and Artistic Reflection on the Dedication of the World's First Saxophone Concerto." *FORUM+* 29, no. 3 (2022): 47–53.

———. "Brussels Connection: An Outline of Research into Early Belgian Saxophone Music, Including the World's First Saxophone Concerto Composed by Paul Gilson." *Clarinet and Saxophone Society of Great Britain*, June 2022.

———. "Attuned to the 'Saxophone Lady': Vincent d'Indy's *Choral Varié*, its context, and its performance." *The Saxophone Symposium* (forthcoming in 2023).

———. *Een ongehoord geluid. De saxofoonklas van het Koninklijk Conservatorium Brussel tussen 1867 en 1904*. Brussels: ASP Editions, 2020.

Bertels, Kurt, and Van den Buys, Kristin. "The Nineteenth-Century Brussels Saxophone School." *The Saxophone Symposium* 43 (2020): 71–87.

Bonds, Mark Evan. "Replacing Haydn: Mozart's 'Pleyel Quartets.'" *Music and Letters* 88 (2007): 201–225.

Bronkin, Bruce Edward. "The Music for Saxophone and Piano Published by Adolphe Sax." DMA diss., University of Maryland, 1987.

Chimenès, Myriam. *Mécènes et musiciens. Du salon au concert à Paris sous la IIIe République*. Paris: Librairie Arthème Fayard, 2004.

Cottrell, Stephen. "Charles Jean-Baptiste Soualle and the Saxophone." *Journal of the American Musical Instrument Society* XLIV (2018): 179–208.

Dimaggio, Paul. "Cultural Entrepreneurship in Nineteenth-Century Boston: The Creation of an Organizational Base for High Culture in America." *Media, Culture and Society* 4 (1982): 33–50.

Gallo, Denise. "Selling 'Celebrity': The Role of the Dedication in Marketing Piano Arrangements of Rossini's Military Marches." In *The Idea of Art Music in a Commercial World, 1800-1930*, edited by Christina Bashford and Roberta Montemorra Marvin, 8–26. Suffolk: Boydell Press, 2016.

Green, Emily H. *Dedicating Music 1785-1850*. Rochester: University of Rochester, 2019.

Greenwood, Nancy Lynne. "Louis Mayeur, His Life and Works for Saxophone Based on Opera Themes." PhD diss., University of British Columbia, 2005.

Gudell, Valerie M. "Georges Longy: His Life and Legacy." DMA diss., The University of Houston, 2001.

Hammes, Andrea Hammes. *Brahms gewidmet: ein Beitrag zu Systematik und Funktion der Widmung in der zweiten Hälfte des 19. Jahrhunderts*. Göttingen: V&R Unipress, 2015.

Hemke, Frederick. "The Early History of the Saxophone." PhD diss., The University of Wisconsin, 1975.

Hubbs, Holly J. "American Women Saxophonists from 1870-1930: Their Careers and Repertoire." PhD diss., Ball State University, 2003.

Lewis, Mary S. "Introduction: The Dedication as Paratext." In *Cui Dono Lepidum Novum Libellum: Dedicating Latin Works and Motets in the Sixteenth Century*, edited by Ignace Bossuyt, 1–11. Leuven: Leuven University Press, 2008.

Locke, Ralph P., Barr, Cyrilla (eds.). *Cultivating Music in America: Women Patrons and Activists since 1860*. Berkeley: University of California Press, 1997.

Mollica, Antonino. "Le saxophone exotique aux XIXe et XXe siècle." In *Une histoire du saxophone par les méthodes parues en France 1846-1942*, edited by Pascal Terrien, 149-173. Sampzon: Editions Delatour France, 2014.

November, Nancy. "Marketing Ploys, Monuments and Music Paratexts: Reading the Title Pages of Early Mozart Editions." In *Late Eighteenth-Century Music and Visual Culture*, edited by C. Eisen and A. Davison, 155-172. Turnhout: Brepols, 2017.

Noyes, James R. "Debussy's 'Rapsodie Pour Orchestre et Saxophone' Revisited." *The Musical Quarterly* 90, no. 3/4 (Fall – Winter 2007): 416-445. http://www.jstor.org/stable/25172879.

———. "Edward A. Lefebre (1834-1911): Preeminent Saxophonist of the Nineteenth Century." PhD diss., Manhattan School of Music, 2000.

Oja, Carol J. "Women Patrons and Crusaders for Modernist Music: New York in the 1920s." In *Cultivating Music in America*, edited by Ralph P. Locke and Cyrilla Barr, 237-263. Berkeley: University of California Press, 1997.

Rose, Stephen. "The mechanisms of the music trade in Central Germany 1600-1640." *Journal of The Royal Musical Assocation* 130 (2005): 1–32.

Smialek, Thomas, Logrande, L.A. "Louise Linden: America's First Saxophone Virtuoso."*The Saxophone Symposium* 38/39 (2016): 1–29.

———. "America's 'Young Lady Saxophonist' of the Gilded Age: The Performances, Repertoire, and Critical reception of Bessie Mecklem." *The Saxophone Symposium* 36/37 (2014): 90–123.

———. "Mrs. B. L. Hackenberger: Bessie Mecklem as Progressive-Era Clubwoman." *The Saxophone Symposium* 45 (2022): 50–74.

———. "Asenath Mann: Boston's Gilded-Age Saxophonist." *The Saxophone Symposium* 45 (2022): 7–41.

Street, William Henry. "Elise Boyer Hall, America's First Female Concert Saxophonist: Her Life as Performing Artist, Pioneer of Concert Repertory for Saxophone and Patroness of the Arts." DMA diss., Northwestern University, 1983.

Van den Braber, Helleke. *Van maker naar mecenas (en weer terug)*. Utrecht: Universiteit Utrecht, 2021.

Walker, Alan Walker. *Reflections on Liszt*. New York: Cornell University Press, 2005.

Webster, James. "One More Time: Mozart's Dedication to Haydn." In *Widmungen bei Haydn and Beethoven*, edited by Bernhard R. Appel and Armin Raab, 121–138. Bonn: Beethovenhaus Verlag, 2015.

Whitesitt, Linda. "Women's Support and Encouragement of Music and Musicians." In *Women and Music: A History*, edited by Karin Pendle, 301–313. Bloomington: Indiana University Press, 1991.

Whitwell, David. *The Longy Club: An Early Wind Ensemble in Boston*. Austin: Whitwell Books, 2011.

Mediography

Bertels, Kurt, Jan Latham-Koenig, and Flanders Symphony Orchestra. *Works for Saxophone and Orchestra by Paul Gilson (1865-1942)*. Etcetera Records, 2020.

Le Guide Musical, January 10, 1878.
Le Guide Musical, September 6,1903.
Le Guide Musical, September 13, 1903.
Le Guide Musical, January 3, 1904.
Le Guide Musical, July 31 and August 7, 1904.
Le Guide musical, June 24, 1906.
Musical America, April 28, 1906.
Musical America, January 1, 1910.
Musical America, February 4, 1911.
Musical America, March 23, 1912.
Musical America, February 7, 1920.
Musical America, May 14, 1921.
The Musical Courier, January 6, 1904.
The Musical Courier, January 25, 1905.
The Musical Courier, April 27, 1910.
The Musical Courier, April 6, 1916.
Samazeuil, Gustave. "Bibliographie." *Le Guide Musical*, November 22, 1903.

PART II
Critical Organology & Social Identity

Exhuming Elise
Rehabilitating Reputations

Adrianne Honnold

ABSTRACT

In the past, scholars have compiled the biographical details of Elise Hall's life but she has not been investigated as a figure whose narrative has been distorted by the constraints rendered by embedded societal power structures. It has not been explicitly demonstrated how language commonly used to discuss Hall has contributed to biases based on gender, ability, and social status and has led to negative value judgments against her and the music she commissioned. This chapter explores Hall and the saxophone through an intersectional, specifically sociocultural lens, examining how the convergence of gender, class, race, positionality, and hierarchical structures have influenced her history and reputation. By enumerating the ways that social identities have contributed to the undervaluing of her performance skills and the saxophone's stature throughout history, both her legacy and the instrument's character are reevaluated and rehabilitated, and the systems that have existed as mechanisms of division are exposed as relics of the past that no longer serve saxophonists and scholars.

Introduction

As I sit in my home office looking at my alto saxophone on its stand in the corner, gleaming in the light from the window and waiting to be played, a series of images and sounds flash through my mind: I see Charlie Parker on album covers, I hear the solo from "Careless Whisper," and I recall snippets of sage advice from my former teacher Debra Richtmeyer. I hear sounds from a broad range of musical genres and recognize aspects of gender, race, and class that are embodied in the inanimate object. From a sociocultural perspective, the saxophone exists as a multi-dimensional artifact that represents a diverse set of socially constructed identities—characteristics that have not been the subject of substantive cultural criticism and have not always been enthusiastically embraced.

The term "intersectionality," coined by Kimberlé Crenshaw, invites us to recognize and consider how social identities relate to one another and collectively define an individual, sometimes serving as a means of marginalization.[1] This notion of the importance of converging identities can be extended to include a musical object such as the saxophone, thus acknowledging that the socially assigned categories of gender, race, and class associated with the instrument have had a profound effect not only on those who play it but also on the scores of people around the world that enjoy listening to it. Historically, these aspects may have contributed to a devaluing of the saxophone in certain contexts. Indeed, the complex set of dynamics surrounding social identities can play a significant part in an examination of music, performers, and instruments, and these dynamics are additionally complicated by considering them in the context of a certain time, place, and set of social and cultural conventions. The Gilded Age (1870-1900) and the Progressive Era (1890-1920) saw the development of foundational arts institutions in the Northeast of the United States, such as the Museum of Fine Arts in Boston (1876) and the Boston Symphony Orchestra (1881), which signaled the emergence of an "American" set of cultural hierarchies.[2] The pioneering saxophonist Elise Hall was actively performing and commissioning music throughout much of this era, and her undertakings happened to overlap with the time period in which the saxophone was developing its long and storied association with American popular music.

Historical and biographical data have been published about Elise Hall since the 1970s, but there are several avenues of inquiry regarding this information and the language used to discuss Hall which warrant scrutiny.[3] She has been described as an amateur, and the music she commissioned assessed as uncomplicated, light, and lacking in virtuosity. Yet these evaluations and even the language used to characterize them are based on beliefs deeply rooted in the patriarchal traditions of classical music, beliefs that emerged in the early seventeenth century to mark gender difference and reflect the formation of social constructions of gender of the time.[4] Hall endured discrimination due to aspects of her identity, and the majority of the gender codes implicit in the histories written about her have gone unmediated.[5]

Concomitant to the methods of inquiry utilized in other chapters in this volume, this chapter takes as its charge the rehabilitation of the narratives that relate to social identity, as well as a closer reading of the structures that impel the saxophone community to fight for relevance and respect. This chapter examines Hall and the saxophone through an intersectional lens, examining how the convergence of gender, class, race, positionality, and hierarchical structures have influenced her narrative history and reputation. By recognizing the systems that have sometimes relegated Hall and the saxophone to liminal spaces, researchers both within and outside the saxophone community can move beyond the anachronistic value judgments prevalent in the classical music milieu and progress toward openly embracing all that the instrument and its players represent in contemporary society and culture.

Background

In the global saxophone community, Hall is viewed as an outlier; there were other women saxophonists performing during the Gilded Age, but Hall stands apart because of the combination of her patronage, performances, and entrepreneurial ventures.[6] Anecdotal evidence gathered from the saxophone community appears to indicate that what is known of her performance ability, in addition to the work that she did to increase the body of the saxophone repertoire in the late nineteenth and early twentieth century, is often viewed with a combination of muted admiration and complacency.[7] There are some fundamental instabilities in the saxophone history which stem from perceptions of Hall and her music. Saxophonists who are familiar with her work seem content to echo the narratives that she was not an accomplished player and the music she played was too simple. The significant time, money, and effort she spent working with renowned composers and performing has been acknowledged by saxophonists and lauded as a foundational element of our heritage. However, the tacit belief that she was not an accomplished player and the undervaluing of the musical works that resulted from her efforts reflect a sense of complacency or even dismissal; scholars have compiled the biographical details of her life, but Hall has not been investigated as a figure whose reputation is colored by the constraints rendered by social identity and hierarchical structures.

The critical task of recognizing that the adverse value judgments levied against her, as well as the music she commissioned, were the result of bias based on gender, ability, and social status, among other things, has not been explicitly examined. A complex assemblage of social identities, along with a uniquely American approach to a life in music, all intersect in the figure of Elise Hall. It is, therefore, necessary to define the relationships between these identities in order to fully understand Hall's legacy and understand certain connotations surrounding the saxophone. These identities impel or galvanize one another in undefined ways and have had a lasting impact on how she is viewed, on the music she commissioned, and—by association—on the saxophone. Further, spatial and temporal factors have played an important part in the formation of aesthetic value judgments.

In the paragraphs below, examinations of intersectionality, positionality, and an approach to dismantling the hierarchies illuminate the ways in which Hall's legacy and history can be rehabilitated. In the process, our past as saxophonists, scholars, and historians is explored and acknowledged, and a path forward is proposed that allows us to come to terms with a broad and diverse view of the way that the saxophone and saxophonists operate in the world.

Positionality: Who's Writing the Histories?

The perspective from which scholars discuss Hall and her music is a consequential part of the story, and therefore it is crucial to briefly explore the idea of positionality. Positionality is defined as the quality of having a position, in various senses, in relation to other people. In sociological terms, positionality is the acknowledgment, or adoption, of a particular position in relation to other people, usually with reference to issues of culture, ethnicity, or gender.[8] To my knowledge, positionality has not been considered in the research surrounding Hall and her music. Those who have studied her have been almost exclusively male, white, and Anglo-American or European.[9] Inevitably, they have brought their own experiences, perspectives, and implicit biases to their work. While it is not necessary for researchers to belong to the same categories of social identity as their subjects, it is important to recognize and attend to the opportunity for potential partiality in these areas.

This approach is inspired by the wave of "New Musicology" of the late 1980s, when scholars such as Susan McClary, Joseph Kerman, Rose Subotnik, and others began to remedy the lacunae in musicological research, from both within and outside of the Western European canonical traditions, by bringing principles from feminism, gender studies, queer theory, and critical theory to the study of music.[10] They published research about music and people that had been left out of the traditional discourse: research that was inclusive of social identity and musical genre, and which explored concepts like positionality and intersectionality. The interdisciplinary nature of the new musicology is invoked here because it presents a multidimensional, holistic approach toward investigating a notable figure like Hall. Research methods primarily rooted in traditional, historical musicology have revealed a certain amount of knowledge surrounding her life and career, but these methods are woefully delimited by a lack of scrutiny regarding long-held and perpetuated biases.

Many saxophonists become familiar with Hall when they play and/or learn about Debussy's *Rapsodie* for the first time, thus positioning her as a secondary figure made notable by her association with a male composer, rather than for her groundbreaking achievements: she was the first woman to play in an American symphony orchestra; commissioned approximately twenty-two works for saxophone; became the president of the Boston Orchestral Club and produced their concerts for many years. In one recent example during an interview about Hall, a male scholar, when asked to provide an overview of her life, opens with an almost immediate assertion that she was not a virtuoso: "Her background is fascinating. As she was learning to play the saxophone, in part to help with some medical issues, she was not a virtuoso player and never thought of herself as a virtuoso player."[11] This overview is problematic for a few reasons, and it perpetuates alleged misinformation related to the facts of Hall's life.[12] Should a musician be introduced to an audience by describing a perceived lack of technical ability? Is virtuosity the first thing that should come to mind? Is it the pinnacle or ultimate achievement of a musician, the prime measure of success or value? In classical music, the answer is (often) yes. This response is due to the connection between male-defined performance practices that have characterized classical musicianship for hundreds of years—traditions that prize virtuosity and technicality above the myriad skills that comprise professional, artistically meaningful performances. In the quote above, the narrative that is presented about Hall prioritizes unfavorable perceptions of her performance abilities thereby diminishing her accomplishments; everything else she did is positioned as subordinate to her "amateur" level of saxophone playing; the remainder of the interview is framed by this perspective. Hall likely considered herself an amateur because of the strictures of classical music and gender of the era. Indeed, the position and title of "professional musician" was not available to her, as will be discussed further below.

Intersections of Identity

To a degree, Hall occupied liminal spaces due to the intersection of her identities and in conjunction with her chosen pursuits. She was an American, a woman, a saxophonist, and a patron; she was also a mother and a contributing member of high society on the East Coast during the Gilded Age/Progressive Era. How did the facets of her life shape the perceptions of those around her and the history that has been told in the years that have passed since her death? Although she does not represent all of the identity markers that have historically converged to marginalize or oppress individuals, Hall was nevertheless subjected to criticism that affected her life and legacy. Groundbreaking scholar and activist Kimberlé Crenshaw's theory of intersectionality is a vital framework with which to approach a discussion of social identity. Originally conceived as a way to understand the oppression of Black women in the American legal system, intersectionality has become a key concept in conversations about racial justice, identity politics, and policing in the United States.[13] Hall was a white woman of British descent but the framework of Crenshaw's theory can be applied in this case in order to re-establish the narrative surrounding her life and legacy and to understand how social structures rendered her work less valuable.

The concept of intersectionality emerged in the 1980s at a time when feminism was largely represented by women who were white and middle-class.[14] The feminist scholars of the time presumed that all experiences with sexism were the same. Crenshaw's paradigm-shifting paper published in the University of Chicago Legal Forum in 1989 upended this notion by demonstrating that women of color experience discrimination not on a "single-axis" as the feminist scholars had posited, but rather at a point where multiple aspects of their identities converge.[15] Crenshaw noted that "this focus on the most privileged group members marginalizes those who are multiply-burdened and obscures claims that cannot be understood as resulting from discrete sources of discrimination."[16] It would be impossible and ill-advised to use intersectionality in this chapter to compare the experiences of a white woman of wealth and privilege or the saxophone itself to those of Black women in the United States. Even so, in the spirit of scholarly inquiry, the concept provides a powerful structure that allows for the examination, or figurative exhumation, of Elise Hall.

Hall is an intriguing figure because her identity cumulatively combines to "other" her in certain ways. The first and most straightforward way is that she played the saxophone—a "ridiculous," "ungraceful," and "queer looking instrument" that had recently been invented by a Belgian but was not fully accepted as a part of conventional Western classical music.[17] The saxophone was new and novel when she started learning it in the late 1800s; it was unknown outside of the marching bands that were popular at the time. As McDonie states in this volume, the fact that Hall played the instrument is the chief reason that we examine her now: the unconventional combination of Hall and the saxophone ensured a level of historical relevance.

Secondly, she was a woman. Women—especially affluent ones—did not traditionally play wind instruments.[18] Wind instruments were, and still are, considered masculine in nature, and it was thought unbecoming of a woman to, as Debussy remarked, "suck at the wooden mouthpiece of this ridiculous instrument."[19] Debussy was referring specifically to Hall in this quote, but she could be seen as a proxy for all women saxophonists. And while Noyes noted that Debussy's tone and demeanor towards Hall softened later, his comments left an impact on critics and musicians of the time who took his words out of context and repeated the sentiment.[20] As Veronica Doubleday noted in a 2008 article entitled "Sounds of Power: An Overview of Musical Instruments and Gender," the very image of a woman playing an instrument like the saxophone is seen as "awkward" or "laughable," and essentially interferes with a man's enjoyment of a woman's face or body.[21]

Thirdly, Hall was an "American," a strong association for her and her family, which is discussed further below. As such, she was tenaciously undertaking the task of increasing the saxophone's concert repertory while attempting to stake a claim for the burgeoning instrument in European classical music.[22] In reference to Hall, Debussy noted "the tenacity of Americans is proverbial," an acknowledgment of the kind of determination that Hall demonstrated but was considered irksome by those outside of American society.[23] She was born in France and was an admitted Francophile, but her family was from the Northeast, as well as mostly long-term residents of Boston despite living in California for a time. This Americanness can be explained thematically as well; her ambition and entrepreneurial spirit aligned with a general ethos, seen at the turn of the century in the United States, which valued a can-do attitude, individuality, fame and fortune, and the lofty pursuit of highbrow cultural prestige. This sensibility would have been challenging in the early years of the twentieth century when the saxophone was finding a home in American popular vernacular styles of music and simultaneously establishing itself as a symbol of American progress and musical independence.[24] When the saxophone was adopted by jazz artists like Sidney Bechet in the late 1910s and 1920s, it began an enduring association with African Americans, a crucial element of its identity that exists today.

Fourth, Hall was a wealthy person. In today's parlance, we might consider her a "one-percenter," a person who possesses more wealth than ninety-nine percent of society. She was able to enjoy all the things that wealth, privilege, and whiteness afforded her at the turn of the century. In congress with other aspects of her identity, this wealth contributed to her status in that it set her apart from the average musician or American, which seems to have alienated her in some ways. In stark contrast to other people or groups that were marginalized due to aspects of identity, her wealth enabled her to achieve a notable level of agency and power. She was able to use these to move about freely in elite musical and social environments that were not open to many people. In Bourdieusian terms, she possessed—and wielded—a considerable amount of economic, social, and cultural capital, the triumvirate of status in society.[25] She possessed each of the individual assets that exist at the apex of a stratified social system that imparts power to a person: language, style of dress, education, intellect, and cultural knowledge.[26]

In relation to Hall's Americanness and wealth, William Street notes that her family considered themselves not immigrants, but colonists. This is a deeply problematic and hostile designation in the twenty-first century—but was an unmistakable point of pride for the family in the 1800s; a meaningful distinction that signaled their wealth and class, and one that set them apart from other inhabitants.[27] Her family name was Coolidge, and she was related to Calvin Coolidge, the thirtieth president of the United States. She came from a family of rich merchants, bankers, and politicians. Hall was a product of generational wealth. They had connections to George Washington (the lilacs growing at his home in Mount Vernon, in Virginia, were planted there by a member of Hall's family and still bloom there today), the Boston Tea Party, and buildings of architectural significance on Harvard's campus. So, Hall's family members were some of the original British colonists, and after generations of serving significant roles in the governance and development of the United States, it was perhaps natural to assume that she and her family thought of themselves as thoroughly American. Of course, there are no royal families in the States, but "founding" families sometimes assume this position in society and mythologize their role in developing the history and culture of the United States. In this way, they are promoting a willful ignorance about and clear discrimination toward the indigenous peoples of North America and engaging in the perpetuation of cultural hegemony. Hall's identity as a wealthy person from a family of colonizers strictly contrasts with the original intentions of intersectionality that helped people understand how class and race often combine to marginalize an individual. A comprehensive exploration of this aspect of Hall is outside the scope of this chapter, but its brief discussion here is critical to understanding the ways that Hall operated in society and culture during her lifetime.

When Hall moved back to Boston from California after her husband's death, she lived next door to Isabella Stewart Gardner, a lively and renowned patron of the arts whose home and remarkable art collection is now the Gardner Museum. As Street notes, she quickly resumed her position in wealthy social circles in Boston at the turn of the century.[28] It is likely that Gardner and others in the social circle in Boston at the time influenced one another's entrepreneurial endeavors. She can perhaps be considered the musical counterpart to Gardner, commissioning well-known composers to write music both in the States and abroad. By many accounts Gardner was stylish, unconventional, and eccentric, similar to the descriptions of Hall.[29]

Despite the attributes of wealth and privilege, Hall's agency and power were undermined by gender constraints. Hall had a great deal of freedom, but she was not free from judgment or discrimination, especially as they continued unchecked after her death. Léon Vallas, a French critic and musicologist, wrote about Hall in his biography of Claude Debussy (1933) and was conspicuously disparaging toward her and the instrument, interpreting the composer's initial reticence and frustration in writing the music that Hall commissioned from him as confirmed bias against her gender and the newish instrument.[30] Indeed, Vallas and other Debussy biographers appear to blame her for his struggles with completing the work.[31] The magnanimity that the biographers afforded Debussy, underscored by male chauvinism, led them to conclude that the fault must lie with the affluent society woman who paid for, and planned to premiere, the piece of music. There is also the fact that composers of the time did not yet know the capabilities of the saxophone, which undoubtedly played a part in Debussy's initial reluctance to undertake the work. This detail is sometimes mentioned by the critics above and appears to be an additional rationale for the unfavorable portrayal of Hall. The *Rapsodie* took over eighteen years to complete, and Debussy was able to collect two paychecks for the work; one from Hall and one from the publisher Durand.[32] In retrospect, the discrimination towards Hall in this scenario is made manifest, especially considering that she never had the opportunity to perform the music.

In 1970, the renowned experimental composer Pauline Oliveros published an essay in the *New York Times* entitled "And Don't Call Them 'Lady' Composers." She notes:

> Many critics and professors cannot refer to women who are also composers without using cute or condescending language. She is a "lady composer." Rightly, this expression is anathema to many self respecting [*sic*] women composers. It effectively separates women's efforts from the mainstream. According to the Dictionary of American Slang, "lady" used in such a context is almost always insulting or sarcastic. What critic today speaks of a "gentleman composer"? ... [I]t is not enough that a woman chooses to be a composer, conductor, or to play instruments formerly played exclusively by men; she cannot escape being squashed in her efforts—if not directly, then by subtle and insidious exclusion by her male counterparts.[33]

Oliveros goes on to say that "women composers are very often dismissed as minor or lightweight talents on the basis of one work by critics who have never examined their scores…"[34] She is putting into words, and publishing in the *New York Times*, the feelings of many women in music, and it is especially relevant in a discussion of Elise Hall, whose playing ability is often disparaged.[35]

In Debussy's correspondence to his wife and editor, he referred to Hall not by name but as "lady," a title often echoed by Vallas. This title may seem appropriate on the surface but was indeed a thinly veiled taunt aimed at ridiculing her and her high socio-economic status in America (a country with no royalty; predisposed to a garish flaunting of wealth). This epithet has followed Hall for approximately one hundred years, and she is sometimes still referred to as "The Saxophone Lady." Although more recently this characterization has shed some of its negative connotations, when the name was initially bestowed upon her it had the effect of reducing her power and agency and linking her to an instrument that was not considered elite; Hall and the saxophone were interlopers in the established world of classical, European music. This title also removes her real name from the narrative, further reducing her cultural capital and agency and rendering her synonymous with novelty. Put simply, the taunt can be read as sexist, classist, and faintly anti-American. To the collective detriment of Hall, the music, and the saxophone, Vallas's contemptuous assessment dominated the narrative for many decades to come.[36] On a positive note, more recent biographical accounts have succeeded in avoiding some of the language that was previously used in reference to Hall. They have incrementally improved the narrative by highlighting the value of the labor that she put into performing and commissioning new works.[37]

In an article thematically similar to the one by Oliveros, the art history professor and author Linda Nochlin observes that this was primarily due to the "white, Western male viewpoint, consciously accepted as *the* viewpoint of the art historian."[38] Nochlin is speaking of positionality, examining the position of the men writing the histories and the position of the women excluded from those histories. She aptly states that the failure of much academic history is to indiscriminately accept value systems simply because that is the way things have been done in the past.[39] Understanding the value systems and the position from which people apply them helps us shift to more inclusive and progressive paradigms of scholarly inquiry.

The final aspect of Hall's identity that contributed to her reputation was her alleged disability, the evidence of which is being debated.[40] The insinuation of an incapacity related to playing the saxophone served as a reason to discredit her in the discourse for decades. Reportedly, she suffered from a hearing impairment that began when she lived in California with her husband. A source in Street's thesis noted that Dr. Hall suggested she learn a wind instrument as a prescription to counteract the progression of the hearing loss that occurred after her recovery from what was possibly typhoid fever, although more recent scholarship refutes this long-held belief.[41] Back in Boston after her husband's passing, Hall performed regularly for almost twenty years, and the supposed increasing deafness, likely due to her advancing age, was never announced publicly. There are accounts of people close to her making reference to the fact that Hall's "musical hearing appeared unhindered."[42] Nevertheless, she was unjustly maligned by Vallas and others after her death for hearing loss, possibly because the assumption bolstered their negative assessments of her playing.

By the time she stopped performing publicly in 1920, she was almost completely deaf, because of her age.[43] Street asserts that the hearing impairment was at least partially responsible for her "eccentric behavior," an arcane term that could have many different meanings.[44] Curiously, Hall's neighbor Isabella Stewart Gardner is also often referred to as eccentric, which could be a catch-all to describe independent, affluent women who were accustomed to doing whatever they wanted at a time when this was not the norm. Perhaps the relative isolation inherent in the lives of wealthy, widowed society figures potentially contributed to this characterization. Both of these women may have engaged in idiosyncratic behaviors, but the language used to describe them can serve to diminish their accomplishments. It is not hard to imagine that going deaf as a musician would have an impact on one's emotional state, but clemency often seems to elude Hall's legacy. Documentation of the existence or impact of a hearing impairment lacks substantive re-examination outside of the Noyes article from 2022, and seems to be a potential direction for future research.

Understanding the Hierarchies: Amateur and Professional

There are two sets of binaries that have been imposed upon the historical narrative surrounding Hall and the saxophone which have not been clearly defined: amateur/professional and classical/popular. These binaries are hierarchical in nature, with professional and classical often placed in opposition to—and above—amateur and popular. When considered in the discipline of music, and more specifically in reference to an American woman in the early twentieth century, these terms are mapped to gender, class, and race. The task of thoroughly examining the two pairs is too broad to comprehensively address in this chapter, so these terms will be briefly defined below for how they have operated in discourse related to the topic of this volume.

The formal definition of professional is "a person that engages in a specified occupation or activity for money or as a means of earning a living, rather than as a pastime; contrasted with *amateur*."[45] Hall produced concerts, commissioned works from well-known composers and then premiered them, performed for years with professional musicians from a major symphony orchestra, and had performances reviewed by critics in major newspapers of the time.[46] Despite all of these accomplishments, she is referred to as an amateur musician. There are two main reasons why she was not considered a professional: she did not accept payment for the concerts in which she performed due to her wealth, and she was a woman. Depending on the perspective and/or a nuanced definition of the word "professional," Hall could be considered a professional because of the amount of work she did producing concerts and performing. In the musical culture of the twenty-first century, there are many people that consider themselves professionals but do not support themselves with money earned from playing. There are quite a few saxophonists who primarily make a living teaching music, either at a university or elementary, middle, or high school. According to the definition mentioned above, they should not be considered professionals. One difference is that music teachers and professors often have a great deal of specialized training, but then again this falls short of the basic definition. Some of the most celebrated jazz musicians of the early and mid-twentieth century did not have formal musical training but were/are considered professionals. For Hall, perhaps the term "semi-professional" should be utilized, to repudiate the gendered notion of "amateur" from this time period, thus acknowledging the many performances that she presented alongside professional, male musicians, in addition to recognizing that she did not accept payment for these performances. It is hard to say whether she would have considered adopting this term. Ultimately, the most suitable and inclusive way to refer to her is simply as a saxophonist.

In the early 1900s, very few women were admitted to conservatories in the United States or Europe due to societal and cultural restrictions, and as a result, there was no path toward winning auditions or joining professional groups such as symphony orchestras and marching bands. In the nineteenth and early twentieth centuries, the position of "amateur" musician was the only one available to women, even though it fails to adequately describe what some women were engaged in at the time. Historian Karen Blair notes that American conventions of masculinity in the late 1800s precluded men from wholeheartedly participating in the arts communities, which left the field open to women. Blair observes:

> The mandate that a proper female be a dilettante, acquainted with the arts only enough to amuse and entertain, lingered well into the twentieth century despite the advent of painting academies, music conservatories, and colleges that provided talented women with the training to match that of men who became the respected artists in America. So firm was the opinion that women were designed to ornament rather than create and interpret that capable women were routinely denied opportunities in the professional art world.[47]

Hall worked closely with Georges Longy, the oboist from the Boston Symphony, and he is often mentioned as the artistic visionary behind the concerts and music that she was performing. However, this excerpt prompts us to reevaluate the relationship between Longy and Hall. It is highly likely that she had more skill and agency than scholars have previously credited her with, and the way they frame the narratives describing the relationship between Longy and Hall represents the subordination of her artistic ideas to those of a male musician that she was working with. Blair goes on to note, "for American women at that time (the Progressive Era, 1890-1930), the distinctions between cultural and political change, and between professional and amateur achievement are artificial."[48]

Women were not "professional" because it was not socially acceptable during the Gilded Age, and there is precedence outside of the music world for gendered implications of the word "amateur." In a study examining the impact of gender on the narratives surrounding women art collectors during the Gilded Age, the author notes that it was common for people to misrepresent art collecting as carried out by women as merely interior design: an overt disavowal of the labor, knowledge, and discernment that women possessed surrounding art and curatorship.[49] Isabella Stewart Gardner is usually classified as an art collector, despite the curatorial duties that she assumed in building her namesake museum. It should be mentioned that the word "amateur" should not be stricken from the record, there are amateurs who engage in activities for mere enjoyment. The salient point is that the way that "professional" and "amateur" are presented as black-and-white binaries, lacking nuance or any gray area, have served as inadequate umbrella terms that leave women out and devalue their creative contributions. Once again, Blair communicates that women were left out due to forces outside of their control; club women like Hall were subject to all manner of social and patriarchal constraints:

> Certainly there were some exceptional women who overcame the domestic obstacles to artistic creation, but they were few in number. No matter how ambitious women might be, to earn a living at their art or merely to work single-mindedly at it, let alone—if they dared express it—to become famous and respected ... they faced tremendous barriers. They inevitably met a male-dominated world of orchestral conductors, newspaper critics, gallery owners, and art collectors who tended to dismiss their work, hamper their development, and exclude them from the customary channels for growth and exposure that male professionals enjoyed.[50]

Understanding the Hierarchies: Classical and Popular

Hall lived at a time when the oppositions between popular and classical music were being codified in the United States, and these distinctions exerted influence on her, the music she commissioned and performed, and the saxophone in a few ways. Ostensibly these two categories appear anodyne, but closer inspection reveals each genre to be closely associated with elements of identity that have served to exclude. As musicologist Susan Cook observes:

> Like so many hierarchical categories, the "popular" and "classical" are *imaginary*, and yet they are powerfully *imagined*. A great deal of energy goes into keeping these categories circulating and often in simplistic and uncritical ways …These categories, like patriarchy itself, were historically created, and every time we use the terms, we call into being something that does not necessarily exist except as a kind of shadow.[51]

> Popular music … [was] the oppositional foil within our constructions of late nineteenth- and early twentieth-century modernism, carries with it a staggering cultural baggage, a trunk full of social codes that have been historically attached to womankind and underprivileged men.[52]

Figuratively speaking, Hall had one foot in the past in terms of the (mostly European) composers and commissioning projects that she engaged with, and one foot in the progressive (American) future by playing the saxophone and engaging in ambitious commissioning and performance projects. The music that the Boston Orchestral Club performed and the manner in which the concerts were presented was irrefutably Western European and classical in style, and that is not up for debate here. What is notable is that these categories often go undefined, while each one encapsulates a set of codes which combine to aesthetically elevate or diminish. Hall, her music, and her legacy are caught in this web. Cook's article is written from a popular music studies perspective, but its message easily translates to Hall's life and career, as well as to other women in music during her time period. She was firmly entrenched in high society, and classical music was a big part of that, but the saxophone was not a traditionally classical instrument, and she was not a man who could pursue a career in that genre. Classical music has developed and maintained its masculine sensibilities over the centuries, and popular music is often associated with the feminine, as outlined below.

Classical music is defined in the Oxford Dictionary as "music written in a Western musical tradition, usually using an established form. Classical music is generally considered to be serious and to have lasting value."[53] The attempt here at defining the term is not meant to be exhaustive and not intended to veer into the territory of genre or aesthetic theory. This definition, as with the definition of "professional" presented above, is limited and perpetuates negative evaluations of its assumed opposite, popular music. Feminist musicologists and cultural critics have engaged in a great deal of discourse that substantially expands upon this definition by detailing the implicit perceptions surrounding classical music.[54] Historically, classical music was seen as high-class or highbrow, masculine, aesthetically valued, intellectual (of the mind), important, and serious.

In terms of the music itself, a revered characteristic in classical music is virtuosity or technical facility. This feature could be in the performance of the music or its composition, and the manner by which it is performed and/or composed could thus be construed as signaling virility, heterosexuality, and ability (contrasted with disability). These attributes emerged from a time when women were discouraged from performing publicly, so naturally, the performance practices were developed by men. As Blair notes above, women of high social standing were meant to only casually learn to play an instrument for the amusement of family and friends or to attract potential suitors, so they would not have had the opportunity to fully immerse themselves in an extensive practice regimen that had been developed and prescribed by male musicians. Thus, it was assumed that their technical skills would not be advanced enough for the conventions of classical music. However, using virtuosity and other male-defined approaches to the study of music as markers for worthiness or value assumes that there were no redeemable qualities in performances by women whose virtuosity was judged (by men) to be lacking. This assumption is wrong for one vital reason: women were denied the opportunity to define any measures of aesthetic value. It is nearly impossible to thrive in an environment where the rules and how to follow them are so narrowly defined. As a result, music that lacked complication and did not require the prescribed level of virtuosity was historically deemed feminine and of lesser value.

The way that classical and popular music have long been situated in tension with one another leads us to the idea that classical is aesthetically superior and is often labeled good while popular music is bad.[55] Popular music is defined as a style considered to have popular appeal,[56] but implicit perceptions of popular music assume that it has little value, or is not aesthetically worthy, and that it is low class or lowbrow, feminine, corporeal (of the body), trivial, insignificant, and fleeting. However, as Levine and Robert Walser demonstrate, simplicity, shallowness, or ephemerality do not define "the popular"; it is defined by the social process of "prescription and negation in the service of competing interests."[57] The aesthetic economies that existed in the United States around the turn of the century, the one in which Hall participated, also were partially stuck in the past and modestly looking to the future. The past included traditional Western European styles, while the future was comprised of American vernacular musics. At the turn of the twentieth century, minstrelsy, vaudeville, marching bands, and ragtime were popular. The popular music industry as we know it today originated with rural folk styles like bluegrass and fiddle tunes from the Southeast, blues from the Mississippi Delta, and jazz from New Orleans and Chicago. After World War I, radios helped to spread and increase the popularity of these uniquely American styles, and with this popularity came visibility and recognition of American individuality. To Europeans, the United States had finally developed its own novel genre traditions that were entertaining, but not high-minded and exclusive like classical music. Interestingly, women and the saxophone participated in many of these styles: women defined the classic blues genre and, in many cases, were the face of early country music; and the saxophone was an essential ingredient in vaudeville, marching bands, and early jazz.[58] For all the enjoyment and flamboyance of these genres in the first two decades of the 1900s, they were still considered lowbrow, populist, and devoid of artistic or aesthetic value.

Several of these popular genres were associated with African Americans, and some of the implicitly negative perceptions of popular music were rendered because of the discriminatory dynamics of race in the United States. By the 1930s the saxophone "craze" was waning, but the instrument's popularity potentially had an impact on the opinion of the European critics and scholars who were writing about Hall in reference to Debussy's *Rapsodie*. An investigation into Hall does not immediately prompt a discussion of race in music in the United States, but as Susan Cook notes, both women and underprivileged men were othered at this time; both groups were marginalized and excluded from Western art/classical conventions.[59] Despite Hall's enterprising work cultivating classical compositions and concerts that included the saxophone, the instrument became more closely associated with popular music and African American players throughout the early and mid-twentieth century. At times, the saxophone was relegated to the domain of parody or novelty, places in which it has intermittently found itself over the last one hundred years.

This abbreviated examination of classical/popular and professional/amateur hierarchical binaries serves as a springboard for future inquiry and criticism of the music, the people, and the legacy not only of Hall but also of the saxophone itself. Additionally, aspects related to male-defined performance practice deserve further investigation, alongside recognition of the value of the artistic perspectives of those who do not identify as men.

Making Space for the Saxophone: We Are Enough

The saxophone also has social identities that warrant analysis, not only in reference to its association with Hall but also due to its increasing connection to mainstream/popular music styles and to the musicians of color who became closely associated with it in the early part of the twentieth century.[60] Musical instruments are the musician's "extra-corporeal voice" as Sonevytsky observed in her article defining a new approach to investigating musical instruments and how they operate in culture, now known as critical organology.[61] Instruments act as expressive intermediaries between the players and the music, and the relationship between the musician and the instrument signals a complementary exchange: the saxophone impacts musicians in particular ways, and the players influence the history and evolution of the saxophone and define how it moves through culture.[62] The social identities of the players and the instrument are linked together; their histories are interwoven. This is the case with Hall and the saxophone: both have been subjected to outmoded value judgments that do not take into consideration a holistic, progressive, inclusive, or generous view of their myriad attributes.

The declamatory statement "we are enough" partially emerged from the findings of an earlier research project for which I had the great fortune to interview several luminaries from the saxophone community, including Lenny Pickett, Mindi Abair, Jeff Coffin, and Branford Marsalis.[63] A shared theme that revealed itself throughout the analysis of the interview data was that saxophonists are fiercely protective of the instrument's reputation and, by association, their own. Why? This sense is largely due to a history of dismissal as a musical instrument that is not taken seriously in certain contexts. Compared to other instruments it is still relatively new, and consequently the pedagogy and repertoire that began to be codified in the twentieth century are still developing in the twenty-first. In terms of hierarchy, the saxophone did not securely establish itself in classical music as its inventor may have hoped; rather, it became the iconographic and aural symbol of jazz and other popular musics in the United States in the first half of the 1900s. The saxophone is popular, is often considered to be "cool," and is quintessentially American from this vantage point, plus—as much as a musical instrument is capable—it exudes ambiguous sexuality. Some combination of these three elements serve to either elevate or diminish the instrument's aesthetic value, depending on your perspective and on the musical genre.

Saxophonists, especially those that identify as classical musicians, have spent the last century concerned with establishing legitimacy: of being taken seriously, of becoming an integral part of classical music and its traditions, and of being considered "objectively good."[64] This goal is aspirational, but the very concept of objectivity in music is an impossibility. Musical subjects (compositions, performances, instruments, etc.) "are formed in culture, and all understandings are intersubjective; there is no way to stand outside cultural understandings, there can be no Archimedean objectivity."[65] Hall laid a firm foundation by building a body of work for saxophonists to perform, but her legacy has been observed through the lens of entrenched sociocultural structures. It is long past time for us—members of the saxophone community—to critically engage with outmoded classical/popular hierarchies that have driven the separation between genres and players and to fully embrace *all* of our histories. Not only that, but it is also time to examine, or rehabilitate, the narratives that emerge from these hierarchical structures specifically in reference to the saxophone and identity, namely, those associated with gender, race, and class. There are strides being made toward inclusivity in the community, but broadly speaking it is long past time that we remove our noses from the grindstone of relentless commissioning and performing, raise our heads, and take a good look around. We are enough. As Hall and many others have proved, we've done the work. We should keep commissioning works and performing them, but we should also avoid the temptation to apologize for the saxophone's symbolic associations that may seem at odds with classical conventions. It is necessary to critically evaluate the instrument, the players, and the repertoire for the ways in which they have operated in broader society and culture, much like similar examinations of the guitar, the accordion, the banjo, and the like.[66] The saxophone, its repertoire, and its players have somehow evaded comprehensive cultural criticism, perhaps because we have been too preoccupied with establishing performance traditions. It is time to explore the ways that the community has not embraced an aggregate appraisal of the saxophone. Both genres and people have been marginalized, and when we confront the ways that some in the saxophone community have been "othered," we can collectively move forward and be richer for it. In calling ourselves out, we will unlock a new level of legitimacy and credibility.

The contributions made by saxophonists around the world, from all walks of life and musical backgrounds, are valuable, and the works they have performed are what make the instrument unique and important regardless of a "lowbrow" or "highbrow" valuation. We do not have to position classical (mapped to masculinity) and popular (mapped to feminine) styles of music and performance in opposition to one another. In the end, the distinction between these two serves to hurt us and repudiates the vast wealth of performance practices and the myriad genres in which the saxophone plays a crucial and beloved role. The saxophone and saxophonists benefit from its broad appeal and seemingly endless adaptability and versatility. Why do we continue to work within these binaries when they are antiquated and problematic? The saxophone is enough; it is worthy. Musicians of any gender, ethnic group, and socioeconomic status, from the past and the present, warrant thoughtful consideration as contributing members of the saxophone community.[67]

Conclusion

Elise Hall—her performances and her music—existed in a liminal space. Her life straddled the turn of the century, and her musical endeavors existed between Europe and America, professional and amateur alike. The intersection of her identities has led some critics and scholars to minimize her skills and accomplishments. The language used to characterize her echoes those phrasings used to describe other enterprising women of the era, and her music has remained unmediated and has been subjected to the perpetuation of anachronistic structures that are historically mapped to gender, race, class, and ability. She may not have referred to herself as a professional or virtuoso, but these descriptors are as much a reflection of the set of complex dynamics surrounding identities, societal constraints, and the subjective, patriarchal conventions of Western classical music as they are historical facts.[68] We now have an opportunity to update this narrative by declaring Elise Hall to be a saxophonist, entrepreneur, patron, and impresario who successfully aided in developing the saxophone repertoire. Just like the saxophone, she demonstrated formidable qualities of versatility and adaptability, which is where their power lies.

NOTES

1. Kimberlé Crenshaw, "Demarginalizing the Intersection of Race and Sex: A Black Feminist Critique of Antidiscrimination Doctrine, Feminist Theory, and Antiracist Politics," *The University of Chicago Legal Forum* 7989, no. 1, Article 8 (1989): 139–167.
2. Lawrence W. Levine, *Highbrow/Lowbrow: The Emergence of Cultural Hierarchy in America* (Harvard University Press, 1988). In this context, "American" specifically refers to the United States.
3. Frederick L. Hemke, "The Early History of the Saxophone" (PhD diss., University of Wisconsin-Madison, 1975).
4. Susan McClary, *Feminine Endings: Music, Gender, and Sexuality* (Minneapolis: University of Minnesota Press, 2002).
5. Susan Cook laments a general lack of mediation in relation to both classical music and gender in her article "'R-E-S-P-E-C-T (Find Out What It Means to Me)': Feminist Musicology and the Abject Popular" (2001).
6. See Smialek, "America's 'Young Lady Saxophonist'" (2014); Smialek and Logrande, "Louise Linden" (2015); and Hubbs, "American Women Saxophonists from 1870-1930" (2003), for more information on Bessie Mecklem, Louise Linden, Etta Morgan, Kathryne Thompson, and others.
7. Fuzzykoala, "Debussy Rapsodie," *Sax on the Web* online forum, May 7, 2007, accessed March 17, 2023. https://www.saxontheweb.net/threads/debussy-rapsodie.58499/#post-503263. This post is an example of one of the saxophone community's active online discussion forums. In this particular forum, users are engaging in a live-

ly exchange about the piece that Hall was most known for commissioning, Debussy's *Rapsodie*. In the discussion several of the users are parroting misinformation in regard to Hall and her disability (it was possibly a hearing impairment that she developed, not a breathing issue), noting her alleged shortcomings as a saxophonist as evidenced by a perceived lack of virtuosity in the saxophone solo part of Debussy's piece.

8. As defined in the *Oxford English Dictionary* (*OED*).
9. William Henry Street, "Elise Boyer Hall, America's First Female Concert Saxophonist: Her Life as Performing Artist, Pioneer of Concert Repertory for Saxophone and Patroness of the Arts" (DMA diss., Northwestern University, 1983); Michael Cappabianca, "Elise Hall: An Interview with Dr. Paul Cohen" (2021); James R. Noyes, "Debussy's 'Rapsodie Pour Orchestre et Saxophone' Revisited," *The Musical Quarterly* 90, no. 3/4 (Fall – Winter 2007): 416–445; Kurt Bertels, "Performing Dedications. A Contextual and Artistic Reflection on the Dedication of the World's First Saxophone Concerto," *FORUM+* 29, no. 3 (2022): 47–53; Léon Vallas, *Claude Debussy: His Life and Works*, trans. Maire O'Brien and Grace O'Brien (Oxford: Oxford University Press, 1933).
10. There are many examples from New Musicology that could be cited here, but three of the most relevant to the topic at hand are McClary, *Feminine Endings: Music, Gender, and Sexuality* (2002, originally published in 1991); Joseph Kerman, *Contemplating Music: Challenges to Musicology* (Boston: Harvard University Press, 2009); Rose Subotnik, *Developing Variations: Style and Ideology in Western Music* (Minneapolis: University of Minnesota Press, 1991).
11. Michael Cappabianca, "Elise Hall: An Interview with Dr. Paul Cohen" (2021).
12. In addition to beginning a conversation about Hall with a statement that undermines her performance abilities, Cohen also mentions a long-held fact that likely inaccurate assumption about Hall's health. In Cohen's defense, previously published materials by Hemke, Street, and others have also maintained this belief. According to James Noyes in his 2022 article on Hall in the *Saxophone Symposium*, there is evidence to suggest that her interest in saxophone was not related to a hearing impairment; this assertion refutes almost all previously published accounts of the reason for her adoption of the instrument. See James R. Noyes, "Elise Hall in Santa Barbara (1889-1898): The Amateur Musical Club and Philharmonic Society," *The Saxophone Symposium* 45 (2022): 78.
13. "Kimberlé Crenshaw on Intersectionality, More than Two Decades Later," Columbia University, accessed February 16, 2023, https://www.law.columbia.edu/news/archive/kimberle-crenshaw-intersectionality-more-two-decades-later.
14. "Intersectionality, Positionality, and Privilege | Infographic | U-M LSA Center for Social Solutions," accessed March 6, 2023, https://lsa.umich.edu/social-solutions/news-events/news/inside-the-center/insights-and-solutions/infographics/intersectionality--positionality--and-privelege.html.
15. Crenshaw, "Demarginalizing the Intersection of Race and Sex," 139–167.
16. Crenshaw, "Demarginalizing the Intersection of Race and Sex," 140.
17. Noyes, "Debussy's 'Rapsodie Pour Orchestre et Saxophone' Revisited," 418.
18. Doubleday, "Sounds of Power"; Koskoff, *When Women Play*; Rita Steblin, "The Gender Stereotyping of Musical Instruments in the Western Tradition," *Canadian University Music Review/Revue de Musique des Universités Canadiennes* 16, no. 1 (1995): 128–144.
19. Stephen Cottrell, *The Saxophone*, 244.
20. Noyes, "Debussy's 'Rapsodie Pour Orchestre et Saxophone' Revisited," 417.
21. Doubleday, *Sounds of Power*, 18.
22. Hall is occasionally lionized for her commissioning efforts in the histories written about her; however, it is important to consider that she was not solely concerned with increasing the saxophone repertoire for posterity. Rather, this work fulfilled her musical ambitions and preserved her social status in the upper-class circles in Boston at the time. Indeed, because of her money and social position, it is plausible that Hall was quite egocentric in the work she did. However, the long-term effects of the music that resulted mostly outweigh any negativity signaled by her self-interest in the commissioning and performing projects she was involved with.
23. Noyes, "Debussy's 'Rapsodie Pour Orchestre et Saxophone' Revisited," 421.
24. Carl Engel, "Charles Martin Loeffler," *The Musical Quarterly* XI, no. 3 (1925): 326.
25. Pierre Bourdieu, *Distinction: A Social Critique of the Judgement of Taste* (Boston: Harvard University Press, 1987) (originally published 1979).
26. Chris Barker, *The Sage Dictionary of Cultural Studies* (London: Sage, 2004).
27. Street, "Elise Boyer Hall," 4. By 'other inhabitants,' I refer to most people living in the United States at the time that were of lower socioeconomic status than Hall and her family.
28. Street, "Elise Boyer Hall," 26.

29. Morris Carter, *Isabella Stewart Gardner and Fenway Court* (Boston: Houghton Mifflin, 1925); Douglass Shand-Tucci, *The Art of Scandal: The Life and Times of Isabella Stewart Gardner* (New York: Harper-Collins, 1998).
30. Vallas, *Claude Debussy*, 161–162.
31. As discussed in Noyes, "Debussy's 'Rapsodie Pour Orchestre et Saxophone' Revisited," 418.
32. Noyes, "Debussy's 'Rapsodie Pour Orchestre et Saxophone' Revisited," 423.
33. Pauline Oliveros, "And Don't Call Them Lady Composers," *New York Times*, September 13, 1970.
34. Ibid.
35. Despite evidence to the contrary; see Andrew Allen's chapter in this volume, "Incomparable Virtuoso," and Noyes, "Debussy's 'Rapsodie Pour Orchestre et Saxophone' Revisited."
36. Noyes, "Debussy's 'Rapsodie Pour Orchestre et Saxophone' Revisited," 417.
37. Notably Cottrell, *The Saxophone*; Noyes, "Debussy's 'Rapsodie Pour Orchestre et Saxophone' Revisited."
38. Linda Nochlin, "From 1971: Why Have There Been No Great Women Artists?" (1971, reposted in a blog 2015).
39. Nochlin, "Why Have There Been No Great Women Artists?"
40. An article from 2022 by Noyes argues that Hall did not take up the saxophone because of a hearing impairment, but because it was on trend for women of the era to do so for good health. See James R. Noyes, "Elise Hall in Santa Barbara (1889-1898): The Amateur Musical Club and Philharmonic Society," *The Saxophone Symposium* 45 (2022): 75–93.
41. Kenneth Radnofsky in Street, "Elise Boyer Hall," 21. This claim is refuted in Noyes, "Elise Hall in Santa Barbara (1889-1898)," 78.
42. Street, "Elise Boyer Hall," 86.
43. As Noyes asserts, her hearing deteriorated because of age-related issues, not necessarily as a result of a specific illness. See "Elise Hall in Santa Barbara (1889-1898)," 79.
44. Street, "Elise Boyer Hall," 87.
45. *Oxford English Dictionary*, "Professional," in *OED Online*.
46. Street's "Elise Boyer Hall," Allen's "Incomparable Virtuoso," and Noyes's "Debussy's 'Rapsodie Pour Orchestre et Saxophone' Revisited" all reference examples of concert programs and newspaper articles that chronicle these activities.
47. Karen J. Blair, *The Torchbearers: Women and Their Amateur Arts Associations in America, 1890-1930* (Bloomington: Indiana University Press, 1994), 2.
48. Blair, *The Torchbearers*, 6.
49. Elizabeth Capel, "'Money Alone Was Not Enough': Continued Gendering of Women's Gilded Age and Progressive Era Art Collecting Narratives," *International Journal of Undergraduate Research and Creative Activities* 6, Article 1 (January 2014): 1–6. https://doi.org/http://doi.org/10.7710/2168-0620.1013.
50. Blair, *The Torchbearers*, 6.
51. Susan C. Cook, "'R-E-S-P-E-C-T (Find Out What It Means to Me)': Feminist Musicology and the Abject Popular," *Women & Music*, Gale Academic Onefile (2001): 141. https://link.gale.com/apps/doc/A82092553/AONE?u=anon~f4158646&sid=googleScholar&xid=9aa0c4c0.
52. Susan C. Cook, "'R-E-S-P-E-C-T (Find Out What It Means to Me)': Feminist Musicology and the Abject Popular."
53. *Oxford Learners Dictionaries*, "Classical Music," https://www.oxfordlearnersdictionaries.com/definition/english/classical-music.
54. To name a few: Theodor W. Adorno, *The Culture Industry: Selected Essays on Mass Culture*, ed. Jay M. Bernstein (New York: Routledge, 2020); Andreas Huyssen, "Mass Culture as Woman: Modernism's Other," *Studies in Entertainment: Critical Approaches to Mass Culture* (1986): 188–208; Naomi Schor, *Reading in Detail: Aesthetics and the Feminine* (New York: Routledge, 2013); McClary, *Feminine Endings*; Kyra Gaunt, *Games Black Girls Play: Learning the Ropes from Double-Dutch to Hip-Hop* (New York: New York University Press, 2006); Robin James, *The Conjectural Body: Gender, Race, and the Philosophy of Music* (Lanham, MD: Lexington Books, 2010); Sheila Whiteley, *Sexing the Groove: Popular Music and Gender* (New York: Routledge, 2013); Susan C. Cook, "Review of 'Musicology and the Undoing of Women,'" *American Quarterly* 44, no. 1 (1992): 155–162. https://doi.org/https://doi.org/10.2307/2713188
55. Susan C. Cook, "'R-E-S-P-E-C-T (Find Out What It Means to Me)'," 141.
56. *Oxford English Dictionary*, "Pop," in *OED Online*.
57. Robert Walser, "Popular Music Analysis," 26.
58. Two widely used texts that detail the history of American popular music are: Larry Starr, Christopher Waterman, and Brad Osborn, *American Popular Music: From Minstrelsy to MP3* (Oxford: Oxford University Press, 2021); John Covach and Andrew Flory, *What's That Sound? An Introduction to Rock and Its History*, (New York: W.W. Norton & Company, 2022).
59. Cook, "R-E-S-P-E-C-T (Find Out What It Means to Me)," 141.

60. The saxophone's lasting associations with cool/kitsch, gender, and race are comprehensively explored in
Adrianne Honnold's doctoral thesis, "'Unacknowledged Ubiquity:' The Saxophone in Popular Music"(PhD
diss., University of Birmingham, 2021).
61. Maria Sonevytsky, "The Accordion and Ethnic Whiteness," *The World of Music* 50, no. 3 (2008): 102.
62. Honnold, "'Unacknowledged Ubiquity,'" 41.
63. Honnold, "Unacknowledged Ubiquity," 2021.
64. Timothy McAllister, interviewed by Nathan Nabb for Saxophone Studio Class – Online! Facebook, April 4, 2020.
65. Robert Walser, "Popular Music Analysis," 23.
66. Kevin Dawe, *The New Guitarscape in Critical Theory, Cultural Practice and Musical Performance* (Farnham, Surrey, England: Ashgate, 2010); Karen Linn, *That Half-Barbaric Twang: The Banjo in American Popular Culture* (Urbana: University of Illinois Press, 1991); Maria Sonevytsky, "The Accordion and Ethnic Whiteness: Toward a New Critical Organology," *The World of Music* (2008); Steve Waksman, *Instruments of Desire: The Electric Guitar and the Shaping of Musical Experience* (Cambridge: Harvard University Press, 2001).
67. To consider space, time, and inclusivity, a saxophone canon that is updated for the twenty-first century might include classic works by composers like Ibert, Creston, and Glazunov, but also compositions by a diverse set of composers that represent all genders, ethnicities, and nationalities, alongside music from a wide range of genres such as Maceo Parker's "Shake Everything You Got," Louis Jordan's "Caldonia," Kathryne E. Thompson's "Bubble and Squeak," Rudy Wiedoeft's "Saxophobia," Charlie Parker's "Confirmation," John Coltrane's "Giant Steps," Candy Dulfer's "Lily Was Here," and Kenny G's "Songbird." Saxophonists have an uneasy relationship with popular artists like Kenny G and others, but as members of the same community we have more similarities than differences; we all strive to express ourselves with this iconic instrument and hope that audiences relate to and enjoy the music we make. For more information on the uneasy relationship that classical and traditional jazz saxophonists have with popular players like Kenny G, see Adrianne Honnold, "Revisiting Kenny G (Colloquy): Aesthetic Abjection – Kenny G from the Saxophonists' Perspective," *Journal of Jazz Studies* (2023).
68. Cappabianca, "Elise Hall: An Interview with Dr. Paul Cohen" (2021).

WORKS CITED

Adorno, Theodor W. *The Culture Industry: Selected Essays on Mass Culture.* Edited and with an introduction by J. M. Bernstein. New York: Routledge, 2020.

Barker, Chris. *The SAGE Dictionary of Cultural Studies.* London: Sage, 2004.

Bertels, Kurt. "Performing dedications. A contextual and artistic reflection on the dedication of the world's first saxophone concerto." *Forum+* 29, no. 3 (2022): 47–53.

Blair, Karen J. *The Torchbearers: Women and Their Amateur Arts Associations in America, 1890-1930.* Bloomington: Indiana University Press, 1994.

Bourdieu, Pierre. *Distinction: A Social Critique of the Judgement of Taste.* Boston: Harvard University Press, 1987.

Butler, Judith. *Gender Trouble.* New York: Routledge, 2002.

Capel, Elizabeth. "'Money Alone Was Not Enough:' Continued Gendering of Women's Gilded Age and Progressive Era Art Collecting Narratives." *International Journal of Undergraduate Research and Creative Activities* 6, Article 1 (January 2014). 1–6. https://doi.org/http://doi.org/10.7710/2168-0620.1013.

Cappabianca, Michael. "Elise Hall: An Interview with Paul Cohen." March 19, 2021. Accessed February 8, 2023. https://wam.rutgers.edu/elise-hall-an-interview-with-dr-paul-cohen/.

Carter, Morris. *Isabella Stewart Gardner and Fenway Court.* Boston: Houghton Mifflin, 1925.

Columbia University. "Kimberlé Crenshaw on Intersectionality, More than Two Decades Later." Accessed February 16, 2023. https://www.law.columbia.edu/news/archive/kimberle-crenshaw-intersectionality-more-two-decades-later. June 8, 2017.

Cook, Susan C. "'R-E-S-P-E-C-T (Find Out What It Means to Me)': Feminist Musicology and the Abject Popular." *Women & Music*, Gale Academic OneFile, 2001. https://link.gale.com/apps/doc/A82092553/AONE?u=anon~f4158646&sid=-googleScholar&xid=9aa0c4c0.

———. Review of "Musicology and the Undoing of Women" by Susan McClary. *American Quarterly* 44, no. 1 (1992): 155–62. https://doi.org/https://doi.org/10.2307/2713188.

Cottrell, Stephen. *The Saxophone.* New Haven: Yale University Press, 2012.

Covach, John Rudolph, and Andrew Flory. *What's That Sound? An Introduction to Rock and Its History*. New York: W.W. Norton & Company, 2006.

Crenshaw, Kimberlé. "A Black Feminist Critique of Antidiscrimination Doctrine, Feminist Theory, and Antiracist Politics." *The University of Chicago Legal Forum* 7989, no. 1, Article 8 (1989): 139–67.

Dawe, Kevin. *The New Guitarscape in Critical Theory, Cultural Practice and Musical Performance*. Farnham, UK: Ashgate, 2010.

DeNora, Tia. *Rethinking Music Sociology*. Cambridge: Cambridge University Press, 2003.

Doubleday, Veronica. "Sounds of Power: An Overview of Musical Instruments and Gender." *Ethnomusicology Forum* 17, no. 1 (2008): 3–39.

Engel, Carl. "Charles Martin Loeffler." *The Musical Quarterly* XI, no. 3 (1925): 311–30. https://doi.org/10.1093/mq/XI.3.311.

Fuzzykoala. "Debussy Rapsodie." *Sax on the Web* online forum, May 7, 2007. Accessed March 17, 2023. https://www.saxontheweb.net/threads/debussy-rapsodie.58499/#post-503263.

Gaunt, Kyra. *The Games Black Girls Play: Learning the Ropes from Double-Dutch to Hip-Hop*. New York: New York University Press, 2006.

Hubbs, Holly. "American Women Saxophonists from 1870-1930: Their Careers and Repertoire," DMA diss., Ball State University, 2003.

Huyssen, Andreas. "Mass Culture as Woman: Modernism's Other." *Studies in Entertainment: Critical Approaches to Mass Culture* (1986): 188–208.

Honnold, Adrianne. "'Unacknowledged Ubiquity:' The Saxophone in Popular Music." PhD diss., University of Birmingham, 2021.

———. "Revisiting Kenny G (Colloquy): Aesthetic Abjection – Kenny G from the Saxophonists' Perspective." *Journal of Jazz Studies* 14, no. 1 (2023):47–58. https://doi.org/10.14713/jjs.v14i1.249.

"Intersectionality, Positionality, and Privilege | Infographic | U-M LSA Center for Social Solutions." Accessed March 6, 2023. https://lsa.umich.edu/social-solutions/news-events/news/inside-the-center/insights-and-solutions/infographics/intersectionality--positionality--and-privilege.html

James, Robin. *The Conjectural Body: Gender, Race, and the Philosophy of Music*. Lanham, MD: Lexington Books, 2010.

Kerman, Joseph. *Contemplating Music: Challenges to Musicology*. Boston: Harvard University Press, 2009.

Koskoff, Ellen. "When Women Play: The Relationship Between Musical Instruments and Gender Style." *Canadian University Music Review/Revue de Musique des Universités Canadiennes* 16(1) (1995): 114–127.

Levine, Lawrence W. *Highbrow/Lowbrow: The Emergence of Cultural Hierarchy in America*. Boston: Harvard University Press, 1988

Linn, Karen. *That Half-Barbaric Twang: The Banjo in American Popular Culture*. Urbana: University of Illinois Press, 1991.

McAllister, Timothy. Interviewed by Nathan Nabb for Saxophone Studio Class – Online! Facebook, April 4, 2020.

McClary, Susan. *Feminine Endings: Music, Gender, and Sexuality*. Minneapolis: University of Minnesota Press, 2002.

Nochlin, Linda. "From 1971: Why Have There Been No Great Women Artists?" *ARTnews.Com* (blog), May 30, 2015. Accessed December 23, 2022. https://www.artnews.com/art-news/retrospective/why-have-there-been-no-great-women-artists-4201/.

Noyes, James. "Debussy's 'Rapsodie Pour Orchestre et Saxophone' Revisited." *The Musical Quarterly* 90, no. 3/4 (Fall – Winter 2007): 416–445.

———. "Elise Hall in Santa Barbara (1889-1898): The Amateur Musical Club and Philharmonic Society." *The Saxophone Symposium* 45 (2023): 75–93.

Oliveros, Pauline. "And Don't Call Them Lady Composers." *New York Times*, September 13, 1970. Accessed February 8, 2023. https://www.nytimes.com/1970/09/13/archives/and-dont-call-them-lady-composers-and-dont-call-them-lady-composers.html.

Oxford Learners Dictionaries. "Classical Music." Accessed February 16, 2023. https://www.oxfordlearnersdictionaries.com/definition/english/classical-music.

Oxford English Dictionary. "Pop." In *OED Online*. Accessed February 16, 2023. https://www.oed.com/view/Entry/147789.

Oxford English Dictionary. "Positionality." In *OED Online*. Accessed February 16, 2023. https://www.oed.com/view/Entry/266539?redirectedFrom=positionality.

Oxford English Dictionary. "Professional." In *OED Online*. Accessed February 16, 2023. https://www.oed.com/view/Entry/152053?redirectedFrom=professional.

Schor, Naomi. *Reading in Detail: Aesthetics and the Feminine*. New York: Routledge, 2013.

Shand-Tucci, Douglass. *The Art of Scandal: The Life and Times of Isabella Stewart Gardner*. New York: Harper-Collins, 1998.

Smialek, Thomas W., and L. A. Logrande. "Louise Linden: America's First Saxophone Virtuoso," 2016. https://scholarsphere.psu.edu/resources/9aa01bfc-540a-447b-b017-c813b8736aed.

———. "America's 'Young Lady Saxophonist' of the Gilded Age: The Performances, Repertoire, and Critical Reception of Bessie Mecklem," 2014. https://scholarsphere.psu.edu/resources/f0d322f6-4a5e-405f-a9db-2c1a4e8ed89d.

Sonevytsky, Maria. "The Accordion and Ethnic Whiteness: Toward a New Critical Organology." *The World of Music* 50(3) (2008): 101–118.

Street, William Henry. "Elise Boyer Hall, America's First Female Concert Saxophonist: Her Life as Performing Artist, Pioneer of Concert Repertory for Saxophone and Patroness of the Arts." DMA diss., Northwestern University, 1983.

Starr, Larry, Christopher Waterman, and Brad Osborn. *American Popular Music: From Minstrelsy to MP3.* 6th edition. Oxford: Oxford University Press, 2021.

Steblin, Rita. "The Gender Stereotyping of Musical Instruments in the Western Tradition." *Canadian University Music Review/Revue de Musique des Universités Canadiennes* 16(1) (1995): 128–144.

Subotnik, Rose. *Developing Variations: Style and Ideology in Western Music.* Minneapolis: University of Minnesota Press, 1991.

Vallas, Léon. *Claude Debussy: His Life and Works.* Translated by Maire O'Brien and Grace O'Brien. Oxford: Oxford University Press, 1933.

Waksman, Steve. *Instruments of Desire: The Electric Guitar and the Shaping of Musical Experience.* Cambridge: Harvard University Press, 2001.

Walser, Robert. "Popular Music Analysis: Ten Apothegms and Four Instances." In *Analyzing Popular Music*, edited by Allan F. Moore, 16–38. Cambridge: Cambridge University Press, 2003.

Whiteley, Sheila. *Sexing the Groove: Popular Music and Gender.* New York: Routledge, 2013.

Instruments Telling History
Engaging Elise Hall through the Saxophone

Sarah McDonie

ABSTRACT

In this chapter, I argue that the saxophone is both the implicit and explicit lens through which we view Elise Hall's musical activity. Hall's reception history is directly shaped by her instrument in ways that have yet to be critically considered. To address this shortcoming, the following chapter explores Hall's legacy and reception history through three paradigms: (1) saxophone as bias; (2) saxophone as epistemology; and (3) saxophone as legacy-builder. My work in foregrounding the saxophone's agency in our historiographic processes is part of a growing body of scholarship that seeks to unsettle conventional assumptions about humankind's centrality in creative work. This goal is especially important in the case of instrumentalists, for whom artistic practice and expression are bounded by the affordances and limitations of their instrument.

Introduction

Repeatedly in letters to his wife Lilly and to colleagues and friends, Claude Debussy referred to Elise Hall as "the saxophone lady." To give an example, Debussy wrote to Lilly during the summer of 1903 in a bout of undisguised frustration: "I do not know why 'the Saxophone Lady' appears to me as the statue of the Commandatore appeared to poor Don Juan!? ... Does it not appear indecent to you, a woman in love with a saxophone ...?"[1] Hall had commissioned Debussy to write a piece for orchestra and saxophone obligato in 1901. Two years later, she found herself frequently checking in with the composer due to his conspicuous hesitancy in completing the piece. What would become *Rapsodie* was ultimately published in 1918 after Debussy's death, seventeen years after he received a commission payment from Hall. Indeed, there is much to be said regarding Debussy's blatant misogyny.[2] We learn through this exchange that for Debussy, however, the saxophone is inextricably linked to Hall's character and identity.

Existing scholarship on Hall's life has thus far focused exclusively on her musical activities and network, with the saxophone as the center of interest.[3] Secondary sources include biographical information about Hall only as part of broader histories of the saxophone and do not interrogate the wider critical, cultural questions that surround Hall's life and work. The edited collection at hand directly addresses this lack of critical engagement. Even so, Hall continues to be framed within the context of saxophone performance. In our historical imaginations, we see Hall and her saxophone together. Like Debussy, we know Hall as the "saxophone lady."

Why does this matter? What began as Debussy's offhand remark regarding Hall's perceived pestering and devotion to her instrument has since become representative of her legacy: Hall is bound to the saxophone in our minds. As discussed below, Hall's connection to the saxophone is so profound that some saxophonists have named a performance competition and a saxophone quartet after her. Legacy is a social relationship; it is built on an exchange between at least two agents, whether people, non-human beings, places, events, or objects. At the center of this exchange of culture and practice is the instrument. The musical instrument mediates the transmission of musical ways of knowing and being across generations of performers and is not passive in this legacy-making process.

Objects that we would typically classify as inanimate have agency and lives all their own: they shape our ideas, move us towards or away from action, and influence our identities. In his introduction to *The Socialness of Things*, Stephen Riggins argues that "objects are a cause, a medium, and a consequence of social relationships" and that we "might speak of people being in dialogue with objects in the sense that it is difficult to construct one's self, and to present that self to others, in the absence of objects which symbolize achieved and desired statuses."[4] If we view the saxophone as a social object, we see that it motivates Hall's investment in music commissioning and participation in her Boston community orchestra, both of which are highly social activities. As a medium, the saxophone channels our understanding of Hall as a historic person, creating a shared space for us to approach her work and legacy. The saxophone is also a consequence of social relationships; its cultural and historical meanings only come from our engagement with the instrument. In fact, what we know as the saxophone is the direct result of layers of meaning that have accrued from countless interactions with people and things. As anthropologist Nicholas Thomas observes, "objects are not what they were made to be but what they have become."⁵ In the case of Hall, the saxophone has become more than an instrument; it is a medium for remembering her, a lens through which we see her life, and a framework for contextualizing her work.

In this chapter, I focus on Hall as a case study to explore how instruments actively participate in our engagement with the past. Hall is a particularly interesting case study for my methodology because most of the existing scholarship written about her is also about the saxophone. Hall's present-day reception and legacy are inseparable from her instrument in ways that have yet to be critically considered. I wonder how our histories might change if we take seriously the role material culture plays in framing our perspectives?⁶ How would our histories of Hall be different if we seriously engaged the saxophone as Hall's co-creator and co-actor in her life and legacy? In response to these questions, I explore different agential aspects of the saxophone's relationship to Hall and to ourselves through three paradigms: (1) saxophone as bias; (2) saxophone as epistemology; and (3) saxophone as legacy-builder. Key to all three paradigms is my argument that the saxophone is the implicit and explicit lens through which we view Hall's musical activity.

It is true that we will never hear Hall perform, and we cannot interview her about her musical experiences. We do not know exactly what she thought of her instrument, the things she loved about it, and the ways it challenged her. Still, objects like the saxophone link us to people of the past through our shared experiences and interactions with that object. In his study of embodied cognition, Jonathan de Souza argues that musical instruments are part of a larger cultural and temporal "already-thereness." By playing instruments that existed in the past, we can step back in time to experience the past that would have remained inaccessible to us otherwise.⁷ Musical instruments do exist outside of us in the present and in the past, but this is not to say that instruments do not change over time, because they do; innovations in keyboards, bore design, and string materials have caused a variety of adjustments to how instruments have been made over the last several centuries. Rather, De Souza is referring to how material culture is always already-there, surrounding us independent of our choosing. This material culture existed before we were born and is part of our culture by default. Musical instruments are part of this pre-existing landscape in which we find ourselves. De Souza uses the piano to exemplify how an instrument can connect us with Beethoven's music, but his argument also applies to the role the saxophone plays in linking us to Elise Hall. When we play instruments, parts of the past become knowable to us because of the shared material and physical experience of playing or hearing a particular instrument.

In this way, De Souza argues, instruments act as mediums of access and connection, bridging the otherwise uncrossable gap of time. The idea of an instrument serving as a time-traveling mediator may seem far-fetched, but I suggest that granting instruments such agency in our creative processes—which includes historiographic activities—more closely aligns with how we experience our relationships both to instruments and to people or events of the past. Since our interest in Hall is centered on the saxophone, we can see and hear what her musical experiences may have been like because of the instrument. In terms of historiography, the instrument structures our narratives about Hall and animates her historical legacy. The saxophone thus has power over our ways of thinking and is not a passive artifactual anecdote in Hall's story. Kevin Dawe speaks to this transformative potential of musical instruments in his article on lute cultures on Crete:

> Musical instruments are invested with the power to transform our world. They are often the driving forces behind ritual transformations that move us from one state of being to another, from one world to another, and provide the means by which another world might be brought into this one. They are a means by which we might carry the past with us, live with the present, and prepare for the future.[8]

The saxophone connects us to Hall, moving us into her time and her into ours. Stories and histories are likewise transformative. Following Dawe's line of thinking, the historical stories we tell keep the past with us, give us guidance about how we might make sense of and find our way through the present, and help us think about our possible futures.[9] Our interpretations of history are often based on objects—their physical characteristics, how we use them, and the stories to which we tie them—so it follows that objects like the saxophone are at the center of historiographic projects.

When we study Hall with an acknowledgement of how our methods are conditioned by her connection to the saxophone, we better understand what we privilege, how we seek and make sense of information, and how we create meaning when addressing historical subjects. Hall as a case study shows us that our knowledge-seeking and meaning-creation processes are rooted in material culture. Historian Joseph Corn notes that historians need to acknowledge the active role objects play in academic work. He argues that "in the context of the debate over when and how scholars learn from things, it behooves us to spell out precisely our debts to objects and to think about how those artifactual apprenticeships, however minor, have shaped our historical questions and interpretations."[10] This chapter aims to trace the saxophone through time and culture in order to do the work of illuminating its significance as a meaningful object.

Saxophone as Bias

Hall's presence in the historical record is tied to the saxophone, which is an obvious point but nevertheless remains uninterrogated. Current scholarship on Hall focuses exclusively on three general categories: Hall's biography, her commissioning projects, and public performances.[11] The saxophone is the context within which scholars and performers alike communicate the value of Hall's life and legacy. Simply put, it is our starting place for asking questions about Hall.

Music critics who attended Hall's performances also focused on the saxophone. Many concert reviews of Hall emphasize how strange yet impressive it was to see a woman playing the saxophone. One such review, titled "A Female Saxophonist," was printed in *Musica* in August 1905. It reads: "The case is rare enough for us to mention. Madame Elise Hall is a perfect virtuoso of the saxophone, an instrument generally played by men." After opening remarks were given at this event, "Hall played a recital… First there was astonishment, then legitimate enthusiasm."[12] This review is not an anomaly; it is very much representative of how both critical and casual audiences perceived Hall's performances.[13] Addressing the question of gender and the saxophone is outside the scope of this paper, but it is important to note that Hall's association with the saxophone in these reviews indicate that she was an outlier, someone audiences did not expect.[14] Both the saxophone and virtuosic performance have masculine associations for audiences of the early twentieth century and today. When we combine these gendered expectations with the newness of seeing and hearing a saxophone perform in an orchestra rather than in a jazz or concert band, we understand why Hall surprised people.

There is another, more subtle form of bias going on here. It shows up in the ways scholars label Hall as a *saxophonist*. The noun "saxophonist" implies a human-instrument fusion, with the human performer taking on her instrument's name. "Saxophonist" represents the assemblage of human and object. The performer and the instrument share an identity—saxophonist, flutist, pianist—in which the words we use to describe an instrument-playing human communicate the ontological status of the musician-instrument hybrid. When we call Hall a saxophonist, we are nominally linking her to the saxophone. It is indicative of how we have come to understand Hall in general. Scholarly accounts like Stephen Cottrell's and William Street's make Hall ancillary to her instrument yet simultaneously render the saxophone invisible as an active agent in Hall's historical narrative. These approaches demonstrate the need for models of historiographic engagement that recognize the feedback loop of influence between human and object, object and human.

One solution is for us to take a closer look at language, as well as to acknowledge that the words we use to describe the world around us have power. *Braiding Sweetgrass* is Robin Wall Kimmerer's sensuously rich testament to the reciprocal relationship between humans and non-human beings and between scientific and indigenous epistemologies. She challenges us to think about the limits of our native languages for recognizing and describing non-human agencies in the world around us. We can find agency in the daffodil, the kingfisher, the rain-washed pebble, and even the brass saxophone. "English doesn't give us many tools for incorporating respect for animacy," she writes. "The arrogance of English is that the only way to be animate, to be worthy of respect and moral concerns, is to be human."[15] We call something an "it" or a "he/she/they." There is little flexibility, nothing to distinguish between different forms of beings or the interrelationships between beings and things. What if nothing was an "it"? Kimmerer suggests that this linguistic move would radically alter how we live. "Grammar is just the way we chart relationships in languages. Maybe it also reflects our relationships with each other. Maybe a grammar of animacy could lead us to whole new ways of living in the world."[16] While Kimmerer is concerned with expanding English speakers' vocabulary for addressing non-human beings, her line of thinking can also encourage us to adopt new ways of considering the dependent relationships humans have with objects.

Scholars working in material culture studies are also looking for ways to expand our understanding of the reciprocal relationship between people and objects. In their contribution to *The Oxford Handbook of Material Culture Studies*, Andrew Jones and Nicole Boivin argue that material agency complicates conventional Western ideas about the boundedness of people and things.[17] In the Western world, we are implicitly taught that a person exists as an independent being, free from entanglement. A pianist plays the piano, for example—the human uses and performs upon the material instrument. Yet what if it is really the other way around? What if the piano plays the human? Perhaps we can find reality somewhere in the middle. Musicians work *with* and *through* their instruments. Jones and Boivin suggest that the concept of material agency is a productive way to engage this dependent and cooperative relationship between humans and objects.[18] "Focusing our analyses upon material agency," they write, "enables us to see that the canonical philosophical terms 'subject' and 'object' are rendered problematic when we start to look in detail at the way in which things and people are combined or attached; agency then becomes a diffuse and performative concept, and objects too are participants in courses of action."[19]

The attachment between human and object is especially paramount in the case of instrumentalists, as Hall shows us. As we have seen in early twentieth-century concert reviews, letters from Debussy to his wife, and in today's academic discourse, Hall and the saxophone are consistently "combined and attached". Hall only comes to us out of the past alongside her instrument.

Musical instruments are not passive lenses through which we view the past; they actively shape our creative historiographical processes. Eliot Bates is clear on this point. In "The Social Life of Musical Instruments," he argues that musical instruments facilitate, mediate, and prevent human activity and relationships.[20] We can see this happening in how we engage with Hall: the saxophone *facilitates* connections between present-day saxophonists and Hall by directing our interest towards her investment in early classical repertoire; the saxophone *mediates* our relationship to Hall because our interest in her begins with our interest in the saxophone; and the saxophone *prevents* us from considering Hall's musical and cultural legacy independent from her instrument. When we focus our attention on these three verbs, it becomes clear that a musician's instrument is not an inert object. Bates argues that we need to directly engage with musical instruments' active presence in the lives of musicians we study, both living and deceased. It is worth quoting Bates here at length:

> I argue for taking objects, and particularly musical instruments, seriously—but not simply as things that humans use or make or exchange, or as passive artifacts from which sound emanates. Much of the power, mystique, and allure of musical instruments, I argue, is inextricable from the myriad situations where instruments are entangled in webs of complex relationships—between humans and objects, between humans and humans, and between objects and other objects. Even the same instrument, in different sociohistorical contexts, may be implicated in categorically different kinds of relations. I thus am arguing for the study of the social life of musical instruments.[21]

The saxophone, Hall, music historians, and present-day saxophonists are all part of these "webs of complex relationships." Within these relational webs, we can make many different observations about the ways the saxophone, Hall, and present-day scholars and performers are connected. To name a few: Hall was seen by her contemporaries as exceptional because she was a woman playing the saxophone—she would not have been an anomaly had she played the piano, for example, so we pay attention to her as a result; because the saxophone was on the periphery of art music practices in the early twentieth century, we position Hall's commissioning efforts within a larger narrative of legitimization; saxophonists today see Hall as part of the larger legacy of classical performance and repertoire.[22] This web of associations and cultural meanings would have been fundamentally different had Hall played another instrument. Each instrument carries an assemblage of cultural imaginaries, stories, and meanings. When we study Elise Hall, we are drawn into the web of meanings created by the saxophone. Because of this association, we are implicitly biased to framing our knowledge of Hall around the saxophone. As a saxophonist, Hall is imbricated in the networks of meaning created by her instrument.[23]

Musical instruments are central to human musical activity, but as Bates's work suggests, conventional approaches to music scholarship do not acknowledge instruments as active collaborators. Nicolas Curry probes these issues in his work on the philosophy of instruments. He directs his critique at how music philosophers have ignored instruments as central to the creation and meaning of musical experience. His work is centered on two main questions: (1) What barriers have prevented music philosophers from positioning musical instruments as central to how people experience music? And (2) What would an approach that takes seriously musical instruments' central role in musical experience look like?[24] This chapter is one response to Curry's second question. It takes seriously the saxophone's role in shaping Hall's reception history and legacy. The facet of musical experience I am exploring here is that of historical understanding. As previously stated, the saxophone is arguably *the* reason why we continue to find Elise Hall worthy of scholarly inquiry. In a very practical way, Hall's connection to the saxophone determines what information has been saved regarding her life and influences how scholars have written about her. By stating this relationship outright, we acknowledge the power of the instrument in shaping history.

The above scholars' work demonstrates that insightful work is being done in organology and material culture studies on the relationships between people and objects. However, a perspective that is still missing is the historical: how we might apply instrument-centered approaches to historical writing? Some scholars such as Jonathan de Souza have made considerable contributions to this approach, but there remains much to be done.[25] Elise Hall presents us with a case study in which this perspective becomes exceedingly valuable because the existing histories of Hall are joint histories of the saxophone. In both academic and public-facing writings about Hall, she is only ever framed as a saxophonist, and this framing is not trivial. It reveals the biased parameters within which we place Hall's life and legacy. Because Hall and the saxophone are entangled in our historical imaginations, we need scholarly approaches that acknowledge and engage this entanglement.

Saxophone as Epistemology

One way for us to directly focus on the collaboration between objects and people is to recognize objects' epistemological value. In the above section, we explored ways that the saxophone frames what and how we study Elise Hall. However, the saxophone has determined not only what we study in connection to Hall, but also the ways we *think* about her. This section explores how we might understand the saxophone as epistemology: how it shapes the questions we ask, the information we seek, and the ways we communicate stories and histories of Hall.

Musical instruments make human knowledge and practice tangible. Ethnomusicologist Kevin Dawe has written extensively this topic:

> Musical instruments not only shape our relationship to the wider world (to the environment, the supernatural and so on) but they can also force us to look within ourselves. Musical instruments, as much as they are our creation, have the power to transform not only our surroundings but also our minds and bodies, and our sense of identity and belonging. They are richly symbolic of our potential to externalise physically and socially our needs, aspirations, allegiances and creative energies. They are one of the ways in which all of these human characteristics can be activated, channelled, sustained and renewed.[26]

The saxophone's dynamic role in shaping Hall's historiography adeptly demonstrates Dawe's claims. As more than just a device for creating musical sound, the saxophone fundamentally influences our relationship to Hall, directing how we gather and organize information about her.

Saxophonists and saxophone historians today find Hall a compelling figure because she invested in the new instrument's classical repertoire at a time when few musicians or patrons thought the saxophone appropriate for formal concert performances, which is reflected in current saxophone scholarship. If music scholars discuss Hall at all, they do so chiefly to consider the saxophone's early history or to explore the tension between popular and "classical" styles of playing already present in saxophone performance practice in the early twentieth century. These approaches are valuable, but they overlook the complexity of Hall's historical reception and wider cultural meanings. For example, Stephen Cottrell's volume discusses Hall for three pages, highlighting her involvement with the Boston Orchestral Club and her contribution to increasing early saxophone repertoire through commissions.[27] What is missing is the intersectional nuance of considering *why* Hall's involvement with the saxophone was remarkable in the early decades of the twentieth century beyond considerations of repertoire. Cottrell's presentation of Hall flattens the complex issues surrounding Hall's amateur status and its gendered associations.

In his book *The Devil's Horn*, Michael Segell does address some of the larger questions such as gender and class surrounding Hall and the saxophone, but only briefly. He discusses Hall in what amounts to two pages, focusing on how audiences consistently found it shocking to see a woman playing the saxophone in public. For him, Hall's most significant accomplishment was that she demonstrated to would-be critics that the saxophone was not an "insufferably lowbrow" instrument but was capable of serious musical performance.[28] However, this may not have been the case. Hall's identity as a woman and an amateur undermined her efforts to be taken seriously as a performer.[29] Virtuosity and professionalism were often coded as masculine.[30]

In terms of historiography, this angle gives us a lot to think about. Current scholarship on Hall may claim to focus on Hall as its central object of study, but a more accurate assessment of the situation would be to say that Hall is a means of understanding more about the history of the saxophone. This perspective is not inherently problematic; it is common practice for historians to focus on people as case studies to tell a story about a particular object, event, time, or place. What can become an issue, however, is when we claim to be writing about a musician when, in fact, we are more focused on the instrument itself and how that person influenced instrumental technique, expanded its repertoire, or exposed new audiences to that instrument. It is a matter of being transparent about what kind of history we are telling. Again, as Corn says, we need to acknowledge our debts to objects and foreground the ways that they directly impact *what* we know and *how* we know.[31]

An instrument-centered epistemology necessitates that we become comfortable with the idea that non-human subjects can have influence and agency in their relations with people and with their environments. Artist, theorist, and media scholar Chris Salter refers to this acting power of non-human subjects as "alien agency."[32] While Salter does not explore musical instruments specifically, his research is consistently concerned with how people partner with technologies, media, nature, and material culture in their artistic, scientific, and daily pursuits.[33] I can't think of a more visible demonstration of artistic human partnership with a non-human entity than the relationship between a musician and their instrument. However, as Salter makes clear, traditional scholarly inquiry in the fields of ethnomusicology, music theory, musicology, and other humanist disciplines, falls short of rigorously engaging with this complex web of agency of objects and people. To address these methodological shortcomings, he offers alternative approaches to art and performance theory that dissolve the Cartesian split between subject and object, recognizing that people and things are part of interdependent and mutually reinforcing systems. How might his concept of alien agency help us understand the role material objects play in framing how we know and write about the more distant past?

Renaissance music scholar Gary Tomlinson offers a compelling answer. In the introduction to his study on music and magic in the Renaissance, Tomlinson discusses how the distant past is an "other" to us, something always beyond our total (or even partial) comprehension.[34] In its persistent unknowability, the past evades our control. It plays with our imaginations. Tomlinson notes that historians often deal with a "sometimes uncomfortable confronting of difference" between themselves and their research subject.[35] This discomfort can be productive. It unsettles our assumptions, prompting us to think in new ways. For example, we can think *with* and *through* objects rather than just *about* them to help us engage with the past.[36] In so doing, the objects become informants of the research and writing process, as we see in the case of the saxophone with Hall. This points to Tomlinson's additional claim that knowledge is mutually negotiated between the researcher and the research subject; knowledge creation is not one-sided. Tomlinson's approach "offers, as an alternative to our usual epistemology of subject interpreting object, an intersubjective conception of knowledge as the rich and messy product of mutually interpreting subjects; thus, it strikes up a productive tension between these conflicting epistemologies."[37] In this dialogic framework, objects become subjects and are invested with agential power. Like Salter's exploration of art that acts and reacts on its own, Tomlinson's conception of the past is one filled with alien agencies. If we want to understand these agencies, we must rely on alternative epistemologies which keep us, as Tomlinson notes, "uncomfortably seated on the fence, suspended between the familiar and the distant, in our interpretations and evaluations."[38]

Our interpretations and evaluations eventually find their way into our stories. This process happens in both academic discourse and in everyday, casual interactions. Ian Woodward explores the centrality of objects in the ways we tell stories in *Material Culture and Technology in Everyday Life: Ethnographic*

Approaches. He argues that objects are not independent of our narration processes but are instead deeply imbricated in the ways we derive meaning from our experiences. This process in turn gives power to these objects.[39] Woodward writes that "narratives allow us to piece together events, making sense of disparate experiences as if they were part of an understandable whole. Importantly, narratives frequently come to life by being embodied in objects. What is even more interesting is that objects frequently structure the very way narratives unfold. Objects stimulate narratives, or they afford us access into them."[40] As is evident in Hall's case, too, the saxophone animates our interest and structures our stories about her. It structures the content of scholarly writing about Hall, determines the contexts in which her name appears (such as in private lessons, performance competitions, and chamber ensembles), and inspires present-day saxophonists through her work as a compelling model for saxophone advocacy. It demonstrates that musical instruments affect the very ways we write history, making possible the stories we tell—and those we do not.

The fragments of surviving information about Hall's life come together in a cogent narrative around the saxophone. William Street's 1983 dissertation is representative of this phenomenon; it has been the most comprehensive work on Hall's life and musical involvement to date.[41] It is a piece of scholarship written by a saxophonist for other saxophonists about a saxophonist. Street's work demonstrates that any project about Elise Hall—including the present contribution—is ultimately a project about the saxophone, a look at the instrument's life through the activities and musical commitments of one particular person in history.

A potential criticism of this approach is that it falls into the trap of determinism. If we push this line of argument too far, we may end up thinking that Hall was nothing more than a puppet controlled by the saxophone. One of the challenges for projects like this one, which aims to de-center the human from historical inquiry, is that the human element could end up being erased altogether.[42] However, this way of thinking is not intellectually satisfactory or respectful towards Hall, or any other historical person we may study. What we need is a middle ground, an approach that allows us to critically engage with the ways objects and non-human beings act on us as humans and how we in turn act on them.

Thinking in terms of networks and collaboration can help us avoid the trap of determinism. Jane Bennett offers us a compelling example of how to do this and why it matters. In her influential book *Vibrant Matter: A Political Ecology of Things*, Bennett introduces the term "thing-power" to describe the ways human-made objects appear to have a life of their own and to act independently of human intervention.⁴³ Through a series of case studies which include objects such as garbage, electricity, and fish oil, Bennett explores the porous boundaries between people and things, the places where "the us and the it slip-slide into each other."⁴⁴ In each case, Bennett does not suggest that humans are controlled by their material possessions or environments. She instead points to how humans and objects form assemblages (a term borrowed from Deleuze and Guattari) that form ecologies.⁴⁵ This approach emphasizes relationships and networks rather than discrete objects. From biological processes such as digestion that depend on bacteria, to hardened algae in shower mats that absorb water, to partnering with our dog to herd sheep, we constantly depend on non-human beings and entities to live and work, independent of whether we acknowledge these partnerships. Bennett's work reminds us that our ways of knowing—and even our ways of being—are embedded in our connections with material culture and non-human beings.⁴⁶

Saxophone as Legacy-Builder

We have seen how the saxophone plays a decisive role in determining what information we seek and deem important about Hall, and this factor becomes especially important when we consider Hall's legacy. The final section considers how Hall shaped and continues to shape the saxophone's legacy just as the saxophone, in turn, shapes hers. Questions of legacy show us that the relationship between Hall, the saxophone, and us is dynamic. The saxophone is not a static, passive figure in Hall's life or in the stories we tell about her but is a co-creator in Hall's historic legacy.

Present-day saxophonists often learn about Hall for the first time when they see her name atop the score of Debussy's *Rapsodie pour orchestre et saxophone*. Beyond this notable work, though, many of the pieces Hall commissioned remain relatively obscure and under-performed. I find this situation ironic considering that both scholars and performers often emphasize the importance of Hall's efforts to increase the saxophone's repertoire. Maybe it is not the music that we value, but the fact that someone cared enough about classical-style saxophone playing to bolster and promote it during the instrument's early history.

In an interview for the Rutgers University's Women in Music series, historian Paul Cohen was asked why the majority of Hall's commissions are never played today. His response was that "there was no legacy for [Hall] because there was no legacy for her."⁴⁷ The second "legacy" refers to students, musical protégés who would have perpetuated Hall's style of playing. Cohen states that all we have left from Hall's musical career are the pieces she commissioned for saxophone. The assumption is that Hall was an amateur performer by choice; her financial situation permitted her freedom to enjoy playing without the need for financial compensation. Consequently, as Cohen points out, Hall did not teach so her musical lineage stopped with her. This may be the case, but it risks oversimplification; this line of thinking seems to indicate that teaching is the only way to build a legacy in classical music. Hall did not directly influence a new generation of saxophone students via private instruction, but she has had a lasting impact on classical saxophonists because of her unwavering commitment to growing the saxophone's repertoire and her energetic work in producing concerts.

Two organizations exemplify this impact: the Elise Hall Saxophone Quartet and the Elise Hall Competition for Emerging Saxophonists. The saxophonists in both organizations recognize Hall's importance in expanding the saxophone's repertoire and in paving the way for other female performers. Hall's legacy may not consist of a direct line of students, but she continues to impact the way saxophonists, especially female-identifying saxophonists, engage with their instrument.

For the members of the Elise Hall Saxophone Quartet, Hall's name resonates with qualities they seek to embody: determination, intelligence, persistence, and passion.[48] The quartet is based out of Italy and is made up of members Isabella Fabbri, Chiara Lucchini, Anna Paola De Biase, and Alessia Berra. When they formed their ensemble in 2006, they chose to name it after Hall as "our tribute to her sincere love for music and the saxophone and to her persistence and enthusiasm for motivating composers to write for the instrument. Thanks to Hall's efforts, we can now enjoy such an important repertoire… In an age where patronage is a rare thing, the push to expand our instrument's repertoire must come from saxophonists themselves. This is one of the primary reasons we named our quartet after Elise Hall."[49] The quartet also makes a point of continuing Hall's commissioning legacy by collaborating with composers throughout the world to enrich their instrument's repertoire: "As the first female musician to leave such an important mark on the saxophone's history, Hall is a model for our own journey of musical discovery and experimentation. It is no coincidence that our group's ear has always leaned towards contemporary sounds and composers, with particular attention to present-day repertoires that merge and combine different musical languages into one sonic narrative."[50] We see, then, that for the quartet members, Elise Hall is synonymous with commitment to the saxophone.

Across the Atlantic, another group of saxophonists likewise recognizes Hall as a model for excellence, dedication, and innovation in the saxophone world.

They founded a young artists competition in Hall's memory, the Elise Hall Competition for Emerging Saxophonists, which is centered around three directives:

1) **CREATE** opportunities for young female-identifying, trans, and non-binary saxophonists to build valuable relationships with other artists and supporters
2) **DEVELOP** programming with consideration of applicant needs, diversity, and innovation
3) **COMMISSION** new works for saxophone by composers from equity-seeking groups[51]

These values and goals reflect Hall's life and musical commitments. She was a member of female-identifying and hearing-impaired communities, both of which had significant impacts on her work as a musician. In fact, it was because of her increasing deafness that Hall took up the saxophone to begin with. As the members of the Elise Hall Saxophone Quartet pointed out, women who aspired to a public-facing life and/or career in the early twentieth century would have met considerable limitations in the few opportunities were available to them. However, Hall was fortunate to have the financial freedom to pursue her musical and philanthropic goals with the saxophone serving as her vehicle for participation in Boston's vibrant music scene. Lastly, the Elise Hall Competition for Emerging Saxophonists aims to continue Hall's legacy of commissioning new works for the saxophone. Investing in the instrument's repertoire and creating performance opportunities is clearly a primary concern and source of motivation for today's saxophonists. Because of her role as both a performer and patron, Hall grounds the identity of this competition, framing its goals for increased inclusivity and equity in today's saxophone community.

These two examples demonstrate that legacy formation is a reciprocal process. Hall contributes to the saxophone's legacy and its cultural meanings just as the saxophone shapes her contemporary and present-day reception histories. Hall and the saxophone are part of a networked system of associations and meanings that inform how we ask and answer historical questions. It is consistent with Dawe's work on the symbolic value of musical instruments, who states that musical instruments "exist in webs of culture, entangled in a range of discourses and political intrigues."[52] The saxophone has become entangled with a myriad of performance practices, social expectations, sonic and visual references, assumptions, and historical narratives that lie beyond the scope of this paper. Still, as for the historical legacy of Elise Hall, the saxophone is the reason we remember her.

Conclusion

The chapter began with the question of how the way we tell history would change if we acknowledge the agency of objects. Because Elise Hall has been connected to the saxophone since her active performing days in the first decade of the twentieth century, she is an ideal case study for this question. In existing scholarship and in the names of young artist competitions and chamber ensembles, Hall is always positioned alongside her instrument, a fact so obvious that it goes unnoticed. Yet what if we choose to notice? How might that alter our perspective?

The point of this chapter is not to offer conclusive remarks regarding Hall's musical activity or biography. Instead, the aim is to expose our own lines of thinking and assumptions about why we find her musical contributions valuable. When we recognize that Hall's legacy consists of a human-instrument assemblage, our approach to understanding her changes. We can see how objects such as musical instruments shape the stories we tell, the things we observe, and what we value. It is necessary to acknowledge the fact that Hall's legacy is intimately bound to the saxophone; by foregrounding the fact that we only engage with one aspect of her life, her personhood and memory are respected.

Approaching Hall from a material culture perspective exposes our own biases and interests. Our histories of her show us that objects like musical instruments have power over the ways we find, organize, and communicate information. Hall's reception history reveals that all this time we have not been interested in her as an individual. Rather, we are interested in Hall's identity as a *saxophonist* and as an advocate and symbol of the saxophone. The underlying ethical issue driving the work for this chapter is that it is disingenuous for us to claim an interest in Hall's life and work without an explicit acknowledgment that this interest stems from the fact that Hall played the saxophone. By directly addressing this issue, we can more clearly see our motivations for studying Hall. We need to be able to articulate and investigate the ways the saxophone shapes how we understand and engage Hall's life and work.

Foregrounding the saxophone's agency in our historiographic processes is ultimately important because it unsettles our assumptions about what we are really studying when we write histories about musicians, especially instrumentalists. Musical instruments are a powerful tool for engaging the past and understanding our own historiographic processes. By virtue of playing the same instrument as someone from the past, we can feel a bond between them and ourselves. Saxophonists today claim that Hall is important to them because of the amount of new music she commissioned, but as we have seen, scholars are quick to point out that most of this repertoire is not well known or performed. Why, then, does Hall matter so much to today's saxophonists? The members of the Elise Hall Saxophone Quartet give us an answer: for many saxophonists—especially for female-identifying performers—Hall symbolizes commitment, passion, perseverance, and vision. Musicians love their instruments, and it seems clear that Hall did, too. The saxophone prompted Hall to advocate for herself as a performer and patron, so much so that she refused to be brushed off by Debussy. Maybe, then, Hall would be proud to know that she has become the "saxophone lady."

NOTES

1. Claude Debussy to his wife, Lilly, on June 4, 1903. Quoted in James R. Noyes, "Debussy's 'Rapsodie Pour Orchestre et Saxophone' Revisited," *The Musical Quarterly* 90, no. 3/4 (2007): 421.
2. For a more in-depth study of the exchanges between Hall and Debussy, see James R. Noyes, "Debussy's 'Rapsodie Pour Orchestre et Saxophone' Revisited," 416–445.
3. Representative examples of existing scholarship on Elise Hall include: Stephen Trier, "The Saxophone in the Orchestra," in *The Cambridge Companion to the Saxophone*, ed. Richard Ingham (Cambridge: Cambridge University Press, 1998), 103; Stephen Cottrell, *The Saxophone* (New Haven: Yale University Press, 2012), 243–246; William Henry Street, "Elise Boyer Hall, America's First Female Concert Saxophonist: Her Life as Performing Artist, Pioneer of Concert Repertory for Saxophone and Patroness of the Arts" (DMA diss., Northwestern University, 1983).
4. Stephen Harold Riggins (ed.), *The Socialness of Things: Essays on the Socio-Semiotics of Objects* (New York: Mouton de Gruyter, 1994), 1–2.
5. Nicholas Thomas, *Entangled Objects: Exchange, Material Culture, and Colonialism in the Pacific* (Cambridge, MA: Harvard University Press, 1991), 4.
6. Jane Bennett asks similar questions about the agency of material culture but in the context of politics. In *Vibrant Matter: A Political Ecology of Things* (Durham, N.C.: Duke University Press, 2010), viii, she asks, "How would political responses to public problems change were we able to take seriously the vitality of (nonhuman) bodies?" This question prompted my thinking about the saxophone's vitality in Hall's reception history.
7. Jonathan de Souza, *Music at Hand: Instruments, Bodies, and Cognition* (New York: Oxford University Press, 2017), 26.
8. Dawe, "Symbolic and Social Transformation," 58.
9. Art historian Jules Prown makes a similar claim in "Material/Culture: Can the Farmer and the Cowman still be Friends?" in *Learning from Things: Method and Theory of Material Culture Studies*, ed. David Kingery (Washington D.C.: Smithsonian Institution Press, 1996), 26: "It is not that the past did not exist. It is that it is irretrievable, a strange, alien place and time. We read the evidence, artifactual or otherwise, to construct a story consistent with our explanation of … development leading to the present. This is not to say that history lacks meaning or value. Through our interpretations of history we construct our present and shape our future."
10. Joseph Corn, "Object Lessons/Object Myths? What Historians of Technology Learn from Things," in *Learning from Things: Method and Theory of Material Culture Studies*, ed. W. David Kingery (Washington, D.C.: Smithsonian Institution Press, 1996), 49.
11. For example, this focus is the case for William Street, Michael Segell, James Noyes, Richard Ingham, and Stephen Trier.
12. "Une femme saxophoniste" *Musica* 4, no. 35, 1 August 1905. Author's translation.
13. Michael Segell also notes that audiences were consistently surprised to see a woman playing the saxophone in his accessible history of the instrument, *The Devil's Horn: The Story of the Saxophone, from Noisy Novelty to King of Cool* (New York: Picador, 2005), 244.
14. This topic is discussed in chapters by Hetrick, Honnold, and Hubbs in this volume.
15. Robin Wall Kimmerer, *Braiding Sweetgrass: Indigenous Wisdom, Scientific Knowledge, and the Teachings of Plants* (Minneapolis: Milkweed Editions, 2013), 56–57.
16. Robin Wall Kimmerer, *Braiding Sweetgrass*, 58.

17. Andrew Jones and Nicole Boivin, "The Malice of Inanimate Objects: Material Agency," in *The Oxford Handbook of Material Culture Studies*, ed. Dan Hicks and Mary C. Beaudry (New York: Oxford University Press, 2010), 333–351.
18. For a gendered perspective on the relationship between people and musical instruments, see Veronica Doubleday, "Sounds of Power: An Overview of Musical Instruments and Gender," *Ethnomusicology Forum* 17, no. 1 (2008): 3–39.
19. Jones and Boivin, "The Malice of Inanimate Objects: Material Agency," 351.
20. Eliot Bates, "The Social Life of Musical Instruments," *Ethnomusicology* 56, no. 3 (2012): 364. Alfred Gell makes similar claims in *Art and Agency: An Anthropological Theory* (Oxford: Clarendon Press, 1998).
21. Bates, "The Social Life of Musical Instruments."
22. For more on aesthetic taste gatekeeping and the connections between art and class, see Lawrence Levine, *Highbrow/Lowbrow: The Emergence of Cultural Hierarchy In America* (Cambridge, MA: Harvard University Press, 1994).
23. For a detailed discussion of the cultural and societal meanings of the saxophone, especially in popular music, see Adrianne Honnold's dissertation "'Unacknowledged Ubiquity': The Saxophone in Popular Music" (PhD diss., University of Birmingham, 2021).
24. Nicholas James Curry, "The Philosophy of Musical Instruments" (PhD diss., University of Illinois at Chicago, 2021), 3.
25. Jonathan de Souza, *Music at Hand: Instruments, Bodies, and Cognition* (New York: Oxford University Press, 2017).
26. Kevin Dawe, "Symbolic and Social Transformation in the Lute Cultures of Crete: Music, Technology and the Body in a Mediterranean Society," *Yearbook for Traditional Music* 37 (2005): 59.
27. Stephen Cottrell, *The Saxophone* (New Haven: Yale University Press, 2012), 243–245.
28. Michael Segell, *The Devil's Horn: The Story of the Saxophone, From Noisy Novelty to King of Cool.* (New York: Farrar, Straus, and Giroux, 2005), 244.
29. Hall's proficiency as a player has also been masked by her association with Longy, with whom she took music lessons, as Cottrell demonstrates in *The Saxophone* (New Haven: Yale University Press, 2012). Cottrell claims that Hall's commissioning efforts "were undoubtedly advised by Longy" (244). This assertion implicitly discredits Hall's abilities to make her own musical choices and negatively affirms her amateur status.
30. For more comprehensive exploration of gender identities and musical performance, see Ellen Koskoff, "When Women Play: The Relationship Between Musical Instruments and Gender Style," *Canadian University Music Review* 16 (1): 114–127; and Veronica Doubleday, "Sounds of Power: An Overview of Musical Instruments and Gender," *Ethnomusicology Forum* 17, no. 1 (2008): 3–39 (2008).
31. Corn, "Object Lessons/Object Myths?", 49.
32. Chris Salter, *Alien Agency: Experimental Encounters with Art in the Making*, afterword by Andrew Pickering. (Cambridge, MA: The MIT Press, 2015).
33. Salter is primarily concerned with activities of research-creation. In *Alien Agency* he writes: "Thinking issues materiality, agency, and vibrancy through words is important, but we also need to be thrown into a lived, bodily, experiential encounter with the material torrent of the world. Such an encounter is the very stuff of artistic practice. What then would it mean to rethink these high-stakes questions about agency, materiality, and stuff from the point of view of making things? From the position of what we term research-creation practice, in which the split between mind-body, epistemology-ontology, human-nonhuman are blurred, messed up, and mixed together?" (5). The non-human or more-than-human world extends far beyond tools, technologies, and media. It is outside the scope of this paper to address how humans interact with and define themselves against the natural and supernatural worlds. To explore these topics, I suggest looking at the work of Eduardo Kohn, Merlin Sheldrake, David Abram, and Jeffery Kripal.
34. Gary Tomlinson, *Music in Renaissance Magic: Toward a Historiography of Others* (Chicago: The University of Chicago Press, 1993), 2–5.
35. Tomlinson, *Music in Renaissance Magic*, 4.
36. For an example of how this methodology (thinking *through* the materiality of objects, or an epistemology of objects) can be applied to an ethnographic project, see Andrea Bohlman, "Making Tapes in Poland: The Compact Cassette at Home," *Twentieth-Century Music* 14, no.1 (2017): 119–134.
37. Tomlinson, *Music in Renaissance Magic*, 6.
38. Tomlinson, *Music in Renaissance Magic*, 19–20.
39. Ian Woodward, "Material Culture and Narrative: Fusing Myth, Materiality, and Meaning," in *Material Culture and Technology in Everyday Life: Ethnographic Approaches*, ed. Phillip Vannini (New York: Peter Lang, 2009), 59–72.
40. Woodward, "Material Culture and Narrative," 59–60.
41. William Henry Street, "Elise Boyer Hall, America's First Female Concert Saxophonist: Her Life

as Performing Artist, Pioneer of Concert Repertory for Saxophone and Patroness of the Arts" (DMA diss., Northwestern University, 1983).
42. N. Catherine Hayles addresses this concern in *How We Became Posthuman: Virtual Bodies in Cybernetics, Literature, and Informatics* (Chicago: University of Chicago Press, 1999). De-centering the human from our artistic interpretations is also one of Chris Salter's concerns throughout his writings.
43. Bennett, *Vibrant Matter*, xvi.
44. Bennett, *Vibrant Matter*, 4.
45. Bennett, *Vibrant Matter*, 4.
46. Bennet claims in *Vibrant Matter* that we need to develop cognitive and perceptual skills to get ourselves out of the rut of comfortable thinking: "What is also needed is a cultivated, patient, sensory attentiveness to nonhuman forces operating outside and inside the human body... Without proficiency in this kind of counterculture thinking, the world appears as if it consists only of active human subjects who confront passive objects and their law-governed mechanisms" (Bennett, *Vibrant Matter*, xiv).
47. Michael Cappabianca, "Elise Hall: An Interview with Dr. Paul Cohen," accessed July 10, 2022, https://wam.rutgers.edu/elise-hall-an-interview-with-dr-paul-cohen/.
48. Elise Hall Saxophone Quartet, email with author, November 2, 2022. Many thanks to Giovanni Zanovello for help with the Italian-English translations.
49. Elise Hall Saxophone Quartet, email with author, November 2, 2022.
50. Elise Hall Saxophone Quartet, email with author, November 2, 2022.
51. "About," *Elise Hall Competition for Emerging Saxophonists*, accessed September 25, 2022, https://www.elisehallsaxophonecompetition.org/about.
52. Kevin Dawe, "People, Objects, Meaning: Recent Work on the Study and Collection of Musical Instruments," *The Galpin Society Journal* 54 (2001): 221.

WORKS CITED

Atfield, Judy. *Wild Things: The Material Culture of Everyday Life*. New York: Berg, 2000.

Auslander, Philip. "Lucille Meets GuitarBot: Instrumentality, Agency, and Technology in Musical Performance." *Theatre Journal* 61, no. 4 (2009): 603–616.

Barad, Karen. "Agential Realism." In *The Science Studies Reader*, edited by Mario Biagioli, 1–11. New York: Routledge, 1999.

Bates, Eliot. "The Social Life of Musical Instruments." *Ethnomusicology* 56, no. 3 (2012): 363–395.

Bennett, Jane. *Vibrant Matter: A Political Ecology of Things*. Durham, NC: Duke University Press, 2010.

Blair, Karen J. *The Torchbearers: Women and Their Amateur Arts Associations in America, 1890-1930*. Bloomington: Indiana University Press, 1994.

Bohlman, Andrea. "Making Tapes in Poland: The Compact Cassette at Home", *Twentieth-Century Music* 14, no.1 (2017): 119-134.

Cappabianca, Michael. "Elise Hall: An Interview with Dr. Paul Cohen." March 19, 2021. Accessed July 10, 2022. https://wam.rutgers.edu/elise-hall-an-interview-with-dr-paul-cohen/.

Cottrell, Stephen. *The Saxophone*. New Haven: Yale University Press, 2012.

Curry, Nicholas James. "The Philosophy of Musical Instruments." PhD diss., University of Illinois at Chicago, 2021.

Dawe, Kevin. "People, Objects, Meaning: Recent Work on the Study and Collection of Musical Instruments." *The Galpin Society Journal* 54 (2001): 219–232.

———. "Symbolic and Social Transformation in the Lute Cultures of Crete: Music, Technology and the Body in a Mediterranean Society." *Yearbook for Traditional Music* 37 (2005): 58-68.

———. *The New Guitarscape in Critical Theory, Cultural Practice and Musical Performance*. Farnham, UK: Ashgate, 2010.

De Souza, Jonathan, *Music at Hand: Instruments, Bodies, and Cognition*. New York: Oxford University Press, 2017.

Doubleday, Veronica. "Sounds of Power: An Overview of Musical Instruments and Gender." *Ethnomusicology Forum* 17, no. 1 (2008): 3–39.

Elise Hall Competition for Emerging Saxophonists. Accessed September 25, 2022. https://www.elisehallsaxophonecompetition.org.

Elise Hall Saxophone Quartet, The. Interview with author via email. November 2, 2022.

Harré, Rom. "Material Objects in Social Worlds". *Theory, Culture, and Society* 19, no. 5/6 (2022): 23-33.

Hayles, N. Catherine. *How We Became Posthuman: Virtual Bodies in Cybernetics, Literature, and Informatics* (Chicago: University of Chicago Press, 1999).

Hicks, Dan, and Mary C. Beaudry, editors. *The Oxford Handbook of Material Culture Studies*. New York: Oxford University Press, 2010.

Honnold, Adrianne Lee. "'Unacknowledged Ubiquity: The Saxophone in Popular Music." PhD diss., University of Birmingham, 2021.

Jones, Andrew, and Nicole Boivin, "The Malice of Inanimate Objects: Material Agency." In *The Oxford Handbook of Material Culture Studies*, edited by Dan Hicks and Mary C. Beaudry, 333–351. New York: Oxford University Press, 2010.

Kimmerer, Robin Wall. *Braiding Sweetgrass: Indigenous Wisdom, Scientific Knowledge, and the Teachings of Plants*. Minneapolis: Milkweed Editions, 2013.

Kingery, David, ed. *Learning from Things: Method and Theory of Material Culture Studies*. Washington, DC: Smithsonian Institution Press, 1996.

Koskoff, Ellen. "When Women Play: The Relationship Between Musical Instruments and Gender Style." *Canadian University Music Review* 16 (1): 114–127.

Locke, Ralph P., and Cyrilla Barr. *Cultivating Music in America: Women Patrons and Activists Since 1860*. Berkeley: University of California Press, 1997.

Lombard, Matthew Guy. "A 'Revolution in the Making': Rediscovering the Historical Sonic Production of the Early Saxophone." DMA diss., University of California, Los Angeles, 2019.

Noyes, James R. "Debussy's 'Rapsodie Pour Orchestre et Saxophone' Revisited." *The Musical Quarterly* 90, no. 3/4 (2007): 416–445.

Salter, Chris. *Alien Agency: Experimental Encounters with Art in the Making*. Afterword by Andrew Pickering. Cambridge, MA: The MIT Press, 2015.

Secrist, Christian Carroll. "Philippe Gaubert's 'Poème Élégiaque pour Saxophone et Orchestre': A Study and Critical Edition." DMA diss., The Ohio State University, 2013.

Segell, Michael. *The Devil's Horn: The Story of the Saxophone, from Noisy Novelty to King of Cool*. New York: Picador, 2005.

Street, William Henry. "Elise Boyer Hall, America's First Female Concert Saxophonist: Her Life as Performing Artist, Pioneer of Concert Repertory for Saxophone and Patroness of the Arts." DMA diss., Northwestern University, 1983.

Thomas, Nicholas. *Entangled Objects: Exchange, Material Culture, and Colonialism in the Pacific*. Cambridge, MA: Harvard University Press, 1991.

"Une Femme Saxophoniste." *Musica* 4, no. 35 (1 August 1905).

Varwig, Bettina. "Embodied Invention: Bach at the Keyboard." In *Rethinking Bach*, edited by Bettina Varwig. New York: Oxford University Press, 2021.

Woodward, Ian. "Material Culture and Narrative: Fusing Myth, Materiality, and Meaning." In *Material Culture and Technology in Everyday Life: Ethnographic Approaches*, edited by Phillip Vannini, 59–72. New York: Peter Lang Publishing, 2009.

PART III

Beyond Elise Hall: Gender, Media & Culture in the 1920s

"He puts the pep in the party"
Gender and Iconography in 1920s Buescher Saxophone Advertisements

Sarah V. Hetrick

ABSTRACT

Despite the contributions of early concert music champions such as Elise Hall, the saxophone has become ubiquitous in popular culture as an icon of racial difference, sexualized masculine desires, and "degenerate" forms of art since its invention in the 1840s. Drawing on the saxophone's novelty and its associations with the exotic, which developed in late nineteenth-century opera and contemporary dance and jazz, saxophone manufacturers in the United States began to market their products as edgy, cool, and virile. In the interest of exploring the ways in which the saxophone craze of the 1920s was a catalyst for the unique sexualization of the saxophone, this chapter utilizes the theories of cultural theorists Stuart Hall and Laura Mulvey, as well as the methods of Arthur Asa Berger, to examine gender in 1920s advertisements from the Buescher Band Instrument Company. The analysis of chronological, mass-circulated saxophone advertisements demonstrates Buescher's application of contemporary advertising methods to promise social, romantic, and financial gains to buyers and to construct narratives that commodified women as an appeal to heteronormative male desires. Through this analysis, we learn that the evolution of capitalist marketing, alongside substantial social growth, uniquely positioned the saxophone as a symbol of "American progress" and, ultimately, masculinity.

Introduction

Though the vision of Adolphe Sax and many efforts by early saxophone advocates such as Elise Hall positioned the saxophone to become a permanent fixture in the realm of concert music and orchestral performance, this legacy would not be linearly achieved.[1] It has been noted by several authors that following its invention in the 1840s, the saxophone quickly achieved ubiquity as a pillar of popular music in the United States.² Due to associations with late nineteenth-century opera, vaudeville acts, and contemporary dance and jazz, the saxophone became known as an icon of racial difference, sexualized masculinity, and even "degenerate" forms of cultural practice.³ An early expression of the saxophone's rapidly growing reputation was documented even in relation to Hall, despite her wealth, social status, and significant contributions as a serious commissioner, performer, and patron. In 1904, Elise Hall's gender and femininity were noted as a peculiarity when Debussy reportedly stated that he was "not impressed when he saw Mrs. Hall in her pink dress and with her 'ungraceful instrument.'"⁴ Again in 1904, the *Boston Daily Evening Transcript* published that "Mrs. Richard J. Hall … played the saxophone solo with a skill fairly astounding to those who appreciate the fact that this is essentially a masculine instrument."⁵ Similarly, in May of 1905, *Musica* printed an article about Hall that stated, "A woman saxophonist, is a case so rare that we thought that we would mention it. Mme. Elise Hall, however, is a perfect virtuoso of the saxophone, an instrument generally played by men."⁶ This presentation of Hall as an oxymoron and the treatment of a woman performing on a wind instrument are no exception, as such activities were not yet socially permissible for most women at the turn of the century. Unlike many other wind instruments, though, the saxophone's association with masculinity evolved throughout the 1900s. The unique sexualization of the saxophone from the 1900s to the present day can be traced through the development of popular culture and mass media in the United States in the early twentieth century, which defined the role of non-male performers in relation to the saxophone and contributed to the ostracism of both the significant role of Hall and the concert saxophone.

    To better understand the saxophone's socio-cultural connotations, as well as the construction and subsequent perpetuation of the saxophone as a masculine instrument, an investigation into the burgeoning mass media/advertising industry that aided in spreading the popularity of the saxophone in the 1920s is desirable. However, research on the saxophone that is refracted through a socio-cultural/identity lens has only recently been initiated, and there is a lacuna in scholarship that addresses gender in advertisements of saxophones, as well as a lack of extensive scholarly work that examines the iconography of the saxophone as it relates to gender. Doubleday, Honnold, Suzuki, Vockeroth, Segell, and Cottrell all refer to the saxophone as it relates to gender in their work, but Vockeroth, Segell, and Cottrell take a perfunctory role in discussing the significance of the saxophone's gender associations.⁷ Doubleday's reference to the topic is brief, while Honnold and Suzuki employ a comprehensive and contemporary examination on gender and the saxophone as an icon.⁸ Suzuki's work presents a case study of women saxophonists and the practice of gender performativity in a male-dominated, sexualized, and racialized discipline.[9]

Among this important work, there is no in-depth analysis of formative early-twentieth century media and the influences that constructed gender norms in relation to the saxophone, the iconography of the saxophone, or the unique sexualization of the saxophone. As such, this chapter will examine 1920s saxophone advertisements from prominent instrument manufacturers, such as Buescher, by utilizing Stuart Hall's encoding/decoding method, Arthur Asa Berger's sociological analysis (as outlined in the fourth edition of *Ads, Fads, and Consumer Culture: Advertising's Impact on American Character and Society*), and Laura Mulvey's "Male Gaze" theory. These frameworks provide a basis for understanding how Buescher prioritized and utilized cultural and social information to create and develop their advertisements, how gender roles were constructed and applied throughout the decade, and how the iconography of the saxophone was influenced through the advertising process. Along with discussing the development of the iconography and cultural heritage of the instrument itself, this chapter provides context for the cultural, economic, and social growth in the early-twentieth century, all of which converged to form inextricable links between the saxophone, masculinity, and heterosexual male desires. This chapter does not explicitly engage with subjects related to Hall and her career, but rather illustrates the atmosphere and general tenor of attitudes toward gender roles and the saxophone which were being codified at the time. Further, this analysis demonstrates the employment of narratives that centered the heteronormative cis-white male experience, commoditized women, and ultimately continued to define the saxophone as masculine far beyond the life and legacy of Hall.[10]

Historical Context

To understand the iconography of the saxophone as it developed in the 1920s, it is paramount to understand the early role of the saxophone as an agent for exoticism in concert and popular music.[11] At the turn of the twentieth century, the saxophone developed a cultural association with novelty, exoticism, and sensuality in Western art music. The instrument was originally intended for use in operas, symphonies, and military bands, and as a product of a well-known instrument maker, it was poised to become a major component in the development of Western art music.[12] However, few composers and performers embraced the instrument and those who did, such as Charles-Jean-Baptiste

Soualle, were quick to exploit its novelty for the sake of exoticism.[13] Soualle was known to adopt the stage name "Ali Ben Sou Alle" for his performances, wearing "oriental" costume, and more to appeal to "growing interest in musical exoticism."[14][15] Additionally, the saxophone was often used in opera and orchestra to evoke non-Western instruments and music, as demonstrated by works such as Georges Bizet's *Les pêcheurs de perles* (1863), George Kastner's *Le Dernier roi de Judah* (1844), Halévy's *Jaguarita L'Indienne* (1855), Meyerbeer's *L'Africaine* (1865), and Jules Massenet's *Le roi de Lahore* (1877).[16] The treatment of the saxophone is similar to that of the cor anglais, as outlined by Derek Scott in "Orientalism and Musical Style."[17] Scott further explains that the cor anglais is used to allude to oriental or exotic style because of its timbre, which is defined as inherently non-Western.[18] In the aforementioned operas, the saxophone is orchestrated to signal stage events that relate to exotic, romantic, or mythical non-Western settings and events.[19] As Annegret Fauser explains, constructions of the exotic were often conflated with eroticism, especially as it relates to the use of the saxophone as a signifier for exoticism, due to its associations with sensuality or sex.

> Musical signifiers of generic exoticism provided couleur locale as surface ornamentation in the … employment of [the saxophone] over generally lush instrumentation. In opera, exotic moments contained in the plot could provide the justification for musical excess, but only within Western musical bounds, whether in the use of sensuous orchestration and unabashedly melodic voluptuousness, or in musical representation of sexual excess. Here the safe and official setting or operatic convention allowed the inclusion of materials that, in other contexts, might have gone beyond the limits of bourgeois acceptability.[20]

These early uses of the saxophone as associated with exoticism narrowly defined the timbre as acceptable for use only in non-programmatic contexts. Further, being made of both brass and reed, the saxophone's ambiguity fostered a sense of androgyny or liminality that ultimately became associated with racial otherness in programmatic contexts and popular genres. This type of orchestration narrowly defined the use of the saxophone and led to an infamy that propelled the saxophone to become well known as a novelty, for romance or sex, in both subsequent artistic output and in popular culture. Further, the use of the saxophone for orchestration trends in Europe in part relegated the instrument to ephemeral or novel forms of entertainment that were considered middle- or low-brow in the United States, likely due to its adoption by Black jazz musicians around this time. It is also important to note that many of the popular forms of entertainment that shaped the development of the saxophone in the United Stated are cultural practices of Black musicians. In this regard, Honnold notes:

> This association with jazz and Black male musicianship shaped how [the saxophone] was received and integrated into other musical genres as well as public culture at large, and questions surrounding its intersecting representations of race, cool/kitsch, and gender/sexuality dialectically relate to perceptions surrounding the instrument's legitimacy, level of prestige, and popularity.[21]

Following the 1872 United States tour of the French *Garde républicaine* and the establishment of the U.S. bands of Patrick Gilmore and John Philip Sousa, the American public was exposed to the saxophone.[22] Not only did these military ensembles fuel interest in the instrument as a hobby and an instrument for more serious study, but their introduction of the saxophone to the public contributed to the instrument's popularization through other mediums of entertainment such as dance bands and vaudeville shows.[23] Cottrell writes that the saxophone's inclusion in vaudeville acts, which were a major venue for entertainment in the early twentieth century, stems from the audience's interest in all things novel, exotic, and unusual.[24] Further, the visual interest in the phallic shape of the saxophone was a significant reason for its "adoption in a variety of popular genres."[25] Michael Segell notes this phenomenon and the saxophone's involvement:

> This was an era of sweeping social change and Americans were eagerly exploring new notions about sex and the role of women. Not surprisingly, it took only a few years for Adolphe Sax's subversive creation to become, in its inimitable attention-grabbing style, the most widely recognized symbol of the racy modern lifestyle and of the emerging music, jazz, that epitomized it.[26]

The overwhelming popularity of the saxophone leading up to and during the 1920s (often referred to as the saxophone craze) was not independent of economic, social, and cultural developments, but a result of inter-war prosperity, exponential growth of the advertising industry, and general social and sexual liberation of society in the United States. As demand for goods increased through the 1920s, so did the investment manufacturers made in advertising, resulting in developments in strategy that reflected and employed shared desires, roles, and expectations in society. Economic prosperity offered advancements in production and availability of goods, new means of production prompted a surge in consumer activity, and new markets developed as social change swept the nation.

Prior to the 1920s, the First World War catalyzed major development in both the advertising industry and its methods. Manufacturers were compelled to halt production of non-essential consumables and pivot to essential and wartime goods. With much of the production in the United States aiding in wartime efforts, companies leaned on institutional advertising that exalted the role of their product in supporting and aiding war efforts.[27] Government programs, such as the Federal Committee of Public Information, employed advertising firms and printing services as the production arm of wartime propaganda. This application temporarily fueled the advertising industry, allowing for exponential growth, development, and influence throughout the economic boom of the 1920s.[28]

Advertising in the 1920s

During the immediate interbellum years, more people than ever before found gainful employment, which consequently generated a large increase in discretionary income for both men and women.[29] This development expanded the entire market and provided advertisers the opportunity to sell and produce more products. A strong infrastructure for mass production allowed an overhaul in the systems of acquisition for consumer goods, as households no longer produced their own goods and instead were able to purchase premade and prepackaged goods easily and quickly.[30]

In addition to the availability of products caused by mass production and an increase in income for consumers, goods such as musical instruments became more accessible using credit and installment payments. By positioning the advancements in advertising alongside the documented marketing efforts of Buescher, we can see the ways in which the saxophone advertisements align with trends and represented changes in the socio-cultural beliefs throughout the saxophone craze of the 1920s. Chris Wharton explains that "by the 1920s 'full-service' advertising agencies were operating, providing the advertising functions such as media planning, research and account management required to create and direct successful twentieth-century advertising campaigns."[31] Additionally, as a familiar tenet of the contemporary United States economy, credit and buy-now-pay-later options were new in their abundance and accessibility to the market, transforming not only the way that consumers purchased goods, but also the promotion and marketing of the goods sold. In the interest of capitalizing on the overwhelming interest in the saxophone and concomitant to the general trends in advertising, both Buescher and Conn began to utilize print media to advertise their saxophones. For example, at the start of the 1920s, C. G. Conn was primarily a marginally profitable, mail-order business, but through the addition of easy-to-play tropes the saxophone was poised to become an attainable hobby for consumers and amateur musicians.[32] Subsequently, Conn responded to the incredible demand for saxophones at this time by allocating 75% of its production to the instrument, adopting an assembly-line production process to lower costs and increase output, while investing heavily in advertising.[33]

In addition to manufacturers' new systems of acquisition, new approaches that changed the strategy of advertising were developed, including the hiring of behavioral psychologists, who conducted quantitative market research to learn more about target demographics and buyer preferences. This research was then utilized by agencies to more effectively influence buyers' purchase decisions.[34] The development of a campaign consisted of a "target consumer, the product concept, communications media, and the advertising message, which is a combination of copy and visuals."[35] This method focused on consumers' interests and desires and prompted the creation of a style of advertisement that mirrored the styles of literary fiction that was popular in widely circulated magazines, using narrative to "strongly dramatize the disadvantages of not using the advertised product and the social incentives for using it."[36] As the market research learned that consumers were interested in "short, powerful narratives with dramatic characters," agencies developed five different formulaic advertising approaches, identified and categorized by Juliann Sivulka as: Melodrama, Friendly Advisor, Modern Testimonial, Tabloid Technique, and Celebrity Endorsement.[37] Further, Peiss explains that, at this time, advertisers utilized methods that systematized desire and attempted to emphasize the differences between the sexes by eliminating notions of difference among women. Through their work, advertisers made it possible for the purchase of goods to evolve into a way of life, where success, popularity, and desire were synonymous with consumption.[38] These changes in advertising strategy are evident in the trajectory of Buescher advertisements: while at the beginning of the decade, advertisements focused on the saxophone itself, by the end of the decade, they had evolved to mostly feature Modern Testimonials, which appealed to consumers through a narrative framework that commodified the promised *results* of buying a saxophone, namely, women—or at least women's attention—and romantic happiness.

Though the advertising industry grew rapidly in the first decades of the twentieth century, it is important to note that their techniques and influence were primarily aimed at a specific demographic: white, middle- to upper-class men. In her examination of advertisers in the 1920s, Katherine Parkin remarks that primarily "white elite men have controlled the advertising industry." A "new professional and managerial class of college-educated, white-collar men [had] spurred the growth of [corporate] marketing and advertising functions," whose "masculine identity lay in an orientation toward efficiency, method, and control" and thus established the thriving advertising industry of the 1920s.[39] At a national level, it has been noted that advertisers contributed to an increasingly hegemonic society, as they actively sought the construction of normative roles that mirrored corporate power structures at this time.[40] As Kathy Peiss notes, this approach detrimentally limited the reach of advertising beyond the target demographic, as most views espoused the narrow, personal experiences and viewpoints of those creating the campaigns. This perspective eliminated the important lenses of consumers' diverse races, ethnic backgrounds, socio-economic statuses, and genders.[41] As a result, many advertisements targeted sales to white, middle- to upper-class consumers—those presumed to have spending power—regardless of readership demographic. Further, advertisements targeting women came through the lens of the advertisers themselves, causing advertisements to feature the modern woman only through a male lens. Simone Davis holds that "as the corporate world became the United States' designated new epic sphere, popular and commercial narratives located masculine self-hood in the persuasive impact one had on others, rather than in the monadic integrity of self-reliance."[42]

In addition to developments in the economy, culture, and entertainment, the social mores of the 1920s diverged from earlier Victorian constraints and represented a general—albeit limited by today's standards—liberation, especially in terms of gender expectations and presentation. Women's efforts at the turn of the century set the trajectory for social, sexual, and financial freedoms that were afforded to women in the 1920s. Modern women, who embraced new freedoms, were primarily from urban areas of the United States and held jobs outside the home. They were often characterized by their appearance and, consequently, labelled "flappers." Einav Rabinovitch-Fox further explains:

> The New Woman ... offered a way not only to understand women's new visibility and presence in the public sphere, but also to define modern American identity in a period of unsettling change. The New Woman image was often positioned in opposition to the Victorian "True Woman" ... [and] did not express a unified message regarding women's changing roles, as those varied by region, class, politics, race, ethnicity, age, time, and historical conditions. The New Woman could be a suffragist or a flapper, a Gibson Girl or a settlement house worker, an actress or a factory laborer, and oftentimes these images and meanings overlapped, allowing women to adopt some characteristics while renouncing others...[43]

Estelle Freedman emphasizes that while most scholarship focuses on the political gains of women in the 1920s, economic and social strides had more impact on the progress toward gender equity. However, the control exercised both explicitly and implicitly by the male dominant society remained, and pervasive discrimination persisted.[44] Within social spheres, this discrimination can be identified in the engendering and negative connotations assigned to ideas associated to the revolution in mores including premarital sex, birth control, drinking, and more. These actions and activities, while legally permissible, still carried the negative critique that they were sinful for women to engage in and that they were responsible for the decline and decay of family life. Thus, women's liberation in the 1920s was often viewed as another movement to be limited or controlled. For the woman who demonstrated freedom without social ruin, there remained an expectation to lead a traditional role as a wife and mother.[45] Freedman acknowledges that the language and laws may have been changing, but the social governance of women's empowerment persisted:

> [Women] in the 1920s began to be presented as flappers, more concerned with clothing and sex than with politics. Women had by choice, the accounts suggested, rejected political emancipation and found sexual freedom. The term feminism nearly disappeared from historical accounts, except in somewhat pejorative references to the Woman's party. While critics claimed that women had achieved equality with men, they issued subtle warnings of moral and family decay.[46]

Further, women who had entered the workforce were perceived as a threat to "husbandly and parental authority."[47] Thus, while the 1920s offered tangible political gains, the degree to which women could act upon their liberation was confined by a cis, white, heteronormative patriarchal expectation. Throughout the analysis of Buescher's advertisements, these limitations become increasingly apparent. Women were presented as modern in their dress and appearance, but this visual attempt to symbolize modernity fell short as the women remain objects in the frame of male desires. As advertising agencies employed narratives that targeted male audiences and centered their own narrow experiences, they defined gender roles via mass consumption in the 1920s. Further, through saxophone advertisements that reinforced the gender binary and commoditized female bodies, the agencies obliquely contributed to the masculinization of the saxophone in broad and long-lasting ways.

Analysis of Advertisements

As methods of advertising developed from the start of the twentieth century to the present day, so have the approaches to analyzing and interpreting media. The advertising profession and related disciplines have yielded substantial research on the development of advertising in the United States. For the present contribution, a discrete methodology adapted from the formative work of scholars Stuart Hall, Arthur Asa Berger, and Laura Mulvey has been adopted in order to understand how the spectacle of gender and the female form was used by Buescher to market saxophones.

Stuart Hall refined The Circuit of Culture as a framework for analyzing cultural artifacts, such as the saxophone, and established the encoding/decoding method which offers a semiotic approach to the analysis of media content. More specifically, this method is used to "examine advertising production, advertising texts, and occurs implicitly in many accounts of advertising production and receptions."[48] Hall outlines a basic structure in the production and consumption of advertisements, where advertisers encode a message, the text is produced, and the audience or consumer decodes the text. Wharton succinctly details this process:

> The advertising framework is first composed of encoding, usually carried out in advertising agencies, which bring together a range of technical and creative abilities and is informed by research and economic considerations. Advertising texts form the middle element of the framework … which enable[s] and constrain[s] the scope and impact of the advertising message. The advertising framework encourages an 'image' of the totality of advertising from message production, presentation through radio, television, billboard, internet, or other advertising forms, to the decoding of the advert by an audience. The decoding takes place within a range of contexts and environments in which a variety of factors can be important.[49]

Hall emphasizes the text in the advertisements as a loop with encoding and decoding as variable outcomes; decoding varies by the reader or viewer, as experiences and backgrounds vary. These different perspectives result in three possible types of decoding: preferred reading, where the reader's "codes, values and assumptions about the world" are congruent with those of the advertiser or the producer; a negotiated reading, where the reader does "not fully accept the meaning of the advert"; and an oppositional reading, where the reader rejects the intended message and is often from a background and perspective that is dissimilar to or juxtaposes that of the producer.[50] While the oppositional reading may seem obtuse, it allows for the "ideological content of the message" to become apparent.[51] Hall explains that this exchange is not linear, but it becomes a loop, where the process of future encoding is dependent on cultural information received from previous decoding.[52] In the immediate context, Hall's framework allows for an analysis to identify Buescher's methods and the ways in which they mirrored methodological trends at the time of publishing. In turn, the construction of gender as both spectacle and acceptable role become revealed. Further, as a future consideration, Hall's framework is essential because the gender stereotypes related to the saxophone are likely to be repeated infinitely unless and until they are examined and actively dismantled.

While Hall's framework offers a more conceptual lens, Berger outlines six practical methods of analysis—including semiotic, psychoanalytic, sociological, historical, political, and myth/ritual analysis—and gives a list of fifteen questions which help the viewer to "direct [their] attention to various matters that might be considered when interpreting a … print advertisement found in a newspaper or magazine."[53] In the interest of brevity, I will primarily utilize the sociological analysis for the Buescher advertisements to understand the elements and ideas used in the composition of ad copy, artwork, and photographs to construct and strategize gender, gender roles, and gender expectations, as well as to identify their desires, interests, and fantasies.[54] Applying the sociological framework to advertisements across the 1920s aids in a current understanding of how the representation of sexuality and gender roles became embedded in society. The saxophone's association with male desires and heteronormative sexuality in the 1920s are demonstrated in this analysis, and Berger's framework is applied to illustrate how sexuality and desire were instrumentalized to appeal to male consumers.

As gaze and its relationship to gender is an important consideration for the advertisements analyzed, I also draw from Laura Mulvey's "The Male Gaze Theory." While Mulvey's theory is often applied to cinema, it is based on the pervasive unconscious power dynamics constructed by a patriarchal and phallocentric society. Mulvey's theory demonstrates that the male gaze holds normative power and privilege in dominant systems of visual representation, where imagery of women can be understood as "a form of objectification which articulates masculine hegemony and dominance over the very apparatus of representation itself."[55] In narrative-based media, such as cinema or advertisements, active and passive roles are assigned by gender which prioritize the scopophilic. Mulvey identifies the male role as the active eye and the woman's role as a passive object to be viewed. Hall explains how the male gaze influences the encoding of meaning, especially as it relates to the saxophone as a phallic object or icon for sexuality:

> Mulvey detailed the way narrative cinema mobilized both the narcissistic aspects of the scopophilic instinct (ego libido) and its voyeuristic and fetishistic components (object cathexis) — essentially those forms of active scopophilia… Mulvey's development of Freudian concepts provides a suggestive way of conceptualizing the moment of articulation between individuals and representational forms. It suggests that the positioning of the individual within the subject-positions established by a particular representation is achieved through the organization of scopophilic drives and the channeling of unconscious identifications. This is also a process that can (depending upon representational conventions) reproduce the positions of sexual difference or gender.[56]

Mulvey's theory allows the analysis of media to consider that gender is posed as voyeuristic spectacle via female form for both the viewer of the advertisement, as well as for the male characters within the image. The male gaze implies the omnipresence of women as passive objects in media, where agency and power over the opposite sex is considered a universal desire of the heterosexual male. Regardless of the sexuality or gender of the viewer, the heterosexual male perspective is forced upon the viewer, ultimately defining and perpetuating roles for a gender binary and sexuality within male dominated society.[57] Throughout the present analysis, I use "the male gaze theory" to understand the encoding and representation of the women in the images and how the women are objectified to appeal to heterosexual male desires.

Findings

Over the course of the 1920s, Buescher, a prominent and successful saxophone manufacturer, capitalized upon the popularity and high demand for saxophones by advertising that the purchase of a saxophone would bring social, romantic, and financial gains. The evolution from selling the saxophone to selling the romantic attention of a woman (or, symbolically, the woman herself) was catalyzed by new cultural constructions of the instrument's social identity and ultimately perpetuated the saxophone as a symbol of masculinity. Extensive survey of advertisements between 1915 and 1930 returned a few categories of advertisements: those that solely market the ease of learning the saxophone, those that feature endorsing artists and popular music ensembles, and those that depict amateurs in social settings. In addition to advertisements that feature a few prominent female-presenting artists and teachers, such as Kathryne E. Thompson, there are a small portion of Buescher and C. G. Conn advertisements featuring female-presenting amateur figures and music ensembles.[58] However, for this chapter, I chose to analyze and include advertisements that represent the vast majority of the ads that were circulated that feature both male- and female-presenting figures in a social setting. Through the analysis of gender roles within a binary, we can best observe the representation of the saxophone as an agent for masculinity and symbol of heterosexual-male desires.

To better understand the advertisements that utilize a social setting to both construct and employ gender roles as a method for incentivizing the purchase of a product, I first look to representative advertisements that establish and constrain the representation of gender. Throughout the 1920s, the use of words like "popular" and "pleasure" are common in almost all Buescher saxophone advertisements. As an example, a 1923 *Redbook* Buescher advertisement touts the copy "double your income, your pleasure, and your popularity." In contrast, similar language is not present in advertisements for other instruments, such as the piano, cornet, and trombone.[59] Instead, the non-saxophone advertisements focus on the mechanics of the instrument or fact-based information regarding the instrument itself.[60] Cottrell shares similar observations in discussing the unique opportunity the saxophone's popularity offered for advertising, noting that "musical instruments are seldom credited with such profound qualities of social transformation" and that as these claims became widespread through media, "the saxophone achieved a reputation as a socially inclusive, fun and undemanding musical instrument."[61] While these types of advertisements do not necessarily include explicit statements on gender, they do tie the saxophone firmly to the social climate and changes of the era, including, by extension, the widely accepted roles for both men and women.

At the turn of the twentieth century, popular performers were very much central to cultural life and to society in the United States, so Buescher often used the popularity of performers to their advantage when trying to sell their saxophones. This method is demonstrated in Buescher's 1924 *Better Homes and Gardens* advertisement (fig. 5.1): the ad includes artist endorsements from Ben Selvin, Clyde Doerr, Tom Brown, Jos. C. Smith, and Donald Clark, and features artist Bennie Krueger with a cutout of his head.[62]

This narrow representation likely reflects the limited budgets of new saxophone companies, like Buescher. To elaborate, many of the same design and copy components were reused with simple modification: the graphic of the

Figure 5.1. Buescher advertisement in *Better Homes and Gardens*, November 1924

hands on the saxophone, for example, appears with interchangeable performers' heads. Though the narrow perspective and lack of diversity in gender and background of advertisers themselves undoubtedly influenced representation regardless, one ramification of cost-cutting measures was that it directly impacted the opportunity to utilize a woman and/or a non-white artist in the advertisements. Many Buescher advertisements in the 1920s followed this model of featuring white male performers and exploiting desired cultural capital, resulting in explicitly defined and perpetuated stereotypes: the saxophonist is popular and almost always a white male.

As the role of a white man in relation to the saxophone was defined by Buescher, so too was that of a white woman. Throughout the decade, the companies began to invest more in their advertisements, introducing the saxophone into a new setting: the domestic sphere, which has definite connotations and expectations regarding gender roles. Intimate, domestic chamber-music settings are commonly used in Buescher's advertisements, where the roles of the two musicians encode socially acceptable relationships between gender and instruments: the male-presenting saxophonist is central, while the female-presenting figure is secondary. In these images the saxophone remains the central focal point of the advertisement, but these additional features build a narrative that prioritizes the desired intangible outcomes of purchasing and playing a saxophone. This attention to the male saxophonist's viewpoint supports the idea that the woman is merely an object of desire rather than an agent in the narrative. Moreover, a lack of identifiable characteristics and the intentional anonymity of women in the images used by Buescher plays into the objectification of the woman. From the heterosexual male perspective, she is a body, interchangeable with any face that suits the individual desires of the viewer. The domestic setting may suggest a dynamic of control over the women, which would be consistent, even subconsciously, with the heterosexual male spectator outlined in Mulvey's theory. Further, by clearly defining the gender roles within this domestic image, the advertiser positions the saxophone as masculine and dominant in the relationship between the two figures.

In figure 5.2, Buescher has begun to employ a romantic subtext that not only is decidedly gendered, but that elicits the saxophone as an agent for masculinity and male desire.[63] The photo used in figure 5.2 is suggestive of romantic attention, where the characters in the photo sit close in an intimate moment away from others. Several photos depict the characters in a social or salon-type setting, where people are dancing, listening to, or playing music. The photo in figure 5.2, however, is taken away from a common living area, and the woman depicted has directed her full attention, as well as her body, towards the saxophone

player in the advertisement. The pair leans toward each other; the woman sits with her legs and arms crossed toward the saxophonist, her gaze fixed upon his face; he angles the saxophone bell directly toward her. Due to its phallic physical nature, the viewer may even interpret the saxophone joining the bodies as a sexual gesture, acting again as a proxy for masculinity and male desire. The intimacy of the setting, which is far more secluded and private than the domestic chamber or salon music settings thus far, indicates that the exchange between characters is meant to be romantic, even sexual in nature. While the text remains focused on popularity and social gain, the photo used is more explicit in underpinning the relationship and closeness that is being used as the primary selling point of the saxophone. At this point, the woman in the photo is central to the advertisement and her body language, and such attention is unique in comparison to the body language and implied relationships seen in earlier advertisements. In the context of Mulvey's theory, the image and suggestive nature of the advertisement again demonstrate the perspective and desires of a heterosexual male. The position of the saxophone as integral to securing these desires, which continues to associate the saxophone with masculinity, sex, and the objectification of women. Figure 5.2, an advertisement from *Cosmopolitan* (which at this time had a general readership), also prioritizes the lifestyle that the saxophone is said to offer the con-

Figure 5.2. Buescher advertisement in *Cosmopolitan*, April 1927

sumer, rather than the product itself. The opening text reads, "Popularity *Plus!* Yours with this most winning of all musical instruments. Step out of the Crowd. Be the popular favorite. Earn your welcome everywhere with a Buescher …" Inferring from the text, as well as the photo, the "*Plus*" in "Popularity *Plus!*" invites the viewer to imagine romantic attention, as suggested from the photo, or it could refer to the financial gain outlined in so many of the advertisements, or it could refer to both.

A 1928 Buescher advertisement from *Cosmopolitan* (fig. 5.3) shows a similar treatment of the saxophone as a vehicle for social gain and, moreover, for the attention of a woman.[64] In this advertisement, the narrative of social gain is indicated in "before" and "after" photos. However, figure 5.3 centralizes the woman depicted in the "after" photo, where the consumer has learned how to play the saxophone. Here, we see the woman smiling at him and the saxophone bridging the bodies of the two figures, reinforcing the relationship between the image and that of the text, which reads, "The First Evening with his *Buescher* – and Three Weeks Later **Going Strong**!" The use of "**Going Strong**" has a gendered subtext, drawing upon expectations or constructions of masculinity, physical strength, and an allusion to sexual virility in an effort to reach the target demographic of the consumer. The text and "before-and-after" imagery suggest that consumers can have the intimate relationship depicted in the picture and described through the text if they purchase the saxophone. Thus, the strategy of the Buescher advertisements to sell the saxophone rely on perceived heteronormative desires of men, consequently imbuing the saxophone with masculine qualities meant to be deployed by male players.

The text continues, "It's just a step from the wallflower's corner to the center of the popularity ring, and an easy step at that. Don't let the other fellows capture all the good times and the smiles of those whose smiles are [worthwhile]. Be the whole show. Take the 'spot' with your Buescher True Tone Saxophone." Buescher has drawn a parallel from the text to the image when they discuss "worthwhile smiles," which refers to the women in the images used who are smiling. The inclusion of "wallflower" as a descriptor with a negative connotation, when juxtaposed with the desire of social relevance, may imply that a passive nature is feminine and thus not a desired quality for men to possess. Further, the text in figure 5.3 also associates "wallflower" to a lack of romantic attention, where "wallflower's corner" is incapable of capturing "the smiles of those whose smiles are worth while [sic]," implying the rejection or absence of a woman's attention. By delineating qualities as feminine or masculine, the advertiser begins to define the qualities possessed or gained by men who play the saxophone. Within the context of Hall's encoding/decoding framework, this introduction and defi-

Figure 5.3. Buescher advertisement in *Cosmopolitan*, February 1928

nition of an undesired quality helps the viewer identify a predictable encoded message: men who play saxophone are popular and masculine.

In another advertisement from *Cosmopolitan* in November 1928, Buescher includes the text, "Other fellows had left him in the social background. Girls avoided him. He was missing all the modern fun. Then, one day, he read an advertisement. It held out a promise of popularity if he would only learn to play a Buescher True Tone Saxophone."[65] Similarly, this text uses language directly referencing women by saying, "Girls avoided him," producing an oxymoron which explicitly tells us that Buescher is claiming that purchasing a saxophone will result in the attention of women; their strategy is confirmed. Additionally, the use of text, "He was missing all the modern fun," in the context of modern cultural and social changes in the 1920s could be simply interpreted as new social freedoms. However, in a decade where new freedoms and social modernity were synonymous with sex and sexual liberation, this text reinforces the notion of selling the attention of women within the framework of sexual desires. Ultimately, this treatment objectifies the women used in the images of the Buescher advertisements and establishes a trajectory for the development of the saxophone as a symbol for sexuality, masculinity, and male desire. Further, while the advertisements analyzed do not necessarily represent any explicit intent to exclude non-male-identifying persons from performing on the saxophone, they do demonstrate a process of capitalism that identified and appealed to demographics that would best secure a successful market share. As such, we see a resultant lack in representation of non-male, non-white persons performing on the saxophone, shaping the public perception and iconography of the saxophone.

Conclusion

Consideration of the saxophone's unique sexualization, ubiquity in popular culture, and relative exclusion from concert music is essential to understanding public perceptions of the instrument. Saxophonists, scholars, and enthusiasts alike look to key performers, the instrument's representation in media, and genres of music that regularly feature the instrument to realize and appreciate its socio-cultural significance. The analysis presented in this chapter offers crucial insight into the formative era of the saxophone's contributions to popular culture and into how the thriving capitalist society of the 1920s situated the saxophone as an icon that represented gender norms and heterosexual male desire. Further, the objectification of women as a marketing mechanism in 1920s saxophone advertisements influenced both the iconography of the instrument and affirmed the general lack in representation of woman saxophonists in mainstream media.

Shadowed by the popular music of the 1920s and the excitement surrounding the saxophone craze, Elise Hall is often noted as the only woman to perform and promote the instrument in concert music. However, many women have been identified as early notable performers thanks to recent scholarship of Hubbs, Smialek, Logrande, and others. Even so, why were there so few women saxophonists? Moreover, why the perceived erasure of these early woman performers? Why does the saxophone community remain overwhelmingly male dominated nearly a century later? While the scope of this chapter may not answer all of these queries, it can speak to the ways in which the musical activities of women like Hall were possibly overshadowed by the popularity of the instrument itself. Moreover, this investigation illustrates how their efforts were undoubtedly impacted by the social order propagandized by the burgeoning mass media industry in the United States. As evidenced through the survey of social, cultural, and economic growth, as well as an analysis of Buescher advertisements, the instrument diverged from the efforts of Hall, her commissions, and the elite Boston orchestral scene, relegating her legacy to the mid-century and later when concert saxophone and academic study of saxophone would resume and where the social climate was more accepting of women instrumentalists. As the development of the saxophone converged with an era where the patriarchal society released its hold on the morality and expression of sexuality, "American" culture was being defined by jazz and Black musicians, and economic growth fueled the accessibility of the "American dream." The saxophone became synonymous with liberation, white, and heterosexual male desires, along with masculinity, rather than with women who labored to commission new concert music and perform in the orchestral concert hall.[66]

NOTES

1. While concert saxophonists continue to advocate for their work as an integral component of concert music, one may argue that the saxophone still has not been widely accepted in classical, concert, and new music idioms. Robert Walser aptly notes: "Classical saxophone playing is an enterprise that is only tenuously established in the academy, and for good reason: it exists nowhere else, and it has virtually no audience beyond the players themselves." Robert Walser, "Popular Music Analysis: Ten Apothegms and Four Instances," in *Analyzing Popular Music*, ed. Allan F. Moore (Cambridge: Cambridge University Press, 2003), 34.

2. Adrianne Honnold, "'Unacknowledged Ubiquity': The Saxophone in Popular Music" (PhD diss., University of Birmingham, 2021); Yuko Suzuki, "You Sound Like an Old Black Man: Performativity of Gender and Race among Female Jazz Saxophonists" (PhD diss., University of Pittsburgh, 2011); Stephen Cottrell, *The Saxophone* (New Haven: Yale University Press, 2013); Michael Segell, *The Devil's Horn: The Story of the Saxophone, from Noisy Novelty to King of Cool* (New York: Picador, 2006).

3. See footnote 271.

4. William Henry Street, "Elise Boyer Hall, America's First Female Concert Saxophonist: Her Life as Performing Artist, Pioneer of Concert Repertory for Saxophone and Patroness of the Arts" (DMA diss., Northwestern University, 1983), 48.
5. Street, "Elise Boyer Hall," 48, 53.
6. Street, "Elise Boyer Hall," 76.
7. Veronica Doubleday, "Sounds of Power: An Overview of Musical Instruments and Gender"; Honnold, "'Unacknowledged Ubiquity': The Saxophone in Popular Music"; Suzuki, "You Sound Like an Old Black Man: Performativity of Gender and Race among Female Jazz Saxophonists."; Segell, *The Devil's Horn: The Story of the Saxophone, from Noisy Novelty to King of Cool.*; Cottrell, *The Saxophone.*
8. See footnote 276.
9. Suzuki, "You Sound Like an Old Black Man: Performativity of Gender and Race among Female Jazz Saxophonists."
10. In a contemporary context, I acknowledge that gender is not binary and that referring to gender as such is not only highly limiting but promotes the erasure of non-binary human beings and the exclusion of their essential perspectives and experiences. This chapter will define gender as a binary for the sole reason that historical advertisements constructed gender within these confines. Furthermore, this chapter aims to offer a starting point for insight into the ways in which the saxophone has a fraught history with racism, misogyny, and the public centering of cisgendered, heterosexual, white male experiences.
11. It is important to note that exoticism, orientalism, and often "novelty" are words used to describe what is the unacceptable appropriation and tokenism of both non-western and Black culture.
12. Richard Ingham, *The Cambridge Companion to the Saxophone* (New York: Cambridge University Press, 1998), 1–15.
13. Cottrell, *The Saxophone*, 113.
14. Cottrell, *The Saxophone*, 113.
15. In addition to addressing Charles Soualle in his monograph on the saxophone, Cottrell details the career and orientalist work of Soualle in a dedicated paper, published in the *Journal of the American Musical Instrument Society*. See Stephen Cottrell, "Charles Jean-Baptiste Soualle and the Saxophone," *Journal of the American Musical Instrument Society* XLIV (2018): 179–208.
16. Jordan Smith, "The Use of Saxophone in the Operas of Massenet," *The Saxophone Symposium* (2015): 36–37.
17. Derek B. Scott, "Orientalism and Musical Style," *The Musical Quarterly* 82, no. 2 (1998): 309-35, accessed April 5, 2021, http://www.jstor.org/stable/742411.
18. Scott, "Orientalism and Musical Style."
19. Annegret Fauser, *Musical Encounters at the 1889 Paris World's Fair* (Rochester: Univ. of Rochester Press, 2009), 140.
20. Fauser, *Musical Encounters*, 140.
21. Honnold, "Unacknowledged Ubiquity," 5.
22. Ingham, *The Cambridge Companion to the Saxophone*, 18.
23. Ingham, *The Cambridge Companion to the Saxophone*, 21.
24. Cottrell, *The Saxophone*, 133–135.
25. Cottrell, *The Saxophone*, 136, 332–333.
26. Segell, *The Devil's Horn*, 86–87.
27. Juliann Sivulka, *Soap, Sex, and Cigarettes: A Cultural History of American Advertising*, second ed. (Boston, MA: Cengage Learning, 2012), 113.
28. Juliann Sivulka, *Soap, Sex, and Cigarettes: A Cultural History of American Advertising*, 113–114.
29. "1920 US Census, Volume 4, Chapter II, Number and Sex of Occupied Persons," United States Census Bureau, December 4, 2015, accessed November 7, 2018, https://www2.census.gov/library/publications/decennial/1920/volume-4/41084484v4ch02.pdf.
30. Sivulka. *Soap, Sex, and Cigarettes*, 120–125.
31. Chris Wharton, *Advertising: Critical Approaches* (London: Taylor and Francis, 2014), 14.
32. Paul Alan Bro, "The Development of the American-made Saxophone: A Study of Saxophones made by Buescher, Conn, Holton, Martin, and H. N. White" (PhD diss., Northwestern University, 1992), 19.
33. Bro, "The Development of the American-made Saxophone," 16.
34. Sivulka, *Soap, Sex, and Cigarettes*, 150–152.
35. Sivulka, *Soap, Sex, and Cigarettes*, 151.
36. Sivulka, *Soap, Sex, and Cigarettes*, 152.
37. Sivulka, *Soap, Sex, and Cigarettes*, 152-158.
38. Kathy Lee Peiss, *Hope in a Jar: the Making of America's Beauty Culture* (Philadelphia, Pennsylvania: University of Pennsylvania Press, 2011).
39. Katherine J. Parkin, *Food Is Love: Advertising and Gender Roles in Modern America* (Philadelphia, Pennsylvania: University of Pennsylvania Press, 2007), 12.
40. Jackson Lears, "From Salvation to Self-Realization: Advertising and the Therapeutic Roots of the Consumer Culture, 1880-1930," in *The Culture of Consumption: Critical Essays in American History, 1880-1980* (New York, NY: Random House, 1988), 1–38.
41. Kathy Lee Peiss, *Hope in a Jar: The Making of America's Beauty Culture*.
42. Simone Weil Davis, *Living up to the Ads: Gender Fictions of the 1920s* (Durham: Duke University Press, 2000), 2.
43. Einav Rabinovitch-Fox, "New Women in Early 20th-Century America."

44. Estelle B. Freedman, "The New Woman: Changing Views of Women in the 1920s," *The Journal of American History* 61, no. 2 (1974): 372–93, accessed March 27, 2021, doi:10.2307/1903954, 376.
45. Estelle B. Freedman, "The New Woman: Changing Views of Women in the 1920s," 377.
46. Freedman, "The New Woman: Changing Views of Women in the 1920s," 379.
47. Freedman, "The New Woman: Changing Views of Women in the 1920s," 379.
48. Wharton, *Advertising: Critical Approaches*, 102.
49. Wharton, *Advertising: Critical Approaches*, 102.
50. Wharton, *Advertising: Critical Approaches*, 103.
51. Wharton, *Advertising: Critical Approaches*, 103–104.
52. Wharton, *Advertising: Critical Approaches*, 103–104.
53. Arthur Asa Berger, *Ads, Fads, and Consumer Culture: Advertising's Impact on American Character and Society* (Blue Ridge Summit: Rowman & Littlefield Publishers, 2011), accessed March 22, 2021, ProQuest Ebook Central, 149–152.
54. Berger, *Ads, Fads, and Consumer Culture*, 159–160.
55. Stuart Hall, Jessica Evans, and Sean Nixon (eds.), *Representation: Cultural Representations and Signifying Practises*, second edition (Los Angeles, CA: Sage Publications Ltd, 2013), 281.
56. Stuart Hall, Jessica Evans, and Sean Nixon (eds.), *Representation: Cultural Representations and Signifying Practises*, second edition (Los Angeles, CA: Sage Publications Ltd, 2013), 312–313.
57. Laura Mulvey, *Visual and Other Pleasures*, 2nd ed. (New York: Palgrave Macmillan, 2009).
58. Bro, "The Development of the American-made Saxophone," 76–77; Advertisement: Buescher Band Instrument Co., *Ladies' Home Journal* 06 (1924): 198; Display ad 88 — no title, *Los Angeles Times (1923-1995)*, December 20, 1923; Advertisement: C. G. CONN, LTD, *Cosmopolitan (1886)* 02 (1922): 144; Display ad 8 — no title, *Los Angeles Times (1886-1922)*, June 21, 1922; Advertisements, *Ladies' Home Journal* 10 (1923): 227.
59. Advertisement: C. G. Conn Ltd., *Cosmopolitan (1886)*, 12 1920, 153; Advertisement: C. C. CONN Ltd., *Cosmopolitan (1886)*, 09 1920, 171; Advertisement: C. G. CONN Ltd., *Red Book Magazine*, 01 1921, 134; Advertisement: C. G. Conn Ltd., *Cosmopolitan (1886)*, 04 1921, 97; Advertisement: CONN BAND, *Better Homes and Gardens*, 06 1928, 46. Advertisement: C.G. Conn, Ltd., *Hearst's International Combined with Cosmopolitan*, 04 1925, 138. Advertisement C. G. CONN, Ltd., *Cosmopolitan (1886)*, 10 1920, 151.
60. Advertisement: C. G. CONN, Ltd., *Cosmopolitan (1886)*, 10 1920, 151.
61. Stephen Cottrell, *The Saxophone*, 155.
62. Advertisement: SAXOPHONE, *Red Book Magazine*, 06 1923, 163.
63. Advertisement: BUESCHER BAND INSTRUMENT CO., *Hearst's International Combined with Cosmopolitan*, 04 1927, 194.
64. Advertisement: BUESCHER BAND INSTRUMENT CO., *Hearst's International Combined with Cosmopolitan*, 02 1928, 201.
65. Advertisements, *Hearst's International Combined with Cosmopolitan*, 11 1928, 200. 44
66. The use of "American" here refers to the colloquial use of the word, often in clichés, and in this context is meant to describe solely the United States.

WORKS CITED

"1920 US Census, Volume 4, Chapter II, Number and Sex of Occupied Persons." United States Census Bureau. December 4, 2015. Accessed November 7, 2018. https://www2.census.gov/library/publications/decennial/1920/volume-4/41084484v4ch02.pdf.

Berger, Asa Arthur. *Ads, Fads, and Consumer Culture: Advertising's Impact on American Character and Society*. Rowman & Littlefield Publishers, 2011.

Bernays, Edward. *Propaganda*. New York: Horace Liveright, 1928.

Bro, Paul Alan. "The Development of the American-made Saxophone: A Study of Saxophones made by Buescher, Conn, Holton, Martin, and H. N. White." DMA diss., Northwestern University, 1992.

Cottrell, Stephen. *The Saxophone*. New Haven: Yale University Press, 2013.

———. "Charles Jean-Baptiste Soualle and the Saxophone." *Journal of the American Musical Instrument Society*, XLIV (2018): 179–208. https://openaccess.city.ac.uk/id/eprint/19911/11/JAMIS44_13_Cottrell.pdf

Davis, Simone Weil. *Living up to the Ads: Gender Fictions of the 1920s*. Durham: Duke University Press, 2000.

de Villiers, Abraham Albertus. "The Development of the Saxophone 1850-1950: Its Influence on Performance and the Classical Repertory." PhD diss., University of Pretoria, 2014.

Doubleday, Veronica. "Sounds of Power: An Overview of Musical Instruments and Gender." *Ethnomusicology Forum 17, no. 1 (2008): 3–39. Accessed February 18, 2021. http://www.jstor.org/stable/20184604.

Eggert, Axel, and Vockeroth, Melanie. *The Saxophone in Advertising*. New York: Peter Lang, 2003.

Endres, Kathleen L., and Therese L. Lueck. *Women's Periodicals in the United States: Consumer Magazines*. Westport: Greenwood Press, 1995.

Fox, Richard Wightman, and Lears, T. J. Jackson. "From Salvation to Self-Realization: Advertising and the Therapeutic Roots of the Consumer Culture, 1880-1930." Essay. In *The Culture of Consumption: Critical Essays in American History, 1880-1980*, 1–38. New York: Random House, 1988.

Freedman, Estelle B. "The New Woman: Changing Views of Women in the 1920s." *The Journal of American History* 61, no. 2 (1974): 372–393. Accessed March 27, 2021. doi:10.2307/1903954.

Hadden, J. C. "Woman and Music." *The Gentleman's Magazine* 294 (1903): 510–516. Retrieved from http://ezproxy.lib.utexas.edu/login?url=https://search-proquest-com.ezproxy.lib.utexas.edu/docview/8557465?accountid=7118

Hall, Stuart, Jessica Evans, and Sean Nixon, eds. *Representation: Cultural Representations and Signifying Practises*. Los Angeles: Sage, 2013.

Hersey, Joanna Ross. "Women Brass Musicians on the Vaudeville Stage." David Werden's Euphonium-Tuba Forum. May 7, 2015. http://www.dwerden.com/forum/content.php/142-Women-Brass-Musicians-on-the-Vaudeville-Stage#.XA25KhNKjOQ.

Honnold, Adrianne. "'Unacknowledged Ubiquity': The Saxophone in Popular Music." PhD dissertation, University of Birmingham, 2021. http://etheses.bham.ac.uk/id/eprint/11843.

Ingham, Richard. *The Cambridge Companion to the Saxophone*. New York: Cambridge University Press, 1998.

Kantor, Michael, and Laurence Maslon. *Make 'Em Laugh: The Funny Business of America*. New York: Grand Central, 2008.

Lampel, Joseph, Jamal Shamsie, and Theresa K. Lant. *The Business of Culture Strategic Perspectives on Entertainment and Media*. Mahwah: Lawrence Erlbaum Associates, 2006.

Landers, James. *The Improbable First Century of Cosmopolitan Magazine*. Columbia: University of Missouri Press, 2010.

Levinsky, Gail Beth. "An Analysis and Comparison of Early Saxophone Methods Published between 1846-1946." DMA diss., Northwestern University, 1997.

Liebman, Roy. *Vitaphone Films: A Catalogue of the Features and Shorts*. Jefferson, NC: McFarland, 2003.

Mulvey, Laura. *Visual and Other Pleasures*. Houndmills, UK: Palgrave Macmillan, 2009.

Parkin, Katherine J. *Food Is Love: Advertising and Gender Roles in Modern America*. Philadelphia: University of Pennsylvania Press, 2007.

Peiss, Kathy Lee. *Hope in a Jar: The Making of America's Beauty Culture*. Philadelphia: University of Pennsylvania Press, 2011.

Rabinovitch-Fox, Einav. "New Women in Early 20th-Century America." *Oxford Research Encyclopedias*. August 14, 2017. Accessed December 2, 2018. https://doi.org/10.1093/acrefore/9780199329175.013.427.

Scott, Derek B. "Orientalism and Musical Style." *The Musical Quarterly* 82, no. 2 (1998): 309–35. Accessed April 5, 2021. http://www.jstor.org/stable/742411.

Seddon, Laura. *British Women Composers and Instrumental Chamber Music in the Early Twentieth Century*. Burlington: Routledge, 2016.

Segell, Michael. *The Devil's Horn: The Story of the Saxophone, from Noisy Novelty to King of Cool*. New York: Picador, 2006.

Sivulka, Juliann. *Soap, Sex, and Cigarettes: A Cultural History of American Advertising*. Boston: Cengage Learning, 2012.

Smialek, Thomas, and L.A. Logrande. "Louise Linden: America's First Saxophone Virtuoso." *The Saxophone Symposium* 38-39 (2016): 1–29.

Smith, Jordan. "The Use of Saxophone in the Operas of Massenet." *The Saxophone Symposium* 36-37 (2015).

Street, William Henry. "Elise Boyer Hall, America's First Female Concert Saxophonist: Her Life as Performing Artist, Pioneer of Concert Repertory for Saxophone and Patroness of the Arts." DMA diss., Northwestern University, 1983.

Suzuki, Y. "You Sound Like an Old Black Man: Performativity of Gender and Race among Female Jazz Saxophonists." PhD diss., University of Pittsburgh, 2011.

Upton, George Putnam. *Woman in Music*. Chicago: A. C. McClurg, 1890.

Walser, Robert. "Popular Music Analysis: Ten Apothegms and Four Instances." In *Analyzing Popular Music*, edited by Allan F. Moore, 16–38. Cambridge: Cambridge University Press, 2003.

Wharton, Chris. *Advertising: Critical Approaches*. London: Routledge, 2014.

Mediography

Advertisement: *Better Homes and Gardens*, November 1924. http://ezproxy.lib.utexas.edu/login?url=https://www-proquest-com.ezproxy.lib.utexas.edu/magazines/advertisements/docview/1926465006/se-2?accountid=7118.

Advertisement: *Better Homes and Gardens*, February 1926. Retrieved from http://ezproxy.lib.utexas.edu/login?url=https://search-proquest-com.ezproxy.lib.utexas.edu/docview/1767280085?accountid=7118.

Advertisement: *The Billboard (Archive: 1894-1960)*, October 08, 1921. http://ezproxy.lib.utexas.edu/login?url=https://www-proquest-com.ezproxy.lib.utexas.edu/magazines/advertisement/docview/1031669916/se-2?accountid=7118.

Advertisement: *The Billboard (Archive: 1894-1960)*, December 18, 1920. http://ezproxy.lib.utexas.edu/login?url=https://search-proquest-com.ezproxy.lib.utexas.edu/docview/1031619595?accountid=7118.

Advertisement: BUESCHER BAND INSTRUMENT CO. *Cosmopolitan (1886)*, December 1924. http://ezproxy.lib.utexas.edu/login?url=https://search-proquest-com.ezproxy.lib.utexas.edu/docview/2038757634?accountid=7118.

Advertisement: BUESCHER BAND INSTRUMENT CO. *Hearst's International Combined with Cosmopolitan*, January 1926. http://ezproxy.lib.utexas.edu/login?url=https://search-proquest-com.ezproxy.lib.utexas.edu/docview/1974004901?accountid=7118.

Advertisement: BUESCHER BAND INSTRUMENT CO. *Hearst's International Combined with Cosmopolitan*, March 1926. http://ezproxy.lib.utexas.edu/login?url=https://search-proquest-com.ezproxy.lib.utexas.edu/docview/1974004949?accountid=7118.

Advertisement: BUESCHER BAND INSTRUMENT CO. *Hearst's International Combined with Cosmopolitan*, April 1927. http://ezproxy.lib.utexas.edu/login?url=https://search-proquest-com.ezproxy.lib.utexas.edu/docview/1974010145?accountid=7118.

Advertisement: BUESCHER BAND INSTRUMENT CO. *Hearst's International Combined with Cosmopolitan*, September 1927. http://ezproxy.lib.utexas.edu/login?url=https://search-proquest-com.ezproxy.lib.utexas.edu/docview/1974001964?accountid=7118.

Advertisement: BUESCHER BAND INSTRUMENT CO. *Hearst's International Combined with Cosmopolitan*, October 1927. http://ezproxy.lib.utexas.edu/login?url=https://search-proquest-com.ezproxy.lib.utexas.edu/docview/1974006582?accountid=7118.

Advertisement: BUESCHER BAND INSTRUMENT CO. *Hearst's International Combined with Cosmopolitan*, November 1927. http://ezproxy.lib.utexas.edu/login?url=https://search-proquest-com.ezproxy.lib.utexas.edu/docview/1974006603?accountid=7118.

Advertisement: BUESCHER BAND INSTRUMENT CO. *Hearst's International Combined with Cosmopolitan*, February 1928. http://ezproxy.lib.utexas.edu/login?url=https://search-proquest-com.ezproxy.lib.utexas.edu/docview/1974008527?accountid=7118.

Advertisement: BUESCHER BAND INSTRUMENT CO. *Hearst's International Combined with Cosmopolitan*, April 1928. http://ezproxy.lib.utexas.edu/login?url=https://search-proquest-com.ezproxy.lib.utexas.edu/docview/1973994985?accountid=7118.

Advertisement: BUESCHER BAND INSTRUMENT CO. *Ladies' Home Journal*, June 1924. http://ezproxy.lib.utexas.edu/login?url=https://www.proquest.com/magazines/advertisement-buescher-band-instrument-co/docview/1876373741/se-2?accountid=7118.

Advertisement: BUESCHER. *Red Book Magazine*, February 1922. http://ezproxy.lib.utexas.edu/login?url=https://search-proquest-com.ezproxy.lib.utexas.edu/docview/1813164583?accountid=7118.

Advertisement: BUESCHER. *Red Book Magazine*, February 1922. Retrieved from http://ezproxy.lib.utexas.edu/login?url=https://search-proquest-com.ezproxy.lib.utexas.edu/docview/1813164583?accountid=7118

Advertisement: C. G. CONN, LTD. *Cosmopolitan (1886)*, February 1922. http://ezproxy.lib.utexas.edu/login?url=https://search-proquest-com.ezproxy.lib.utexas.edu/docview/2034251461?accountid=7118. Display Ad 88 – no title. *Los Angeles Times (1923-1995)*, December 20, 1923. http://ezproxy.lib.utexas.edu/login?url=https://www.proquest.com/historical-newspapers/display-ad-88-no-title/docview/161577047/se-2.

Advertisement: *Cosmopolitan (1886)*, April 1920. http://ezproxy.lib.utexas.edu/login?url=https://search-proquest-com.ezproxy.lib.utexas.edu/docview/2034261365?accountid=7118.

Advertisement: *Hearst's International Combined with Cosmopolitan*, November 1928. http://ezproxy.lib.utexas.edu/login?url=https://search-proquest-com.ezproxy.lib.utexas.edu/docview/1974001236?accountid=7118.

Advertisement: *Ladies' Home Journal*, October 1923. http://ezproxy.lib.utexas.edu/login?url=https://www-proquest-com.ezproxy.lib.utexas.edu/magazines/advertisements/docview/1866675330/se-2?accountid=7118.

Advertisement: LYON & HEALY HARP. *Town & Country*, June 01, 1922. http://ezproxy.lib.utexas.edu/login?url=https://www-proquest-com.ezproxy.lib.utexas.edu/magazines/advertisement-lyon-healy-harp/docview/2101204553/se-2?accountid=7118.

Advertisement: *Red Book Magazine,* October 1923. http://ezproxy.lib.utexas.edu/login?url=https://www-proquest-com.ezproxy.lib.utexas.edu/magazines/advertisements/docview/1767283578/se-2?accountid=7118.

Advertisement: SAXOPHONE. *Red Book Magazine,* June 1923. http://ezproxy.lib.utexas.edu/login?url=https://www-proquest-com.ezproxy.lib.utexas.edu/magazines/advertisement-saxophone/docview/1807545501/se-2?accountid=7118.

Advertisement: *Town & Country,* March 01, 1924. http://ezproxy.lib.utexas.edu/login?url=https://www-proquest-com.ezproxy.lib.utexas.edu/magazines/advertisements/docview/2103723509/se-2?accountid=7118.

Bell. "New Acts this Week: JUVENILITY (8)." *Variety (Archive: 1905-2000),* November 04,1921. http://ezproxy.lib.utexas.edu/login?url=https://www-proquest-com.ezproxy.lib.utexas.edu/magazines/new-acts-this-week-juvenility-8/docview/1475787020/se-2?accountid=7118.

Display Ad 7 – no title. *Los Angeles Times (1923-1995),* July 31, 1923. http://ezproxy.lib.utexas.edu/login?url=https://search-proquest-com.ezproxy.lib.utexas.edu/docview/161528992?accountid=7118.

Display Ad 8 – no title. *Los Angeles Times (1886-1922),* June 21, 1922. http://ezproxy.lib.utexas.edu/login?url=https://search-proquest-com.ezproxy.lib.utexas.edu/docview/161092878?accountid=7118.

Display Ad 31 – no title. *Los Angeles Times (1923-1995),* February 24, 1924. http://ezproxy.lib.utexas.edu/login?url=https://www-proquest-com.ezproxy.lib.utexas.edu/historical-newspapers/display-ad-31-no-title/docview/161615720/se-2?accountid=7118.

Display Ad 39 – no title. *New York Times (1857-1922),* August 23, 1922. http://ezproxy.lib.utexas.edu/login?url=https://search-proquest-com.ezproxy.lib.utexas.edu/docview/99421363?accountid=7118.

Levick, M. B. "OUR MOANING SAXOPHONE IS NOW CALLED IMMORAL." *New York Times (1923-Current File),* September 13, 1925. http://ezproxy.lib.utexas.edu/login?url=https://search-proquest-com.ezproxy.lib.utexas.edu/docview/103482818?accountid=7118.

Mark. "New Acts this Week: RUTH GLANVILLE and CO. (1)." *Variety (Archive: 1905-2000),* October 22, 1924. http://ezproxy.lib.utexas.edu/login?url=https://www-proquest-com.ezproxy.lib.utexas.edu/magazines/new-acts-this-week-ruth-glanville-co-1/docview/1505660367/se-2?accountid =7118.

"THE STORY OF THE SAXOPHONE." *The Billboard (Archive: 1894-1960),* September 17, 1921. Retrieved from http://ezproxy.lib.utexas.edu/login?url=https://search-proquest-com.ezproxy.lib.utexas.edu/docview/1031659028?accountid=7118.

Intersections of Gender, Genre, and Access

The Enterprising Career of Kathryne E. Thompson

Holly J. Hubbs

ABSTRACT

As Elise Boyer Hall endeavored to expand the saxophone's concert repertoire on the East Coast of the United States, a growing trend within vernacular music drew in other female performers who would similarly champion the saxophone's mainstream acceptance within popular genres. The story of one woman in particular, the Los Angeles-based Kathryne E. Thompson (c.1889-1957), illustrates the level of success that an enterprising female saxophonist could achieve within popular music. Wildly successful during the 1920s, Thompson has been virtually forgotten by modern musicians and audiences. During her career, which spanned approximately two decades, she composed, published, concertized, and founded her own teaching studio which ultimately grew to more than 100 students. Thompson was also frequently featured as a soloist on Los Angeles radio and directed the "Southern California Saxophone Band," one of the most popular ensembles of its kind during the 1920s. Thompson made it clear in interviews in *Jacobs Band Monthly* that while she wrote and performed vernacular music, she was a technically well-trained performer—setting herself apart from what she describes as the many "raw recruits" who were "honking" on the instrument during the American amateur saxophone craze of the 1920s. Like Hall two decades earlier, Thompson would strive in her career to expand the saxophone's repertoire and reputation. By weaving together the stories of Hall, Thompson, and other women like them, we begin to have a more nuanced and comprehensive understanding of the immense—yet until recently almost invisible—impact that women have collectively made on the musical culture of America.

Introduction

In a 2021 interview about Elise Boyer Hall, saxophone historian Paul Cohen noted that Hall's circumstances as "a single woman with significant financial resources and high social status" were unique and quite likely opened doors for her that remained closed for other women of her time.[1] That this book celebrates Hall's legacy in advancing the saxophone's role in American music culture is a testament to the lasting implications of her efforts, as well as the trails she blazed for others. Yet there were other women who also achieved thriving professional careers as saxophonists, composers, and performers during the late nineteenth and early twentieth centuries in the United States, and their lives are also worthy of rediscovery. For example, the Los Angeles-based saxophonist Kathryne Thompson, like Hall fifteen years earlier, made tremendous efforts to increase the saxophone's repertoire and reputation but was left out of the historical record. This chapter, which explores details about Thompson's career, begins by examining the place of women in music-making culture more broadly and aims to contextualize the legacies of Hall and Thompson within a lineage of female musicians and composers whose lives are only now being revisited and reinserted into historical accounts.

Many saxophonists, while they may be familiar with the story of Hall's commission of the *Rapsodie pour saxophone et orchestre* by Claude Debussy, know very little about her life and larger impact. Even fewer still have encountered the story of Thompson's successful career or played her entertaining pieces like *Bubble and Squeak* or *Valse Minah*.

Thompson, who was born a generation after Hall in 1889, enjoyed a flourishing career in the Los Angeles area during the 1910s and '20s. Whether she knew of Hall's achievements is unclear, but it is possible. By the time Hall retired from playing around 1918, Thompson had already been performing professionally for almost a decade, including in collaboration with virtuoso saxophonist Edward Lefebre. That Lefebre was engaged in performances in Boston and other East Coast locations around the turn of the twentieth century could indicate that he knew both Hall and Thompson in his lifetime.[2]

While facets of their stories are similar, the impact of Hall's and Thompson's legacies on the instrument's repertoire differ in terms of genre. Hall was a saxophonist in the classical tradition, living a generation before the post-WWI proliferation of popular American vernacular musical styles such as ragtime and jazz.[3] Thompson played and composed what she considered "ragtime" and other popular music styles such as fox trots, waltzes, and parlor songs. Differences aside, both Hall and Thompson loved the saxophone and during their careers remained undaunted advocates for the instrument. A cursory glance shows us that both Hall and Thompson expanded the saxophone repertoire, while a closer examination of their musical accomplishments illustrates more profound commonalities, such as their personal commitment to aesthetic value and their efforts to increase the saxophone's profile within their communities.

I discovered Thompson while pursuing research for my doctoral dissertation, a survey of the lives and music of late nineteenth- and early twentieth-century American women saxophonists.[4] Everything about Thompson's story immediately resonated with me. She, like me, was originally from Illinois, and began playing saxophone early in her life. Unlike me, however, she took the plunge into Los Angeles entertainment culture while she was only in her twenties. She performed and improvised 1920's ragtime and was quite demonstrative in interviews that saxophone players must fight against their association with amateurish, unpracticed playing technique. Thompson once said in an interview, when referring to unstudied playing, "if I thought for one single second that his sourtone, out-of-tune raucous, bilious-sounding saxophone playing were anything but a process of infantile development, I assuredly would sell my saxophone at once."[5] The more her story came alive through my research and conversation with her family, the more I wanted to reintroduce her compositions to the saxophone-playing community.

The Impact of Women on Musical Cultures

As twenty-first-century concert audiences and readers become more familiar with women of the past, it is important to contextualize their stories, and since women's achievements often pave the way for other women's achievements, there is merit in recognizing the career accomplishments of female musicians within the continuum of those that came before and after them. To set the stage for a closer look into the lives of Hall and Thompson, then, let us first take a step back to consider the status of women in late-nineteenth and early-twentieth-century music more generally. That women music-makers of the past came to find opportunities within music at all, considering the restrictive conventions of pre-twentieth-century gender roles, demonstrates their persistence and creativity. Despite their efforts and achievements, however, it is only in the early twenty-first century that accounts of women such as Hall, Thompson, and myriad others are being more fully considered as part of the historical narrative.

That few people are familiar with the accomplishments of women of the past is perhaps unsurprising, considering that their achievements have been omitted from written histories for centuries. Numerous under-celebrated women music-makers—prolific performers and composers like Barbara Strozzi, Fanny Hensel-Mendelsohn, Amy Cheney Beach, and Florence Price—are only now, in the twenty-first century, beginning to enter the canon of Western art music history. The cultural impact of these composers' contributions continues to be reevaluated and, as in the case of Florence Price, their works are rediscovered and more frequently programmed in concert. The brief discussion of a few historical women that follows serves as a reminder that history is a dynamic and mutable narrative that is constantly revised and rewritten, and recasting historiographies to include accounts of women's musical achievements is necessary and long overdue.

Despite their largely undocumented contributions throughout history, women have always been present in various aspects of music-making and patronage. A widely-accepted narrative tells us that before the twentieth century, women were mostly confined to the domestic sphere and therefore had little access to professional domains. As early as the ninth century, however, Kassiani the Hymnographer (c.810-865, sometimes referred to as Kassia of Constantinople), a Byzantine abbess, composed hymns still used today in Byzantine liturgy. In the twelfth century, the German Benedictine abbess and polymath Hildegard von Bingen (1098-1179) penned one of the largest bodies of chant by any Medieval composer, but her work was largely forgotten or disregarded until the 800th anniversary of her death, in 1979, when the New London Consort began to perform her music. For Kassia and Hildegard, access to the music-making realm came through the necessity of liturgical music within women's religious houses, but what about those with secular lives?

In a time when institutional access was not guaranteed for secular women, financial privilege, social class, and marital status could open doors that might have otherwise remained closed. In the case of Strozzi, Hensel-Mendelsohn, and Cheney Beach, opportunities were facilitated (although sometimes simultaneously tempered) through a combination of their social class and the efforts of influential or financially supportive men in their lives. Strozzi was aided by her adoptive—and most likely illegitimate biological—father's connections and musical involvement in seventeenth-century Venice. Mendelssohn Hensel's talent was supported by her more famous brother, Felix, if only marginally tolerated by their father. Cheney Beach's musical prodigiousness, which became evident very early in her life, was nurtured by her parents and later tolerated, yet limited, by her surgeon husband, Henry Aubrey Beach.

Composer Florence Price forged a more atypical path to artistic achievement in music. As a mixed-race African American woman born in the late nineteenth-century American South, Price faced profound disadvantages compared to women like Beach or Hensel. After a relocation to Chicago from Arkansas, Price found compositional fulfillment as a part of the Chicago Black Renaissance during the 1930s and '40s. Price's trajectory and the current renaissance of her work are exceptional in many ways. The accidental discovery in 2009 of a trove of her manuscripts in an abandoned house in St. Anne, Illinois, avoided the permanent loss of her work and began an avalanche of rediscovery. Price's story is also unique in that unlike other female composers whose efforts were facilitated by men in their lives, she enjoyed her biggest successes later in life, after divorcing an abusive husband and struggling as a single mother.[6]

Although they were separated not only by generational differences but also by various demographic factors including race and class, women such as Price, Beach, Hensel, and Hall were significantly influenced by European composers and styles and shared a common goal of thriving in Western classical musical environments. Classical music has long been associated with the European elite, and much classical art music was commissioned by and for members of the wealthy classes of Western Europe. It is therefore not surprising that having been born in Paris, Hall also had strong European ties and engaged mostly French composers when commissioning new works. Hall's interest and participation in Parisian society reflects an American elite's view of France as the pinnacle of high culture, and she worked hard to imbue the saxophone and its compositions with this ethos in her hometown of Boston.

During Hall's lifetime, however, Americans' musical tastes were increasingly drawn away from European classical styles, as listeners' proclivity for commercial American vernacular styles continued to grow. Hall also lived during a time of great change in women's roles in music. Whereas in 1870, women musicians performed primarily on piano, harp, or guitar—as women were expected to play only on instruments that allowed them to look graceful while performing—by 1900 there were professional all-women orchestras. Organized in 1888, the Boston Fadette Orchestra gave over 6,000 concerts between 1890 and 1920. Caroline B. Nichols, their conductor of over thirty years, is yet another of the many musical high-achievers waiting to be rediscovered and duly lauded for her achievements. Census data from between 1870 and 1910 document the trend of increasing numbers of professional women music-makers. The 1870 United States Census Report documents 16,010 women employed in the music field, a number that rose dramatically every decade, until reaching 139,310 by 1910.[7]

In 1904, noted music critic and journalist James Huneker proclaimed the "death" of nineteenth-century stereotypes of women in music:

> Passed away is the girl who played the piano in the stiff Victorian drawing rooms of our mothers… The new girl is too busy to play the piano unless she has the gift; then she plays with consuming earnestness. We listen to her, for we know that this is an age of specialization, an age when woman in coming into her own, be it in nursing, electoral suffrage, or the writing of plays.[8]

Women were not, however, always readily welcomed in their new musical roles. Women musicians of all types—not just saxophone performers—struggled for recognition in their male-dominated field during the late nineteenth and early twentieth centuries. In 1888, after attending a series of concerts by the talented trumpeter/cornetist Anna Berger Lynch, George Bernard Shaw—under his critic pseudonym Corno di Bassetto—wrote, "I do not know why a lady should play the cornet," after which he conceded that her double-tonguing technique verged on "unattainable." Despite his penchant for humor within reviews, Shaw was undoubtedly impressed by Berger's playing, also writing that her "keenness of blare rivals Mr. Howard Reynolds."[9] Reynolds was a popular orchestral cornet soloist in London, an impressive comparison.

When women played instruments that were considered non-standard for them, they made themselves vulnerable to sexist ridicule. In 1906, one critic for *Musical America* stated:

> For the sake of the veneration in which all women should be held it is to be hoped that none of them will … take to playing the trombone, the French horn or the gigantic Sousaphone for, as Byron once said: "seeing the woman you love at table is apt to dispel all romance." And seeing a woman get red in the face blowing into an instrument is just as likely to prove an unpleasant shock.[10]

Because appearances played such a significant role in the way women were judged and perceived, many of those who did become successful soloists concerned themselves with the issue of whether it was most advantageous to emphasize or de-emphasize their gender.[11]

Marion Fairchild Nickell, in a 1928 article for *Musical America,* stated "although women have made significant contributions as performers, educators, patrons, writers, etc., they have yet to 'make their mark.'"[12] Eight years later, English composer Marie Wurm commented on women's overly demure nature as a disadvantage in their struggle for recognition in music, writing "women themselves do not promote their works enough."[13] Even as late as 1938, women were still receiving gender-biased criticism for their performance on the saxophone. An article titled "Why Women Musicians are Inferior," printed in *Downbeat* magazine in that year, states, "Have you ever heard a woman saxist who didn't get a quavering tone with absolutely uncontrolled vibrato?"[14] The popular big band bandleader Peggy Gilbert published a response in the same year, writing:

> A woman has to be a thousand times more talented, has to have a thousand times more initiative even to be recognized as the peer of a man. Why? Because of that age-old prejudice against women, that time-worn idea that women are the weaker sex.[15]

Author Sarah Mendelsohn writes that Gilbert and other women performers of her time just wanted "to play their music," but were forced to fit a mold, protect their physical appeal, and smile simultaneously while playing. Within the burgeoning popular music industry in which saxophonists like Thompson and Gilbert performed, male promoters and managers believed that stereotypically attractive women would bring more paying audiences to venues.

That women performers of popular music have long been subject to image-based criticism likely takes few readers by surprise. A look back into Hall's own personal story reveals that within the classical realm, she too was not immune to criticism and setbacks. In a June 8, 1903, letter to his friend, composer Andre Messager, Claude Debussy wrote, "the tenacity of Americans is proverbial," referring to Hall. Debussy likely felt desperate to navigate his current situation with Hall, who had commissioned and pre-paid for a composition in the summer of 1901 and would famously not receive a manuscript for over a decade. Debussy's reticence, letter correspondence about the project, and Hall's undying patience have become an indelible part of the mythology of the *Rapsodie*. Debussy desperately needed the money that Hall's commission provided, but he was at sea for the "newest and most appropriate combinations" for what he called an "aquatic" instrument.[16] A few days earlier, on June 4, 1903, in a letter to his first wife Lily, Debussy wrote, "Does it not appear indecent to you, a woman in love with a saxophone?" referring to Hall.[17] While Debussy's unduly harsh opinion of the saxophone was likely exacerbated by his frustrations with his own procrastination, his appraisal of Hall as an example of a "tenacious" American woman seemed suitable. Hall, like other American women musicians before and after her, would have to remain steadfast in her resolve to engage as a performing artist and cultural patron.

Hall was born to a prominent, wealthy Boston family and later became an even wealthier widow with distinct advantages that facilitated her access to a life of music-making. When reexamining Hall's life from a twenty-first-century perspective, one cannot overlook the ways in which her social class and abundant financial resources provided a privileged level of access to her role as performer and patron. Despite her socio-economic advantages however, Hall—as a woman over forty years old before even taking up the saxophone—was nevertheless subject to gender and age biases as were other women of her time. That Debussy once referred to her as an "old bat who dresses like an umbrella" could not illustrate this point further.[18] Despite this type of cruel reception, however, Hall and women like her paved their own way, through persistence and determination.

After helping to found the Boston Orchestral Club in 1899 with her friend, mentor and saxophone teacher George Longy, Elise Hall became president of the club in 1902. Longy, who had become the principal oboist with the Boston Symphony Orchestra a year earlier in 1898, founded a number of instrumental groups during his time in Boston. "Music clubs" grew greatly in number and popularity in late-nineteenth-century America and provided access to amateur and semi-professional music making for many women. The performance repertoire of many municipal music clubs began to blur the line between strictly classical music or strictly popular music concerts, often combining parlor song and dance music arrangements with classical works. During the second half of the nineteenth century, many women established local music clubs around the United States, both urban and suburban. These clubs, which fulfilled a social as well as a musical function, provided music teachers and performers a chance to work with other musicians and extend their social contacts. Music clubs presented concerts given by members; raised money to buy new instruments and bring in guest artists; and commissioned new solo, chamber, and orchestral works. Members were also encouraged to perform and compose, and many had their works performed in concert.[19] Because of their widespread popularity, music clubs inspired many women to compose and publicly perform who otherwise would not have done so.

Hall's Boston Orchestral Club, which flourished into the twentieth century, was comprised of both amateurs and professionals. The orchestra performed concerts a few times a year, selecting their own repertoire, which was coached by Longy. Considering Elise Hall's interest in saxophone and her key role as a founder and then president of the club, it is logical that Hall sought orchestral repertoire that would allow her to perform with the orchestra.[20] In his interview about Hall, Cohen posits that Hall's intent was less to have concertos written for herself, but rather to have orchestral works that included significant roles for the saxophone.[21]

As American music clubs grew in number and reach thanks to the efforts of patrons such as Hall, vernacular musical styles also continued to rise in popularity. By the 1910s and '20s, marches, ragtime, parlor song, and early Dixieland jazz music began to overtake opera and longer-form classical genres in mainstream popularity. As the saxophone's popularity spread, partly fueled by its association with these vernacular styles, an explosion of amateur saxophone playing ensued, as increasingly more middle-class Americans wanted not only to experience music as listeners, but as performers as well. As shorter-form, commercial music genres flourished among mainstream audiences, many saxophonists—Thompson and her well-known contemporary Rudy Wiedoeft included—created their own arrangements and original pieces in these genres. First published in 1916, Felix Arndt's novelty ragtime song "Nola" had already grown wildly popular by the time Thompson adopted its saxophone arrangement as her signature song in the early 1920s. During this time, piano and sheet music sales soared, local concert bands grew in number, and more Americans sought private music instruction. The saxophone, which perhaps more than most instruments has negotiated various identities within both classical and popular music, took center stage as an instrument on the rise within both the amateur and popular music-making communities.

The saxophone was quickly adopted by many aspiring performers during the American "saxophone craze," which began around 1915. In his book *That Moaning Saxophone*, author Bruce Vermazen captures the spirit of the growing saxophone frenzy as the instrument's reputation was elevated beyond "novelty noisemaker" status through the popularity of the Six Brown Brothers, who were a saxophone-playing sextet who became one of America's most well-known minstrel and vaudeville groups.[22] Joe Murphy writes that between 1921 and 1924, the saxophone outsold all instruments in the United States. In 1921, the Southern California Music Company offered a series of free lessons with their star teacher, Kathryne Thompson, for every saxophone purchased at the store. By 1926, the national saxophone mania had reached such epic proportions that Kansas City, Missouri, was forced to pass a saxophone curfew, by which it became illegal to play the saxophone within the city limits between the hours of 10:30 p.m. and 6:00 a.m.[23] By 1930, over one million saxophones existed throughout the world.[24]

As the popularity of vernacular music styles increased in America, so did the saxophone's popularity, gradually associating the instrument's reputation largely with that of a jazz instrument. This connection enticed some young

Figure 6.1. Kathryne Thompson on the cover of Felix Arndt's *Nola* (New York: Sam Fox Publishing Co., 1924)

players to choose a path toward jazz or other commercial vernacular styles, rather than classical music, in their pursuit of a performing career. This was the case for Thompson, despite the fact that she complained of being labeled as a "raw recruit, who is able to 'get by' because he can twist around on one foot and 'honk' a few wavy accordion-pleated tones that sound more like a bleating lamb than a musical instrument."[25] She made it clear in interviews that there should be a distinction between amateur playing and those who "studied" saxophone, clearly placing herself in the latter category despite not having ever attended a conservatory or degree program in music. In a 1923 interview for *Jacobs Band Monthly*, when asked about her opinion of amateur jazz players, Thompson remarked that "in every art there must be an element of commercialism. Of course ragtime is jazz to the well-schooled, artist-musician."[26] Thompson's multi-dimensional career also foreshadowed the type of multitasking that many freelance musicians would have to manage in order to have successful careers, balancing her performing career with a thriving teaching studio, composing original works, performing with famous saxophonists like Jascha Gurewich and Lefebre, and hosting a weekly radio program on one of the most popular stations in Los Angeles.

Kathryne Thompson's Enterprising Career

The youngest of five siblings, Kathryne Elizabeth Thompson was born in Illinois, probably in 1889, although various accounts of the year of her birth exist. As William Henry Street discusses in his dissertation on Hall, many late nineteenth- and early twentieth-century women felt compelled for various reasons to disguise their age, making it difficult for researchers to discern an accurate birth year.[27] Regardless of her exact age, by 1900 Kathryne Thompson's father had died and her mother Caroline had relocated the family to California.

The earliest records of Thompson performing on saxophone appear in 1903, at the Los Angeles YMCA, where she was listed on a program as "Kitty" Thompson. Sometime between 1905 and 1909, Thompson met and began study with saxophonist Lefebre, who became her ally and advocate during the last years of his life. By 1909, then seventy-five-year-old Lefebre had toured in Los Angeles and had engaged Thompson and two other women, Florence Makay and Ida Weber, as quartet members. Born in The Netherlands in 1835, saxophone virtuoso Lefebre had gained fame and spread the saxophone's popularity in the United States during the 1890s while playing with the John Philip Sousa band. Lefebre was also the first saxophonist to make a phonograph recording as a soloist, and in the late stages of his life he enjoyed a touring and freelance career, primarily with his Lefebre Saxophone Quartette.[28] By May of 1909, Kathryne, around twenty years of age, had the opportunity to perform with Lefebre as his second alto saxophonist in what was billed as Lefebre's Los Angeles Saxophone Quartet. After their performances in 1909, Thompson and Lefebre developed a professional relationship that would last until Lefebre's death in 1911. After this point in her career, Thompson would similarly champion her own female students and provide them with commercial live and radio performance opportunities as Lefebre had done for her. In doing so, Thompson was able to perpetuate the significance of mentorship that was integral to the codification of performance practice on the nascent saxophone. The growing network of mentorship was especially crucial in jazz styles, for which techniques were only just developing, and these networks were critical for the development and proliferation of saxophone pedagogy.

Between 1911 and 1918, Thompson engaged in an active performance schedule. Perhaps it had been Lefebre's influence that had provided her with initial opportunities, but by the end of the decade, it was Kathryne's own professional savvy and performance ability that enabled her reputation to grow. Although no marriage record can be found, we know that by 1916 Kathryne had married her first husband, because her name appears as "Thompson-Higham" in concert announcements in both 1916 and 1917. The January 1917 issue of *Musical Monitor* contains an announcement that "Katherine [sic] Thompson-Higham" had played a concert in Schubert Club, and that "Mrs. Higham" performed saxophone solos which were "received with great appreciation."[29] During this six-year period, she had numerous performing engagements with Navassar Ladies Band, Moore's Band, Brinks Cabaret, Gamut Club, Schubert Club, and the Los Angeles Women's Orchestra. Extant programs from these appearances show that Thompson was performing her own original works, plus novelty ragtime pieces (like her signature version of Felix Arndt's *Nola*), parlor songs, and light classical pieces.

By 1918, Kathryne's career began to extend more toward teaching, while she still engaged in many live performances. Thompson began her saxophone teaching career at the Frank J. Hart Southern California Music Company, with which she would have a long relationship of both teaching and publication.[30] At some point during this year Kathryne began again appearing using only her maiden name, though it is unclear from records whether she became widowed or divorced; the following census lists her simply as "single."[31] If she remained married at the beginning of this year, however, it was a career pivot common for a married woman of her time to focus more on teaching than on an active performance schedule.

Figure 6.2. Advertisement for Frank. J. Hart Southern California Music Company offering free lessons from Kathryne E. Thompson for every saxophone purchased at the store. *Los Angeles Times*, July 19, 1921, p. II1.

The Southern California Music Company (SCMC) was the main dealer of Buescher saxophones in the Los Angeles area and served a large number of students for private instruction. It is unclear how Thompson came into her employment by the SCMC; perhaps her access, in this case, came because of a shortage of teachers due to those deployed into service for the First World War. At the end of the war, however, Thompson remained in her teaching position, and by 1921, the SCMC offered a series of free lessons with Thompson with every sale of a saxophone through the store.[32] This interwar period of the growing popular music industry, the rising number of amateur music makers, and the proliferation of the saxophone's popularity in America undoubtedly contributed to Thompson's growing professional success as both a performer and teacher. Kathryne, who had adopted the stage name "Kitty" early in her playing career, was known to give her female students unusual and sometimes gender-focused stage names for use in vaudeville careers. One of Kathryne's students, Mary Gillespie, was deemed "America's Little Pavlova" by Thompson, referring to the famous Russian ballerina who was famous for her role in *Swan Lake*.[33] Perhaps this practice was an attempt to capitalize on or exploit the fact that both the saxophone and the women playing them were novel; perhaps it was necessary for exposure and certainly a shrewd marketing move by Thompson.

Her relationship with Southern California Music Company would for years be fruitful for Thompson, as it would be with their printing services, through which Thompson would go on throughout the 1920s to publish both method books and solo saxophone sheet music. In total, Thompson published five method books: *Thompson Practical Studies, The Modern Way: A Short Method for Saxophone Beginners, The Thompson Progressive Method for the Saxophone, Practical Studies in Bass Clef,* and *The Ragtime Saxophonist*. She also composed several solos for alto saxophone with piano (often with second alto saxophone obbligato), and these will be discussed further below.

In 1922, Thompson's popularity spread after she began a relationship with KHJ radio station in Los Angeles. KHJ was one of the first radio stations in the city of Los Angeles and aired its first broadcast in April of 1922. During what would become regular engagements on KHJ, Kathryne often performed with members of her studio as a quartet, most notably with her star student Lillian Althouse. Whether Thompson was paid or performed regularly for no or little pay is uncertain, as many early radio performers were compensated poorly, if at all.[34] There were many positive reviews of her radio performance and her popularity broadened despite the persistence of gendered comments in reviews and concert announcements. A printed 1923 announcement for that evening's radio broadcast boasts, "Make those saxophones behave, Kathryne, Lillian."

Thompson performed again with Althouse for a Hollywood Bowl performance in 1923, and the same year she appeared as a soloist with saxophonist Jascha Gurewich and the Southern California Saxophone Band. Gurewich must have been somewhat close with Thompson, as he composed and performed a piece, "Kathryne," as a dedication to her, which he sometimes performed at concerts as a duet version with Thompson.[35] An announcement in the *Los Angeles Times* from June 3, 1923, states,

> He played his own compositions exclusively, delighting the Saturday night audience of listeners. His first selection was "Ida Ballet," called the most pretentious modern saxophone composition published for saxophone. Other splendid numbers were "Kathyrne," romance, dedicated to Kathryne E. Thompson, who accompanied him, "Sunrise," "Emily," "Heartbreaking," and "Slaptonious," the last being a jazz encore.[36]

1923 was a banner year in Thompson's career, as by November of that year she assumed leadership of the Southern California Saxophone Band. It was through this unique orchestral-sized saxophone ensemble that Kathryne made perhaps her greatest impact, by changing public perception about the instrument as a honky, shrill-sounding noisemaker into something pleasing that, in an ensemble combination, could present orchestrated arrangements of classical as well as popular music. In the band's varied repertoire were opera and overture arrangements (such as Verdi's "Anvil Chorus" from *Il Trovatore* and Franz van Suppe's "Poet and Peasant" overture), arrangements of popular songs (like Carrie Jacobs Bond's "The Hand of You"), and various fox-trots and other dance music. *Los Angeles Times* writer Claire Forbes Crane wrote in 1924, "The saxophone is the true instrument of this era, and no greater exponents could be found than the Southern California Saxophone Band. Beautiful smooth tone, peppy rhythms, and faultless pitch distinguish all the members."[37]

The same year, in 1924, Thompson was balancing a full plate of professional activity. In this year, her photo was featured on the Sam Fox Publishing (New York) sheet music edition of Felix Arndt's wildly popular song "Nola". The caption to her photo reads, "Featured with great success by Kathryne E. Thompson," illustrating that her popularity had by this time spread beyond Los Angeles. She remained at the helm of the Southern California Saxophone Band for the entire year. The Los Angeles Chamber of Commerce also sponsored Thompson, along with the Sorority Six all-women dance band, to perform in Hawaii as a tourism and commerce initiative. It was around this time that Kathryne married for the second time. Her husband Lewis D'Ippolito was a New Jersey saxophonist and music teacher, who was also six years her junior. The couple would continue to collaborate professionally for the remainder of Thompson's career, including founding their own "Thompson-D'Ippolito School" for private saxophone instruction, which enrolled over 100 students.[38] She also shared her daily radio show, "The Thompson Progressive School for Saxophone," with Lewis, which featured performances of her own pieces, plus other popular solos of the time by H. Benne Henton, Edward Barroll, Gurewich, and Clay Smith.

During April 1927, Thompson performed for radio with the Golden State Band while six months pregnant. She gave birth to her daughter Caroline in July, and was back on radio by September. Her return to KHJ was short-lived, however, as both a change in ownership and changes within the Federal Broadcasting Commission resulted in different programming on the station in 1928. Mary Huneker writes that the Radio Act adopted that year, while it was created to "clean up the airwaves," consolidated a few commercial East Coast stations and cleared the way for large networks such as CBS and NBC to broadcast nationally. Smaller stations like KHJ subsequently revamped their programming in order to compete with their East Coast rivals.[39]

At this point in her career, now a mother and without her standing radio gig, Thompson's professional life began to dissipate. In late 1927, she and her husband closed their private music school, and Lewis D'Ippolito began a job at Long Beach High School. Within a year Kathryne gave birth to their second daughter, Kitty Lou, after which Kathryne's performing career would not continue. She and her husband would again collaborate in 1930 on the *D'Ippolito Modern Way Method for Band and Orchestra*, and Kathryne's final professional publication came in the early 1940s in the form of a collaboration with Freddie Martin on his saxophone technique book. After this date, little is known of Thompson, and she died in 1957, at age 68.

Compositions

Thompson's compositional output, while stylistically typical of music that was fashionable in the 1920s, is briefly mentioned here but worthy of rediscovery and further investigation. She published several solo works for saxophone, including *Barcarolle, Bubble and Squeak, Carolyn Melodie* (dedicated to her mother Carolyn), *Reverie, Romance, Song of Spring, Valse Caprice,* and *Valse Minah* (dedicated to her brother Minah Thompson); at least one song for voice and piano, *Waiting for You*; and some simplified arrangements for saxophone quartet. While no modern volume of Thompson's music has yet been compiled, her original sheet music editions and method books can still be found for sale periodically at online auctions and vintage sheet music sites.

A closer look at one of her original pieces, *Valse Minah*, reveals characteristics that give us insight into not only Thompson's writing style but also her playing ability, as we know she frequently performed her own pieces. *Valse Minah*, published in 1922, was available in editions for E-flat alto, C-melody, and B-flat tenor saxophones. The piece, which includes an optional second saxophone obbligato part, exhibits frequently fast-moving eighth-note lines and fast-articulated passages, set in a fast *valse caprice* tempo. The piece also has a rapid-fire *vivo* coda section (Ex. 6.1). Modern saxophonists might recognize characteristics of music by Rudy Wiedoeft (1893-1940) within Thompson's writing style. The popular Wiedoeft, who set the virtuosic standard of his time and was partially responsible for the saxophone craze of the 1920s, was a contemporary of Thompson's, and she likely knew of his music. That Wiedoeft's works such as *Valse Erica* and *Valse Vanité* bear some resemblance in style to Thompson's and have been widely performed and recorded by saxophonists might suggest that Thompson's music is worthy of inclusion in contemporary programming.

Thompson's *Bubble and Squeak* for saxophone and piano (fig. 6.3) also features a second alto saxophone obbligato line that is not included in the score pictured here (ex. 6.2). *Bubble and Squeak* presents the saxophonists with rapid tonguing passages at a fast, cut-time *tempo vivo*, and a slower *poco moderato* section that then returns to the first *vivo* theme.[40]

Example 6.1. From *Valse Minah* by Kathryne E. Thompson
(Pittsburgh: Volkwein Brothers, 1939)

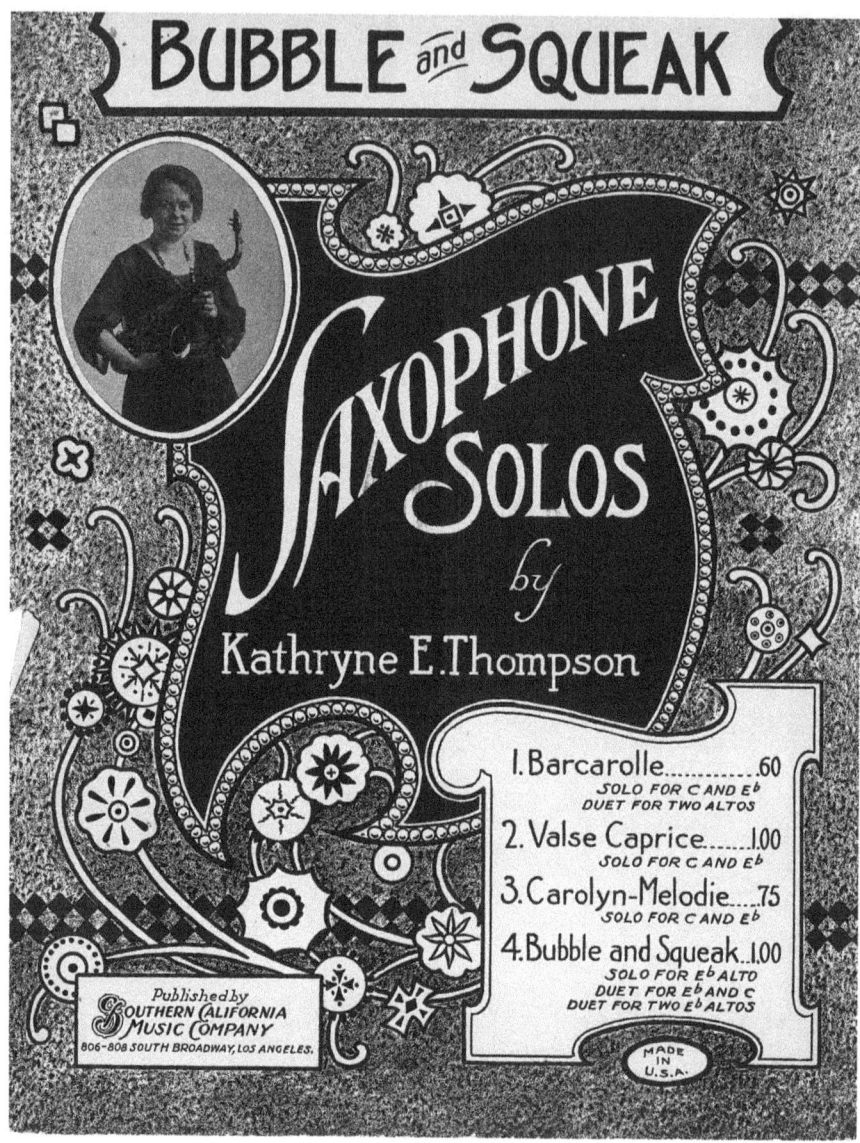

Figure 6.3. Cover of *Bubble and Squeak* by Kathryne E. Thompson (Southern California Music Company, 1923)

Example 6.2. From *Bubble and Squeak* by Kathryne E. Thompson (Southern California Music Company, 1923)

Conclusion

Little is known of Thompson's life after she ended her playing career, so her story presents unanswered questions. It could be that Thompson decided to stop performing in order to remain at home with her children, as that was a choice many professional women were pressured to make after becoming mothers. Whether she had regrets about leaving her thriving career behind, however, is impossible to know. Perhaps she felt compelled by her husband, or societal norms in general, to "settle down," or maybe it was her own personal choice. Perhaps she felt she had achieved enough professionally and yearned for a pivot into a more domestic life. Regardless, in her case this decision does not diminish the importance of what she achieved as a professional saxophonist who left behind not only a legacy of new compositions but also a legacy of saxophone protégés whom she mentored and inspired.

Despite the differences in their chosen musical genres and life circumstances, Elise Boyer Hall and Kathryne Thompson shared a passion for the saxophone, and both served as early twentieth-century role models for other women who aspired to a life in music. Similar to Hall, Thompson was yet another woman neglected for her achievements and contributions to the saxophone's popularity and repertoire. Both Hall—through her commissions and work with the Boston Orchestral Club—and Thompson—through her work with Southern California Saxophone Band, compositions, and extensive private studio—significantly contributed to the saxophone's rise in prominence in early twentieth-century America. Only when we draw comparisons to their histories, along with those of women like Anna Berger Lynch, Peggy Gilbert, and Florence Price, can we begin to have a more comprehensive understanding of the almost invisible yet immense impact that women have collectively made on the musical culture of the United States.

NOTES

1. Michael Cappabianca, "Elise Hall: Interview with Paul Cohen," accessed September 9, 2022, https://wam.rutgers.edu/elise-hall-an-interview-with-dr-paul-cohen/.
2. James R. Noyes, "Edward A. Lefebre (1835-1911): Preeminent Saxophonist of the Nineteenth Century" (PhD diss., Manhattan School of Music, 2000).
3. This paper uses the definition of the term "popular music" as defined by the editors of *Encyclopedia Britannica*, as any commercially oriented music principally intended to be received and appreciated by a wide audience.
4. Holly J. Hubbs, "American Women Saxophonists from 1870-1930: Their Careers and Repertoire" (PhD diss., Ball State University, 2003).
5. Edward C. Barroll, "The Saxophone Hall of Fame," *Jacobs Band Monthly* (Boston, MA), March 1923, 75.
6. Alex Ross, "The Rediscovery of Florence Price," *The New Yorker*, February 5, 2018.
7. Judith Tick, "Passed Away is the Piano Girl: Changes in American Music Life, 1870-1900,"

in *Women Making Music,* ed. Jane Bowers and Judith Tick (Urbana, IL: University of Illinois Press, 1986.), 327.
8. James Huneker, *Overtones* (New York: privately printed, 1904), 286.
9. George Bernard Shaw, *London Music in 1888-1889 as Heard by Corno Di Bassetto (later Known as Bernard Shaw) with Some Further Autobiographical Particulars* (London: Constable and Co., 1937), 127.
10. "The New Woman in Music," *Musical America,* April 28, 1906, 8.
11. Beth Abelson Macleod, *Women Performing Music: The Emergence of American Women as Instrumentalists and Conductors* (Jefferson, NC: MacFarland & Company, Inc., 2001), 3.
12. Marion Fairchild Nickell, "Music as a Field for Women," *Musical America,* September 1928, 14.
13. Marie Wurm, "Women's Struggle for Recognition in Music," *Etude* 54, no. 11 (November 1936): 687.
14. "Why Women Musicians are Inferior?" *Downbeat,* February 1938, 4.
15. Peggy Gilbert, "How do you Blow a Horn Through a Brassiere?" *Downbeat,* April 1938, 3.
16. James R. Noyes, "Debussy's 'Rapsodie Pour Orchestre et Saxophone' Revisited," *The Musical Quarterly* 90, no. 3/4 (Fall – Winter 2007): 422.
17. Noyes, "Debussy's 'Rapsodie Pour Orchestre et Saxophone' Revisited," 422.
18. Noyes, "Debussy's 'Rapsodie Pour Orchestre et Saxophone' Revisited," 421.
19. Christine Ammer, *Unsung: A History of Women in American Music,* 2nd ed. (Portland, OR: Amadeus Press, 2002), 288.
20. Michael Cappabianca, "Elise Hall: An Interview with Dr. Paul Cohen," accessed July 10, 2022, https://wam.rutgers.edu/elise-hall-an-interview-with-dr-paul-cohen/.
21. See footnote 354.
22. Bruce Vermazen, *That Moaning Saxophone: The Six Brown Brothers and the Dawning of a Musical Craze* (Oxford: Oxford University Press, 2004).
23. Ted Hegvik, *The Legacy of Rudy Wiedoeft,* accessed September 12, 2022, http://www.garfield.library.upenn.edu/essays/v12p071y1989.pdf.
24. Joseph Murphy, "Saxophone Instruction in American Music Schools Before 1940," *The Bulletin of Historical Research in Music Education* 18, no. 1 (September 1996): 6.
25. Edward Barroll, "Saxophone Hall of Fame," *Jacobs Band Monthly* (Boston, MA), August 1922, 78.
26. Ibid.
27. William Street goes on to explain that documents exist that indicate Hall's birth year as late as 1862, but it was likely 1853. See William Henry Street, "Elise Boyer Hall, America's First Female Concert Saxophonist: Her Life as Performing Artist, Pioneer of Concert Repertory for Saxophone and Patroness of the Arts" (DMA diss., Northwestern University, 1983).
28. Thomas W. Smialek, "The First Solo Saxophone Recording Reconsidered," *The Saxophone Symposium* 36/37: 1–28.
29. *Musical Monitor* was published monthly in Chicago by the National Federation of Music Clubs, beginning around 1911. In each issue, a country-wide "round-up" of notable concerts is listed.
30. The Southern California Music Company, founded in 1880, is likely the oldest music store in Los Angeles, and the second oldest in the state of California. The company is still operating under the same name in Glendale, CA.
31. The California census of 1920 lists Thompson as being single, neither widowed nor divorced.
32. *Los Angeles Times,* July 19, 1921.
33. E. Garfield, "Current Comments: Sax Discrimination," *Essays of an Information Scientist* 4 (1979-1980): 653.
34. Mary Huntimer, "Kathryne E Thompson: Her Life and Career as a Leading Saxophonist in Los Angeles from 1900-1927" (PhD diss., University of Kansas, 2012).
35. One unhappy critic from the March 7, 1924, *Brooklyn Standard Reviewer* wrote "Gurewich's 'Kathryne' was an obvious inconsequentiality and, like the remaining numbers on the programme, in no way indicated a genuine worth in the instrument."
36. Display Ad 31, *Los Angeles Times,* June 3, 1923, II1.
37. Claire Forbes Crane, "Saxophone is Ruler of Air," *Los Angeles Times,* June 4, 1924, A10.
38. Joe Murphy, "Saxophone Instruction in American Music Schools Before 1940," *The Bulletin of Historical Research in Music Education* 18, no. 1 (September 1996): 6.
39. Huneker, *Overtones,* 14.
40. When making a recording of Kathryne's music in 2007, I had a wonderful time recording both alto parts with the help of modern editing technology!

WORKS CITED

Ammer, Christine. *Unsung: A History of Women in American Music*. 2nd ed. Portland, OR: Amadeus Press, 2022.

Arndt, Felix. *Nola*. New York: Sam Fox Publishing Co., 1924.

Barroll, Edward. "The Saxophone Hall of Fame." *Jacobs' Band Monthly* (Boston, MA), March 1923.

Cohen, Paul. "Vintage Saxophones Revisited." *Saxophone Journal* 14 (July/August 1989): 8–10.

———. "Early Women Saxophone Professionals." *Saxophone Journal* 15 (July/August 1990): 8–13.

Garfield, E. "Current Comments: Sax Discrimination." *Essays of an Information Scientist* 4 (1979-1980): 653.

Huntimer, Mary. "Kathryne E. Thompson: Her Life and Career as a Leading Saxophonist in Los Angeles from 1900-1927." DMA diss., University of Kansas, 2012.

Hubbs, Holly. "American Women Saxophonists from 1870-1930." DMA diss., Ball State University, 2003.

Huneker, James. *Overtones*. New York: privately printed, 1904.

Macleod, Beth Abelson. *Women Performing Music: The Emergence of American Women as Instrumentalists and Conductors*. Jefferson, NC: MacFarland & Company, 2001.

Mendelsohn, Sarah. "'To The Women For Pulchritude; To The Men For Jazz': Sexism in Post-World War II Jazz." Honors thesis, Georgetown University, 2021.

Murphy, Joseph. "Saxophone Instruction in American Music Schools Before 1940." *The Bulletin of Historical Research in Music Education* 18, no. 1 (September 1996): 1–12.

Noyes, James R. "Debussy's 'Rapsodie Pour Orchestre et Saxophone' Revisited." *The Musical Quarterly* 90, no. 3/4 (Fall – Winter, 2007): 416–445.

———. "Edward A. Lefebre (1835-1911): Preeminent Saxophonist of the Nineteenth Century." PhD diss., Manhattan School of Music, 2000.

Pool, Jeanie. "Researching Women in Music in California." In *California's Musical Wealth*, ed. Stephen M. Fry (Southern California Chapter Music Library, 1988). 126.

Thomas Smialek. "The First Solo Saxophone Recording Reconsidered." *The Saxophone Symposium* 36-37: 1–28.

Street, Henry William. "Elise Boyer Hall, American's First Female Concert Saxophonist: Her Life as Performing Artist, Pioneer for Concert Repertory for Saxophone and Patroness of the Arts." DMA diss., Northwestern University, 1983.

Gee, Harry. *Saxophone Soloists and Their Music, 1844-1985*. Bloomington: Indiana University Press, 1986.

Tick, Judith. "Passed Away is the Piano Girl: Changes in American Musical Life, 1870-1900." In *Women Making Music*, edited by Jane Bowers and Judith Tick, 325–348. Urbana, IL: University of Illinois Press, 1986.

———. "Women as Professional Musicians in the United States, 1870-1900." *Yearbook for Inter-American Musical Research Intl.* 9 (1973): 95–133.

Mediography

Cappabianca, Michael. "Elise Hall: Interview with Paul Cohen." March 19, 2021. Accessed September 9, 2022. https://wam.rutgers.edu/elise-hall-an-interview-with-dr-paul-cohen/.

Crane, Claire Forbes. "Saxophone is Ruler of Air." *Los Angeles Times*, June 4, 1924.

Gilbert, Peggy. "How Do You Blow a Horn Through a Brassiere?" *Downbeat*, April 1938.

Hegvik, Ted. *The Legacy of Rudy Wiedoeft*. Accessed September 12, 2022. http://www.garfield.library.upenn.edu/essays/v12p071y1989.pdf..

"How Can You Blow a Horn Through a Brassiere?" *Downbeat*, May 1938.

"The New Woman in Music." *Musical America*, April 28, 1906.

Nickell, Marion Fairchild. "Music as a Field for Women." *Musical America*, September 1928.

Ross, Alex. "The Rediscovery of Florence Price." *The New Yorker*, February 5, 2018.

Thompson, Kathryne E. *Bubble and Squeak*. Los Angeles, CA: Southern California Music Company, 1923.

———. *Practical Studies in Bass Clef for Saxophone*. Los Angeles: F.J. Hart Southern California Music Company, 1922.

———. *The Ragtime Saxophonist: Suggestions and Models for 'Ragging' On Saxophone*. Los Angeles: Kathryne Thompson, 1920.

———. *Valse Minah*. Pittsburgh, PA: Volkwein Bros, 1939.

"Why Women Musicians are Inferior?" *Downbeat*, February 1938.

Wurm, Marie. "Women's Struggle for Recognition in Music." *Etude* 54 (November 1936): 687, 746.

"YMCA Educational." *Los Angeles Times*, May 20, 1903.

Epilogue

Elise Hall and the Saxophone
Updated Narratives and Future Considerations

Kurt Bertels & Adrianne Honnold

There are several parallels that exist between Elise Hall and the saxophone and a certain liminality that defines both. As Stephen Cottrell and others have noted, the saxophone is quintessentially American, despite its European provenance, and much the same origin story can be used to describe Hall. She was an admitted Francophile enamored with European art music, but her innovative, entrepreneurial spirit was distinctively American. She capitalized on the democratic, inclusive, and egalitarian societal ethos of the United States at the turn of the century to carry out her dreams of building a repertoire of music to perform. This is the same ethos that the saxophone came to embody: it symbolized modernity and progress to the American people. In the early decades of the twentieth century, the saxophone's path teetered and eventually toppled head first into the American popular side of the cultural fence that it had straddled, whereas Hall's path remained steadfastly beholden to the European, classical past. This was due in part to class structures; the saxophone's reputation as something lowbrow was building exponentially, whereas Hall was an inveterate member of the upper echelons of the elite, wealthy society. This divergence also somehow evokes that which is so attractive about the instrument; its polysemy is likely the saxophone's greatest strength, and it is the precise thing that makes it—and the people like Elise Hall who are inextricably linked to it—so challenging to comprehensively examine. This volume initiates the process of critically engaging with a historical subject whose life and career warrant investigation from a contemporary perspective, and we, the editors, hope that it inspires others to carry on the important work of revisiting and reframing canonical subjects in the history of music, musicians, and the saxophone.

As stated in the introduction of this volume, the collective endeavors of scholars in recent years have yielded substantial evidence to support the significant contributions made by numerous women in music history, whether as composers, patrons, or performers, despite the gender biases prevalent in historical narratives. Key references in saxophone studies have considered Hall as a historical figure who developed her own career as a musician and patron at the beginning of the twentieth century. These investigations mainly focused on Hall's biography concluding that she was a true pioneer, particularly as one of the very first female saxophone soloists. As a Francophile and president of the Boston Orchestral Club, she was actively engaged in the musical and cultural life of the United States and France. She commissioned twenty-two compositions between 1900 and 1920 from internationally renowned composers from France, Belgium, and the United States. Her musical journey was characterized by a passion for entrepreneurship and the relatively new saxophone, and it has left an indelible mark on this under-studied corner of music history.

With this volume, we aimed to expand the existing knowledge about Hall's life and career by exploring historical and sociocultural factors that have not been extensively studied in the past, as well as to amend some aspects of her historical record. We posed the questions: How can we understand her legacy today? How did intersectional factors that form her identity shape perceptions of the saxophone? What are the specific ways that gender has affected her legacy? To answer these queries and explore relevant contiguous topics from the era and environment in which she existed, we featured three main parts divided into two chapters each, featuring different viewpoints. The central theme that connects all the contributions by our co-authors is the examination of gender as it relates to the saxophone. When Hall's musical journey began in the late nineteenth century, the saxophone was an unconventional instrument, especially for a woman and someone of her stature. Undeterred by societal expectations and gender norms, Hall fearlessly embraced the saxophone, recognizing its limitless potential for artistic expression. Through her dedication and commitment, she excelled at performing and elevated the instrument to new heights, captivating audiences with virtuosity and musicality. In addition to her notable achievements as a performer and entrepreneur, Hall's philanthropic initiatives warrant recognition. Hall demonstrated a keen appreciation for the transformative potential of music in the community, as evidenced by her establishment and financial support of the Boston Orchestral Club. This organization served as a platform for predominantly female amateur musicians, drawn from her extensive transnational network, to come together and engage in musical pursuits.

Hall accomplished many things that deserve examination, but it should be reiterated that she was human and not a sacrosanct figure. She came from a renowned upper-class colonial family, a source of pride that likely endowed her with an innate sense of "Americanness" despite the fallacy and implicit violence of such a claim. She was a white woman born into privilege that afforded her the luxuries of time and money to pursue an active career in music. Likewise, Hall presumably employed these privileges to increase her power and agency and achieve her own musical goals. This is not an inherently malevolent way to use one's influence, but it needs to be stated in order to paint a full picture of who she was and the circles in which she operated. The individuals and institutions that she was involved with were not available to many people at the time; the cultural capital that she possessed separated her from other female saxophonists (and other musicians) because of this access and her financial independence. The power and influence that she may have imposed on the institutions that she was involved with and the media of the time is potentially worthy of further consideration beyond the pages of this volume.

In order to link the research carried out for this volume to future avenues of inquiry, we provide a final overview of each chapter followed by potential next steps. Delving deeper into Hall's legacy makes us realize there is still much territory for future lines of inquiry that remains unexplored.

At present, a notable research gap exists with regard to undertaking a critical analysis of Hall's transnational patronage and performance practice, particularly in relation to her identity as a woman and the reception she received, taking into consideration her hearing impairment. The exploration of Hall's role as a patron-performer and of the impact of her distinctive performance style on the aesthetics of compositions written specifically for her remains largely unexplored. Additionally, there is a lack of comprehensive investigation into the genesis of the musical works commissioned by Hall, as well as their intended functions and occasions. Conducting a thorough contextual and artistic study in this area might provide valuable insights into the multifaceted relationships between Hall as a patron-performer and the composers she collaborated with. Such an investigation would shed new light on the dynamics of artistic creation within the framework of Hall's patronage and contribute to a deeper understanding of the social, cultural, and musical contexts that shaped her career. Furthermore, it would offer a fresh perspective on the intersections of gender, ability, and artistic expression in the realm of classical music during Hall's time, thereby enriching our understanding of the broader historical and cultural significance of her contributions as a female saxophone player.

In part I of this volume, we examined the extensive coverage of reviews of Hall's performances, which provides valuable insights into her reception as a female saxophonist, the commissioned works she presented, and the perception of the saxophone at the beginning of the twentieth century. It is noteworthy that, despite the prevailing social norms, contemporary journals refrained from making negative comments about Hall's playing abilities. Yet it is worth considering whether the societal expectations of the time hindered journalists from highlighting any shortcomings of upper-class women, or if Hall herself played a significant role in shaping her portrayal in the press. These lingering questions serve as fertile ground for further research in the realm of patronage studies and critical reception studies, thereby posing challenges in evaluating the contextual background and reliability of historical sources pertaining to Hall's reception.

One of the defining aspects of Hall's career was her unwavering determination to challenge the status quo and break down barriers. Working within a male-dominated industry, she faced numerous obstacles including prejudices based on gender and the burgeoning instrument she played. However, Hall refused to let traditional expectations confine her, and instead, she used her talent, passion, and substantial resources to shatter stereotypes and carve a path for future generations of female musicians.

As Andrew Allen's chapter has clearly demonstrated, her contributions as a performer have been historically undervalued. Examination of contemporary reviews reveals that her performances were equal to other saxophonists of her time, if not of a higher caliber. Indeed, the persistent and prevailing negative perception of Hall as a performer is both anachronistic and unsupported. The assumption—perpetuated by (male) historians throughout the twentieth century—that Hall was a mediocre performer has led to a gross underestimation of her contributions to the saxophone history. However, a closer examination of professional reviews from reputable journals and periodicals in the United States and France reveals overwhelmingly positive evaluations of Hall's artistic performances. Indeed, despite the misogynistic tone of many of the reviews, her abilities consistently garnered praise, often surpassing those of her professional counterparts on the same programs. Also, the repertoire choices she made demonstrated a broader artistic ambition compared to her contemporaries. Despite being the only female instrumentalist in professional spaces, Hall operated in various capacities as an orchestral saxophonist, chamber musician, and soloist, collaborating with esteemed classical musicians, many of whom were principal players in the prestigious Boston Symphony Orchestra. Their repeated choice to perform on stage with Hall strongly suggests that unfavorable assessments of her skills were unfounded. This volume unequivocally reclaims the notion that Hall was an accomplished performer, by all counts a professional, despite the subjectivities imposed after her death by Debussy's biographer Vallas and others who followed him.

In addition to her performance career, Kurt Bertels' chapter goes beyond Hall's impact extending beyond her own performances. Indeed, she also played a pivotal role in the growth and development of the saxophone as a new instrument in the field of Western classical music. Recognizing the need for quality repertoire for the saxophone, she actively sought out composers and collaborated with them to create new works. This undertaking expanded the instrument's repertoire and helped establish the saxophone's legitimacy in the classical music world. Many saxophone works were initially created by Adolphe Sax's acquaintances who were unfamiliar with the instrument's unique capabilities. After this first phase, the emergence of repertoire was mainly composed by early saxophone educators and international soloists based on their own pedagogical aims and concert experiences. After the nineteenth century, Elise Hall broke away from the predominantly solo or saxophone and piano repertoire of the period, amassing a collection of compositions that ranged from chamber music to concertante works for saxophone and orchestra. In contrast to her predecessors and contemporaries, she was the only woman active in the field of strictly classical music.

Hall's role as a patron-performer reveals her active engagement within transnational networks of composers and performers, spanning the United States and Europe. Future research endeavors could focus on the transnational mobility of the pioneering first-generation saxophonists, exploring the influence of transnational exchanges on performance practices within diverse national and institutional contexts. Just like the inventor, Adolphe Sax, who relocated from Dinant, Belgium to Paris, France to promote and teach his revolutionary instrument, it is known that numerous first-generation saxophonists also embarked on travels to teach and perform, thereby establishing the groundwork for a vibrant and global saxophone culture. The history of the saxophone serves as an exemplary case study for examining transnational dynamics between performers and composers, as well as their impact on the early saxophone's performance practices.

In part II, Hall and the saxophone are viewed from a few standpoints that have not previously been investigated. Approaches informed by critical organology, intersectionality, material culture, and the exploration of social identities provide frameworks that enable further understanding of the relationships between Hall, the saxophone, and her current legacy. Adrianne Honnold argues in her chapter that Hall existed in a liminal space, straddling the nineteenth and twentieth centuries, the European and North American continents, and professional and amateur musical environments. In addition to these bifurcations, elements of her identity have converged to subvert her reputation and devalue her performance capabilities and the significant work she did to produce concerts. Although often referenced by members of the saxophone community, anecdotal evidence shows a somewhat dismissive regard for her abilities and the aesthetic quality of the music she performed. This apathy has persisted for almost a century and stems from aspects of her identity, class structures, and systemic marginalization of women and their work in classical music. By enumerating elements of her personal identity and the ways that patriarchy and positionality have played a part in the historiographies, her legacy is rehabilitated. She was a real person, imperfect in many ways, but this exploration of identity results in a more comprehensive view of her life and work and exposes some of the ways that the saxophone community has been uncritical in assessing its own biases.

Further research could be undertaken to investigate specific ways that the saxophone has been imputed with aspects of class and race. For instance, the instrument's associations with predominantly Black, male players that developed in the late 1920s and 1930s have been acknowledged and partially addressed, but warrant additional scrutiny. Additionally, these identity associations are also tangentially related to male-defined performance practices that remain foundational to saxophone pedagogy. What if—instead of saxophonists being held to standards that devalue performance qualities that are considered feminine or non-masculine in some way—new, inclusive standards were fully and objectively embraced? What would that look like?

Sarah McDonie's chapter also considers bias, though from a viewpoint that prioritizes the saxophone as an implicit and explicit lens through which we view Hall's musical activities. In other words, the saxophone informs and circumscribes what and how we study her, thereby challenging assumptions related to the centrality of the musician in creative work. Saxophonists and scholars have overlooked the power of the instrument in providing layers of meaning garnered from innumerable interactions with people and things, rendering the meaningful object invisible. However, as Bates, Dawe, and other critical organologists have noted, instruments have significant social value and act as intermediaries that connect us to the past, present, and future. In the case of an examination of Hall, the saxophone acts as a bias, epistemological foundation, and legacy-builder. Situating the instrument as the crucial object through which we study Hall allows us to acknowledge its agency and its existence as a frame for the historiographic process; the saxophone is an active collaborator and the primary driver of interest in the life and career of Hall.

In part III, Sarah Hetrick examines the ways in which the saxophone partially developed its sexualized reputation through participation in the burgeoning mass media industry and the development of commercial popular culture production in the United States in the 1920s. This approach represents an exploration of the instrument's social life that complements those examined in chapters 3 and 4. The saxophone's symbolic association with a distinctly American form of modernity and progress, owing (in part) to its ubiquity in the popular music of the time, helped it become desirable to countless would-be musicians, as is demonstrated in advertisements for the sale of the instrument in the 1920s. The story in the ads was geared towards—and sold to—almost exclusively white men who had the purchasing power that drew the attention of the manufacturers. This capitalistic endeavor that catered to the male gaze substantially contributed to the saxophone's masculine gender association. The sound and shape of the saxophone are generally considered quite ambiguous and androgynous; it was the media and advertising industries that propagandized the instrument for their benefit that contributed to the instrument's entrenched masculinity. In analyzing examples of the print advertisements from this period, we are able to see the ways that the saxophone was—and remains—a strong signifier of socially assigned characteristics.

The exploration of Hall's narrative serves as a crucial precedent to unveil and understand previously unexplored avenues for rediscovering other female saxophonists from that era. With a chapter by Hully Hubbs, our volume presents for the very first time an exhaustive study on Kathryne Thompson, who like Hall shared a love for the saxophone and played a significant role as an early twentieth-century role model for aspiring female musicians. Despite their differences in performance style or socioeconomic status, both Hall and Thompson have been overlooked for their contributions to the saxophone's popularity and repertoire. Through Hall's commissions and work with the Boston Orchestral Club, and through Thompson's involvement with the Southern California Saxophone Band, compositions, and extensive private studio, these women significantly influenced the saxophone's rise in prominence in the United States during this time period. Through their correlated histories, we gain a more comprehensive understanding of the profound yet often overlooked impact that women collectively had on the musical culture of the time.

Hall's legacy continues to resonate in the global saxophone community long after her passing. Her pioneering spirit and unwavering determination have inspired generations of musicians to push boundaries and challenge conventions. Today, countless saxophonists owe their success to Hall's trailblazing performance and commissioning efforts, which have in some ways become archetypal in the classical saxophone community. Most significantly, her influence can be witnessed in the ever-increasing representation of women in the field. Elise Hall's musical contributions have had a significant impact, just a few of which are explored here. Her journey serves as a testament to the power of perseverance, passion, and a refusal to be confined by societal expectations. Through her unparalleled talent, unwavering dedication, and commitment to breaking down barriers, she has left an enduring mark on the history of music. As we reflect on her remarkable life and career, let us celebrate her legacy and continue to strive for equality and inclusivity in the world of music.

About the Authors

Dr. Kurt Bertels is a postdoctoral researcher at LUCA School of Arts (KU Leuven), Koninklijk Conservatorium Brussel, and Royal Conservatoire Antwerp, Belgium. A saxophonist, he performs both in Belgium and abroad as soloist and as a member of various ensembles. He has participated in national and international CD, radio, and television recordings, including *The Saxophone in 19th-Century Brussels* (2020) and *Works for Saxophone and Orchestra by Paul Gilson* (2020). His research focuses on dedicating music in early twentieth-century music, with a particular focus on patronage and transnationalism in music. He has published several articles and a monograph, *Een ongehoord geluid* (2020), on the history and performance practice of the early saxophone. Affiliated with Utrecht University's Chair of Patronage Studies, he works on Elise Hall's saxophone collection.

Dr. Adrianne Honnold is an assistant professor of music at Lewis University, where she teaches courses in popular music studies and applied saxophone. She has performed as a saxophonist throughout the United States and Europe, and holds degrees in music education, saxophone performance, and ethnomusicology/popular music studies. Her research engages with methods from critical organology and the sociology of music to explore the nature of the relationship between music and identity.

Dr. Andrew J. Allen serves as an associate professor of music and coordinator of woodwinds, brass, and percussion at Georgia College & State University. Allen has premiered more than two dozen works for the saxophone in performances throughout North America and Europe. His articles have appeared in *The Saxophone Symposium*, *Saxophone Today*, and *The NACWPI Journal*, among many other publications. He is assistant editor of *The Saxophone Symposium* and is president-elect of the North American Saxophone Alliance.

Dr. Sarah V. Hetrick serves as an assistant professor of saxophone at the University of Arkansas, where she teaches applied saxophone and chamber music. Sarah is an active solo and chamber musician and has been invited to teach, perform, and share her research throughout the United States.

Dr. Holly J. Hubbs currently holds the William F. Heefner Endowed Chair of Music at Ursinus College, where she teaches music history and directs the wind and jazz ensembles. Hubbs holds music degrees from Quincy University and Western Illinois University, and she received her doctoral degree in saxophone performance from Ball State University.

Sarah Adele Kirkman McDonie is a PhD candidate in musicology with a minor in media studies at Indiana University – Bloomington. Her research is informed by a deep sense of wonder at the small things in the world. Her sensitivity to questions of the spiritual and the unusual drives her work on cybernetics and experimental performance art, performance theory, and ecological systems theory. Sarah is an alumna of the Diverse Intelligences Summer Institute and is the executive director for the nonprofit Reimagining Opera for Kids.

Index

Abair, Mindi: 97
Advertising industry: 128, 131, 132, 133, 134
Althouse, Lillian: 166
American progress: 87, 127
Arndt, Felix: 161, 162, 164, 167

Barr, Cyrilla: 60
Bak, Adolf: 40, 47
Balakirev, Mily: 47
Barroll, Edward: 167
Bates, Eliot: 111, 112
Beach, Amy Cheney: 156, 157
Beach, Henry Aubrey: 156
Bechet, Sidney: 87
Bennett, Jane: 116, 117
Berger, Arthur Asa: 127, 136, 137
Berger Lynch, Anna Berger: 158, 172
Berra, Alessia: 118
Bizet, Georges: 34, 44, 45, 130
Blair, Karen: 92, 93, 95
Boivin, Nicole: 110
Boston Orchestral Club: 17, 31, 33, 34, 35, 42, 47, 48, 49, 59, 66, 68, 71, 74, 85, 94, 114, 160, 172, 178, 183
Boston Pops: 40
Boston Symphony Orchestra (BSO): 17, 29, 34, 35, 40, 42, 44, 45, 46, 50, 51, 66, 72, 82, 160
Brinks Cabaret: 164
Brooke, Arthur: 42
Brown, Allen: 45
Brown, Tom: 139
Buescher: 23, 127, 129, 132, 133, 136, 137, 138, 139, 140, 141, 142, 143, 144, 145, 146
Buescher Band Instrument Company: 127
Bull, Anna: 32
Butler, Morgan: 50

Caplet, André: 17, 38, 41, 50, 63, 65, 67
Carnegie Hall: 64
C. G. Conn: 132, 133
Chauvet, Alexis: 41
Chimènes, Myriam: 60
Clark, Donald: 139
Coffin, Jeff: 97
Cohen, Paul: 117, 118, 154, 160
Colonization: 18, 24

Combelle, François: 63
Cook, Susan: 94, 96
Coolidge, Calvin: 88
Corn, Joseph: 108, 114
Cortot, Alfred: 31
Cottrell, Stephen: 16, 31, 59, 72, 110, 114, 128, 131, 139
Couvent des Oiseaux: 40
Covent Garden: 35
Crenshaw, Kimberlé: 82, 86
critical organology: 22, 23, 24, 79, 97, 181, 185
Critical theory: 84
cultural studies: 22, 23, 181
Curry, Nicolas James: 112

Davis, Simone Weil: 134
Dawe, Kevin: 108, 113, 119, 182
Deafness: 91, 119
De Biase, Anna Paola: 118
Debuchy, Albert: 40
Debussy, Claude: 17, 18, 30, 34, 58, 60, 63, 66, 68, 70, 84, 86, 87, 89, 90, 96, 105, 106, 111, 117, 121, 128, 154, 159, 160
Demersseman, Jules: 62
de Souza, Jonathan: 107, 108, 112
de Voto, Alfred: 40
Dimaggio, Paul: 60
D'Indy, Vincent: 17, 37, 40, 42, 58, 60, 63, 65, 66, 69, 70, 71, 72, 73,
D'Ippolito, Lewis: 167
Disability: 16, 90, 95
Discrimination: 24, 82, 86, 88, 89, 135
Doerr, Clyde: 139
Doubleday, Veronica: 87, 128
Downes, Olin: 45
Ducasse, Jean: 47
Dupin, Paul: 63, 68
Durand et fils: 70

Elise Hall Collection of Saxophone Music by 20th-Century Composers: 59
Elise Hall Competition: 118, 119
Elise Hall Saxophone Quartet: 118, 119, 121
Epistemology: 105, 106, 107, 113, 114, 115
Eroticism: 130
Exoticism: 129, 130

Fabbri, Isabella: 118
Fairchild Nickell, Marion: 158
Faucett, Bill: 60
Fauré, Gabriel: 60
Fauser, Annegret: 130,
Feminine: 19, 37, 94, 95, 98, 143, 182
Feminism: 84, 86, 135
Feminist musicology: 19, 22, 23
Ferir, Emile: 47, 49
Fétis, François-Joseph: 62
Forbes, Claire: 167
Franck, César: 42, 47
Frank J. Hart Southern California Music Company: 164, 165
Freedman, Estelle B.: 135
Frisch, Povla: 50

Gamut Club: 164
Garde républicaine: 131
Gardner Museum: 88
Gaubert, Philippe: 49, 63, 66, 68
Gender associations: 21, 128, 183
Gender norms: 129, 145, 178
Gender performativity: 129
Gender stereotype: 32, 137
Gender studies: 23, 84
Gideon, Henry: 50
Gietzen, Alfred: 40
Gilbert, Peggy: 159, 172
Gilibert, Charles: 35
Gillespie, Mary: 165
Gilmore, Patrick: 131
Gilson, Paul: 17, 57, 58, 60, 63, 68
Golden State Band: 167
Green, Emily: 67
Grisez, Georges: 40
Grovlez, Gabriel: 50, 63, 68
Gudell, Valerie: 31, 72
Gurewich, Jascha: 163, 166, 167
Gymnase musical militaire: 62, 73

Hain, Frank: 40
Hale, Philip: 44
Halévy, Jacques: 130
Hall, Richard J. (Dr. R. J. Hall): 16, 17, 33, 47, 50, 65, 66, 69, 71, 74, 90, 128
Hall, Stuart: 127, 129, 136
Hearing impairment: 16, 17, 90, 91, 179
Helleberg, John: 40
Hemke, Frederick: 31, 59, 72
Henton, H. Benne: 167
Hensel-Mendelsohn, Fanny: 156, 157
Heteronormative: 127, 129, 135, 137, 143
Higginson, Henry: 33
Highbrow: 24, 87, 95
Huber, Ernest: 49

Huneker, James: 158
Huneker, Mary: 167
Huré, Jean: 50, 63, 69, 72

Iconography: 23, 127, 128, 129, 145
Intersectionality: 82, 84, 85, 86, 88,

Jacobs, Carrie: 167
Jones, Andrew: 110

Kassiani the Hymnographer (Kassia of Constantinople): 156
Kastner, George: 130
Keller, Joseph: 40
Keller, Karl: 40
Kerman, Joseph: 84
Kimmerer, Robin Wall: 110
Köhler, Ernesto: 33
Krueger, Bennie: 139

Lalo, Edouard: 47
Lazzari, Sylvio: 47
Lefebre, Edouard: 62, 154, 163, 164
Legacy-builder: 105, 107, 117, 182
Lenom, Clément: 40
Levine, Lawrence: 95
Locke, Ralph: 60
Loeffler, Charles Martin: 17, 38, 40, 63, 64, 69,
Logrande, L.A.: 17, 146,
Longy, Georges: 17, 29, 31, 33, 34, 35, 38, 40, 41, 42, 45, 47, 50, 58, 63, 65, 69, 71, 72, 93, 160
Longy Club: 29, 31, 35, 36, 38, 39, 40, 47, 72
Longy Miquelle, Renee: 50
Lorbeer, Heinrich: 40
Los Angeles Saxophone Quartet: 164
Los Angeles Women's Orchestra: 164
Lowbrow: 24, 95, 96, 98, 114, 177
Lucchini, Chiara: 118

MacDowell Club Orchestra: 50
Makay, Florence: 163
Male chauvinism: 89
Male-dominated: 21, 38, 93, 129, 158, 180
Male gaze theory: 129, 137
Maquarre Daniel: 40
Maquarre, André: 42
Marsalis, Branford: 97
Martin, Freddie: 168
Masculine: 21, 86, 94, 95, 109, 114, 127, 128, 129, 134, 137, 141, 143, 145, 182, 183
Masculinity: 17, 23, 92, 98, 127, 128, 129, 138, 139, 141, 142, 143, 145, 146, 183
Massenet, Jules: 130
Material culture: 22, 23, 107, 108, 110, 112, 115, 117, 120, 181
Mayeur, Louis: 62

McClary, Susan: 19, 84
Mendelsohn, Felix: 156
Mendelsohn, Sarah: 159
Messager, Andre: 159
Metropolitan Museum of Art: 64,
Metropolitan Opera: 35, 64
Meyerbeer, Giacomo: 130
Misogyny: 30, 37, 51, 105
Mollica, Antonino: 59
Moore's Band: 164
Moreau, Léon: 47, 63, 66, 69, 72
Mouquet, Jules: 63, 72
Mule, Marcel: 30, 42
Mrs. Hall's Concerts: 29, 33
Mulvey, Laura: 127, 129, 136, 137, 138
Murphy, Joe: 161
Museum of Fine Arts in Boston: 82

Navassar Ladies Band: 164
Neuls-Bales, Carol: 32
New England Conservatory (NEC): 12, 58, 59, 63, 68, 73
New London Consort: 156
New Musicology: 84
New York Philharmonic: 64
Nichols, Caroline B.: 157
Nochlin, Linda: 90
Noack, Sylvain: 47, 49
Noyes, James: 16, 17, 30, 72, 86, 91

Oliveros, Pauline: 89, 90
Ondricek, Karl: 40
Opéra-Comique: 35, 41

Paris Conservatory: 35, 38
Parker, Charlie: 81
Parkin, Katherine: 133
Patriarchy: 94, 182
Patronage, patronage studies, patronage theory: 20, 21, 22, 24, 57, 59, 60, 64, 69, 74, 83, 118, 156, 179, 180
Peiss, Kathy: 133, 134
Pessard, G.: 41
Pickett, Lenny: 97
Playing ability: 33, 89, 168
Positionality: 81, 82, 84, 90, 182
Powell, Verne: 50
Price, Florence: 156, 157, 172

Queer theory: 84

Rabinovitch-Fox, Einav: 134
Rabuad, Henri: 42
Race: 23, 81, 82, 88, 91, 96, 98, 99, 131, 134, 156, 157, 182
Racial difference: 127, 128
Raine, Sarah: 19

Raschèr, Sigurd: 30, 42
Rettberg, August: 40
Reynolds, Howard: 158
Richtmeyer, Debra: 81
Riggins, Stephen: 106
Rimsky-Korsakov, Nikolai: 42
Roussel, Albert:49
Royal Conservatoire de Bruxelles: 62

Salle Pleyel: 40, 41
Salter, Chris: 114, 115,
Santa Barbara Amateur Music Club: 33
Santa Barbara Philharmonic Club: 33
Sax, Antoine-Joseph ('Adolphe'): 15, 61, 62, 73, 127, 131, 181
Saxophone craze: 127, 131, 132, 146, 153, 161, 168
Saxophone Lady: 90, 105, 106, 121
Saxophone pedagogy: 164, 182
Schmitt, Florent: 17, 49, 63, 72
Schubert Club: 164
Schuecker, Heinrich: 40
Scott, Derek B.: 130
Segell, Michael: 114, 128, 131
Selvin, Ben: 139
Sensuality: 129130
Sexualization: 127, 128, 129, 145
Shaw, George Bernard (Corno di Bassetto): 158
Singelée, Jean-Baptiste: 62
Sivulka, Juliann: 133
Six Brown Brothers: 161
Smialek, Thomas: 17, 146
Smith, Clay: 167
Smith, Jos. C.: 139
Social identity: 22, 23, 79, 82, 83, 84, 86, 138
Société de Musique de Chambre pour instruments à vent: 72
Société Nationale de Musique: 37, 71
Sonevytsky, Maria: 97
Sorority Six: 167
Soualle, Charles ("Ali Ben Sou Alle"): 62, 130
Sousa, John Philip: 131, 163
Southern California Music Company: 161, 164, 165, 170, 171
Southern California Saxophone Band: 153, 166, 167, 172, 183
Sporck, Georges: 63
Stewart Gardner, Isabella: 64, 88, 91, 93
Strauss, Richard: 60
Stravinsky, Igor: 60
Street, William Henry: 16, 20, 31, 50, 59, 88, 90, 91, 110, 116, 163
Strong, Catherine: 19
Strozzi, Barbara: 156
Subordination: 93
Subotnik, Rose: 84
Suzuki, Yuko: 128

Thomas, Nicholas: 106
Thompson-D'Ippolito School: 167
Thompson, Kathryne E.: 23, 139, 153, 154, 155, 159, 161, 162, 163, 164, 165, 166, 167, 168, 169, 170, 171, 172
Thompson, "Kitty": 163, 165
Tomlinson, Gary: 115
Torchet, Julien: 41, 71

Vallas, Léon: 16, 30, 32, 51, 89, 90, 91, 180
van den brabrer, Helleke: 69, 73
Vannini, Augusto: 40
van Suppe, Franz: 167
Vermazen, Bruce: 161
Vernacular music/styles: 87, 96, 153, 154, 157, 161, 163
Virility: 95, 143

Vockeroth, Melanie: 128
von Bingen, Hildegard: 20, 156

Walser, Rober: 95
Washington, George: 88
Weber, Ida: 163
Wharton, Chris: 132, 136
Whitessitt, Linda: 58
Whitwell, David: 31
Wiedoeft, Rudy: 168
Woodward, Ian: 115, 116
Woollett, Henry: 42, 47, 49, 50, 63, 67, 72,
Wurm, Marie: 158

Young, Benjamin: 49

Milton Keynes UK
Ingram Content Group UK Ltd.
UKHW022244120424
441043UK00008B/166